Bubble Value at Risk

Bubble Value at Risk

Extremistan and Procyclicality

Max C.Y. Wong

To my heavenly Father who gave me this assignment

Acknowledgements

This book has benefited from the valuable comments of various practitioners and academics. I am most grateful to Michael Dutch for his generous proof-reading of the manuscript; John Chin and Brian Lo for their comments. The book was further enriched by reviews and suggestions from Paul Embrechts from ETHZ.

The production of the book involved many excellent individuals. I thank Lim Tai Wei for grammatical edit suggestions, Sylvia Low for web-design and the cover design team in Beijing: Michael Wong, Kenny Chai, Liu DeBin and Xiao Bin.

I am grateful to my wife, Sylvia Chen, for her patience and for taking care of the children during this project.

Contents

Preface   xiii

Part I Background

1. Introduction
   1.1 The evolution of riskometer   4
   1.2 Taleb's extremistan   6
   1.3 The Turner procyclicality   7
   1.4 The commonsense of bubble value-at-risk (buVaR)   8

2. Essential mathematics
   2.1   Frequentist statistics   17
   2.2   Just assumptions   21
   2.3   Quantiles, VaR and tails   28
   2.4   Correlation and autocorrelation   31
   2.5   Regression models and residual errors   37
   2.6   Significance tests   40
   2.7   Measuring volatility   43
   2.8   Markowitz portfolio theory   48
   2.9   Maximum likelihood method   51
   2.10 Cointegration   52
   2.11 Monte Carlo method   55
   2.12 The Classical decomposition   58
   2.13 Quantile regression model   62
   2.14 Spreadsheet   65

Part II Value-at-Risk Methodology

3. Preprocessing
   3.1 System architecture   71
   3.2 Risk factor mapping   74
   3.3 Risk factor proxies   79
   3.4 Scenario generation   81
   3.5 Basic VaR specification   83

4. Conventional VaR methods
   4.1 Parametric VaR   88
   4.2 Monte Carlo VaR   94
   4.3 Historical simulation VaR   98
   4.4 Issue: Convexity, optionality and fat tails   101
   4.5 Issue: Hidden correlation   107
   4.6 Issue: Missing basis and beta approach   109
   4.7 Issue: The real risk of premiums   111
   4.8 Spreadsheet   113

5. Advanced VaR methods
   5.1 Hybrid historical simulation VaR   115
   5.2 Hull-White volatility updating VaR   117
   5.3 Conditional autoregressive VaR (CaViaR)   118
   5.4 Extreme value theory VaR   121
   5.5 Spreadsheet   127

6. VaR reporting
   6.1 VaR aggregation and Limits   129
   6.2 Diversification   131
   6.3 VaR analytical tools   132
   6.4 Scaling and Basel Rules   136
   6.5 Spreadsheet   140

7. The physics of risk and pseudoscience
   7.1 Entropy, leverage effect and skewness   143
   7.2 Volatility clustering and the folly of i.i.d.   149
   7.3 "Volatility of volatility" and fat-tails   149
   7.4 Extremistan and the fourth quadrant   153
   7.5 Regime change, lagging riskometer and procyclicality   156
   7.6 Coherence and expected shortfall   159
   7.7 Spreadsheet   161

8. Model testing
   8.1 Precision test   163
   8.2 Frequency back test   165
   8.3 Bunching test   167
   8.4 Spreadsheet   169

9. Practical limitations of VaR
   9.1 Depegs and changes to "Rules of the game"   171
   9.2 Data integrity problems   173
   9.3 Model risk   174
   9.4 Politics and gaming   176

10. Other major risk classes
    10.1 Credit risks (and Creditmetrics©)   179
    10.2 Liquidity risk   184
    10.3 Operational risk   189
    10.4 The problem of aggregation   194
    10.5 Spreadsheet   197

Part III The Great Regulatory Reform

11. Regulatory capital reform
    11.1 Basel I and Basel II   201
    11.2 The Turner Review   205
    11.3 Revisions to Basel II market risk framework   208
    11.4 New liquidity framework   212
    11.5 The new Basel III   213
    11.6 The ideal capital regime   215

12. Systemic risk initiatives
    12.1 Soros' reflexivity, endogenous risks   219
    12.2 Crashmetrics©   224
    12.3 New York Fed CoVaR   229
    12.4 The Austrian model and BOE RAMSI   232
    12.5 The global systemic risk regulator   238
    12.6 Spreadsheet   240

Part IV Introduction to Bubble Value-at-Risk (BuVaR)

13. Market BuVaR
    13.1 Why an alternative to VaR   243
    13.2 Classical decomposition, new interpretation   245
    13.3 Measuring the *bubble*   248
    13.4 Calibration   252
    13.5 Implementing the inflator   255
    13.6 Choosing the best tail risk measure   257
    13.7 Effect on joint distribution   261
    13.8 The scope of BuVaR   262
    13.9 How good is the BuVaR buffer?   263
    13.10 The brave new world   266
    13.11 Spreadsheet   269

14. Credit BuVaR
    14.1 The credit bubble VaR idea   271
    14.2 Model formulation   274
    14.3 Behavior of response function   277
    14.4 Characteristics of credit BuVaR   279

14.5 Interpretation of credit BuVaR   281
14.6 Spreadsheet   282

15. Acceptance tests
    15.1 BuVaR visual checks   283
    15.2 BuVaR event timing tests   297
    15.3 BuVaR cyclicality tests   303
    15.4 Credit buVaR parameter tuning   304

16. Other topics
    16.1 Diversification and basis risks   311
    16.2 Regulatory reform and buVaR   313
    16.3 BuVaR and the banking book. Response time as risk   315
    16.4 Can buVaR pick tops and bottoms perfectly?   317
    16.5 Post-modern risk management   317
    16.6 Spreadsheet   318

17. Epilogue: Suggestions for future research   319

References   321

Index   327

Preface

This is a story of the illusion of risk measurement. Financial risk management is in a state of confusion. The 2008 credit crisis has wreaked havoc on the Basel pillars of supervision by highlighting all the cracks in the current regulatory framework that had allowed the credit crisis to fester, and ultimately leading to the greatest crisis since the Great Depression. Policy responses were swift— UK's *Financial Services Authority* (FSA) published the *Turner Review* which calls for a revamp of many aspects of banking regulation, the *Bank of International Settlements* (BIS) speedily passed a Revision to its Basel II, while the Obama administration calls for a reregulation of the financial industry reversing the Greenspan legacy of deregulation.

The *value-at-risk* risk measure, VaR, a central ideology for risk management, was found to be wholly inadequate during the crisis. Critically, this "riskometer" is used as the basis for regulatory capital—the safety buffer money set aside by banks to protect against financial calamities. The foundation of risk measurement is now questionable.

The first half of this book develops the VaR riskometer with emphasis on its traditionally-known weaknesses, and talks about current advances in risk research. The underlying theme throughout the book is that VaR is a faulty device during turbulent times and by its mathematical sophistication misled risk controllers into an illusion of safety. The author traces the fundamental flaw of VaR to its statistical assumptions—of normality, i.i.d. and stationarity—the "gang of three".

These primitive assumptions are very pervasive in the frequentist statistics philosophy where probability is viewed as an objective notion and can be measured by sampling. A different school of thought, the Bayesians, argues for subjective probability and has developed an entire mathematical framework to incorporate the observer's opinion into the measurement (but this is a subject matter for another publication). We argue that the frequentist's strict mathematical sense often acts as a blinder that restricts the way we view and model the real world. In particular, two "newly" uncovered market phenomena— extremistan and procyclicality—cannot be engaged using the frequentist mindset. There were already a few other well-known "market anomalies" that tripped the VaR riskometer during the 2008 crisis. All these will be detailed later.

In Part IV of the book, the author proposes a new risk metric called *bubble VaR* (buVaR) which does not invoke any of the said assumptions. BuVaR is not really a precise measurement of risk; in fact it presumes that extreme loss events are unknowable (extremistan) and moves on to the more pressing problem—how do we build an effective buffer for regulatory capital that is countercyclical, and that safeguards against extreme events.

This book is an appeal (as is this preface) to the reader to consider a new paradigm of viewing risk—that one need *not* measure risk (with precision) to protect against it. By being obsessively focused on measuring risk, the risk controller may be fooled by the many pitfalls of statistics and randomness. This could lead to a false sense of security and control over events which are highly unpredictable. It is ultimately a call for good judgment and pragmatism.

This book is intended to reach out to the top management of banks (CEOs and CROs), to regulators, to policy makers and to risk practitioners—not all of whom may be as quantitatively inclined as the specialized risk professional. But they are the very influencers of the coming financial reregulation drama. We are living in epic times and ideas help shape the world for the better (or for worst). It is hoped that the ideas in this book can open up new and constructive research into countercyclical measures of risk.

With this target audience in mind, this book is written in plain English with as few Greek letters as possible, the focus is on concepts (and illustrations) rather than mathematics. Because it is narrowly focused on the topic, it can be self-contained. No prior knowledge of risk management is required; pre-university level algebra and some basic financial product knowledge are assumed.

A word on the use of Excel: All the spreadsheets used in this book can be downloaded from the companion website:

www.bubble-value-at-risk.com

Excel is an excellent learning platform for the risk apprentice. Monte Carlo simulations are used frequently to illustrate and experiment with key ideas, and where unavoidable, VBA functions are used. The codes are written with pedagogy (not efficiency) in mind.

Max C. Y. Wong

PART *I*

BACKGROUND

Chapter 1

Introduction

The 2008 global credit crisis is by far the largest boom-bust cycle since the Great Depression (1929). Asset bubbles and manias have been around since the first recorded tulip mania in 1637, and in recent decades have become such a regularity that they are even expected as often as once every 10 years (1987, 1997, 2007). Asset bubbles are in reality more insidious than most people realize for it is not the massive loss of wealth that it brings (for which investor has not entertained the possibility of financial ruin) but because *it widens the social wealth gap*; it impoverishes the poor. The 2008 crisis highlighted this poignantly—in the run-up to the US housing and credit bubble, the main beneficiaries were bankers (who sold complex derivatives on mortgages) and their cohorts. At the same time, a related commodity bubble temporarily caused a food and energy crisis in some parts of the developing world, notably Indonesia, the fourth most populous nation in the world and an OPEC member (until 2008). When the bubble burst, ten trillion dollars of US public money was used to bail out failing banks and to take over toxic derivatives created by banks. On their way out, CEOs and traders of affected banks were given million dollar contractual bonuses, even as the main economy lost a few million jobs. Just as in 1929, blue collar workers bore the brunt of the economic downturn in the form of unemployment in the US.

The ensuing zero interest rate policy and quantitative easing (printing of dollars by the Fed) induced yet other bubbles—commodity prices are rising to alarming levels and asset bubbles are building up all over Asia, as investors chase non-US dollar assets. We see home prices skyrocketing well beyond the reach of the average person in major cities. The wealthy are again speculating in homes, this time in East Asia. In many countries, huge public spending on infrastructure projects that is meant to support the headline GDP caused a substantial transfer of public wealth to property developers and cohorts. The lower income and under-privileged are once again left behind in the tide of inflation and "growth".

The danger of an even larger crisis now looms. The US dollar and treasuries are losing credibility as reserve currencies because of rising public debt. This means that "flight-to-quality", which has in the past played the role of a pressure outlet for hot money during a crisis, is no longer an appealing option.

If there is a lesson from the 2008 crisis, it is that asset bubbles have to be reined in at all costs. It is not just John Keynes' "animal spirits" at work here—the herd tipping the supply-demand imbalance—but the spirit of "mammon"—unfettered greed. There is something fundamentally dysfunctional about the way financial institutions are incentivized and regulated. Thus, a global regulatory reform is underway, led by the UK, EU and US, with a target deadline of 2012. Our narrow escape from total financial meltdown has highlighted the criticality of systemic risks in an interconnected world; we can no longer think in isolated silos when solving problems in the banking system. The coming reregulation must be holistic and concerted.

One major aspect of the reform is in the way risk is measured and controlled. The great irony is that our progress in risk management has led to a new risk: the risk of "risk assessment". What if we are wrong (unknowingly) about our measurement? The crisis is a rude wake-up call for regulators and bankers to reexamine our basic understanding of what risk is and how effective are our regulatory safeguards.

We start our journey with a review of how our current tools for measuring financial markets risk were evolved. In this chapter, we will also give a prelude to two important concepts that grew out of crisis response—extremistan and procyclicality. These will likely become the next buzz words in the unfolding regulatory reform drama. The final section offers, *bubble VaR*, a new tool researched by the author which regulators can explore to strengthen the safeguards against future financial crises.

1.1 The Evolution of Riskometer

"Necessity is the mother of inventions" (Plato, Greek philosopher, 427-347 BC)

Ask a retail investor what are the risks of his investment portfolio and he will say he owns USD30,000 in stocks and USD70,000 in bonds, and he is "diversified" and therefore "safe". A lay investor thinks in notional terms, but this can be misleading since two bonds of different duration have very different risks for the same notional exposure. This is because of the convexity behavior peculiar to bonds. The idea of duration, a better risk measure for bonds, was known to bankers as early as 1938.

In the equities world, two different stocks of the same notional amount can also give very different risk. Hence, the idea of using volatility as a risk measure was introduced by Harry Markowitz (1952). His mean-variance method not only canonized standard deviation as a risk measure but also introduced correlation and diversification within a unified framework. And modern portfolio theory was born. In 1963, William Sharpe introduced the single factor beta model. Now investors can compare the riskiness of individual stocks in units of beta relative to the overall market index.

The advent of options introduced yet another dimension of risk which notional alone fails to quantify, that of non-linearity. The Black-Scholes option pricing model (1973) introduced the so-called *Greeks*, a measurement of sensitivity to market parameters that influence a product's pricing, an idea that has gone beyond just option instruments. Risk managers now measure sensitivities to various parameters for every conceivable product and impose Greek limits on trading desks. The use of limits to control risk-taking gained acceptance in the mid 1980's but sensitivity has one blind spot—it is a local risk measure. Consider, for example, the delta of an option (i.e. option price sensitivity to a 1% change in spot) that has a strike near spot price. For a 10% adverse move in spot, the real loss incurred by the option is a lot larger than what is estimated by delta (i.e. 10 times delta). This missing risk is due to non-linearity, a behavior peculiar to all option products. The problem is more severe for options with complex (or "exotic") features.

The impasse was solved from the early 1990's by the use of stress tests. Here, the risk manager makes up (literally) a set of likely bad scenarios—say a 20% drop in stocks and a 1% rise in bond yield—and computes the actual loss of this scenario. While this full revaluation approach accounts for loss due to non-linearity, stress testing falls short of being the ideal *riskometer*—it is too subjective and it is a static risk measure—the result is not responsive to day-to-day market movements.

Then in 1994, JP Morgan came out with Riskmetrics©, a methodology that promotes the use of value-at-risk (VaR) as the industry standard for measuring market risk[1]. VaR is a user-determined loss quantile of a portfolio's return distribution. For example, if a bank chooses to use a 99%-VaR, this result represents the minimum loss a bank is expected to incur with a 1% probability.

---

[1] There are claims that some groups may have experimented with risk measures similar to VaR as early as 1991.

By introducing a rolling window of say 250 days to collect the distributional data, VaR becomes a dynamic risk measure that changes with new market conditions.

In 1995 the Basel Committee of Banking Supervision enshrined VaR as the de facto riskometer for its *Internal Model* approach for market risk. Under Basel II, all banks are expected to come up with their implementation of VaR (internal) models for computing minimum capital.

1.2 Taleb's Extremistan

The idea of *extremistan* was made popular by Nassim Taleb, author of the New York Times best seller, *The Black Swan*[2]. The book narrates the probabilistic nature of catastrophic events, and warns of the common misuse of statistics in understanding extreme events of low probability. It is uncanny that the book came out a few months before the subprime fiasco that marked the onset of the credit crisis.

The central idea is the distinction between two classes of probability structures—*mediocristan* and *extremistan*. Mediocristan deals with rare events that are *thin tailed* from a statistical distribution perspective. Large deviations can occur but they are inconsequential. Take for example the chance occurrence of a ten-foot bird, which has little impact on the ecosystem as a whole. Such distributions are well described by the (tail of) bell-shaped Gaussian statistics or modeled by random walk processes. On the other hand, extremistan events are *fat tailed*—low probability, high impact events. *Past occurrences offer no guidance on the magnitude of future occurrences.* This is a downer for risk management. The effect of the outcome is literally immeasurable. Some examples are World Wars, flu pandemic, ponzi schemes, wealth creation of the super rich, a breakthrough invention, etc.

A philosophical digression—mediocristan and extremistan are closely associated with scalability. In mediocristan, the outlier is not scalable—its influence is limited by physical, biological or environmental constraints. For example, our lone ten-foot bird cannot invade the whole ecosystem. Extremistan, in contrast, lies in the domain of scalability. For example, capitalism and free enterprise, if unrestrained by regulation, allow for limitless upside for the lucky few able to leverage off "other people's money (or time)". Because of scalability, financial

---

[2] Taleb, 2007, *The Black Swan: The Impact of the Highly Improbable.*

markets are extremistan—rare events of immeasurable devastation or *Black Swans* occur more often than predicted by thin tailed distributions.

Another reason why financial markets are more extremistic than nature is because they involve thinking participants. The inability of science to quantify its cause and effect has pushed the study of this phenomenon to the domain of behavioral finance, with expressions such as herd mentality, animal spirits, madness of the crowd, reflexivity, endogeneity of risk and positive feedback loops.

VaR is a victim of extremistan. Taleb, a strong critic of VaR, sees this method as a potentially dangerous malpractice[3]. The main problem is financial modelers are in love with Gaussian statistics where simplistic assumptions make models more tractable. This allows risk modelers to quantify (or estimate) with a high degree of precision, events which are by nature, immeasurable (extremistan). That can lead to a false sense of security in risk management. Taleb's extremistan, vindicated by the 2008 crisis, has dealt a serious blow to the pro-VaR camp.

This book introduces, *bubble VaR* (buVar), an extension of the VaR idea that denounces the common basic statistical assumptions (such as stationarity). It is fair to say that the only assumption made is that one cannot measure the true number. It is hypothetical and it is a moving target. In fact, we *need not* measure the true expected loss in order to invent an effective safeguard. This is what buVaR attempts to achieve.

1.3 The Turner Procyclicality

The idea of procyclicality is not new. In a consultative paper, Danielsson et al. (2001)[4] discussed procyclicality risk in the context of using credit ratings as input to regulatory capital computation as required under the Internal Rating Based (IRB) approach. Ratings tend to improve during an upturn of a business cycle and deteriorate during a downturn. If the minimum capital requirement is linked to ratings—requiring less capital when ratings are good—banks are encouraged to lend during an upturn and cut back loans during a downturn. Thus, the business cycle is self-reinforced artificially by policy. This has damaging effects during a downturn as margin and collateral are called back from other banks to meet higher regulatory minimum capital.

---

[3] See the discussion "Against Value-at-risk: Nassim Taleb replies to Phillip Jorion", Taleb, 1997.
[4] Danielsson et al, "An Academic Response to Basel II", Special Paper 130, ESRC Research Centre, 2001.

This danger is also highlighted in the now famous *Turner Review*[5] named after Sir Adair Turner, the new FSA chief tasked to reform the financial regulatory regime. The review has gone furthest to raise public awareness of hard-wired procyclicality as a key risk. It also correctly suggested that procyclicality is an inherent deficiency in the *VaR measure* as well. Plot any popular measure of VaR throughout a business cycle and you will notice that VaR is low when markets are rallying, and spikes up during a crisis.

This is similar to the *leverage effect* observed in the markets—rallies in stock indices are accompanied by low volatility and sell downs are accompanied by high volatility. From the reasoning of behavioral science, fear is a stronger sentiment than greed.

However, this is where the analogy ends. The leverage effect deals with the way *prices* behave, whereas VaR is a *measurement* device (which can be corrected). The Turner Review says our VaR riskometer is faulty—it contains hard-wired procyclicality. Compounding the problem is that trading positions are recorded using mark-to-market accounting. Hence, in a raging bull market, profits are realized and converted into additional capital for even more investment just as (VaR-based) regulatory capital requirement reduces. It is easy to see that this is a recipe for disaster—the rules of the game encourage banks to chase the bubble.

To mitigate the risk of procyclicality, the Turner Review calls for a longer observation period—the so-called "through the cycle" rather than "point in time" (what VaR is doing currently) measures of risk—as well as more stress tests. Some critics[6] argue that the correct solution is not simply to make the capital charge larger or more penal for banks, but also more timely. It is unavoidable that VaR based on short histories is procyclical, precisely because it gives a timely forecast. Efforts to dampen procyclicality by using a longer history will worsen the forecast; it is no longer market sensitive and timely.

As we shall see, buVaR addresses the procyclicality problem, by being countercyclical in design and yet without sacrificing timeliness.

1.4 The Commonsense of Bubble Value-at-Risk (buVaR)

The idea of buVar came from a simple observation: when markets crash, they fall downwards, rather than upwards (?). Yes, this basic asymmetry is overlooked by present day measures of risks. Let's think along.

---

[5] FSA, 2009, The *Turner Review- a regulatory response to the global banking crisis.*
[6] RiskMetrics Group, 2009, "VaR is from Mars, Capital is from Venus."

Even in the credit crisis in 2008 when credit spreads "crashed" upwards, that event came after a period of unsustainable credit spread compression. So, to be more precise, a market crash happens only after an unsustainable price rally or decline—often called a "bubble"—and in the opposite direction to the prevailing trend.

If this is a universal truth and there is overwhelming evidence that it is, then does it not make sense that market risk at point C is higher than at points A, B and D? (Figure 1-1). We know this intuitively and emotionally as well; suppose you do not have any trading views, then a purchase (or sale) of stocks at which level would make you lose sleep? Because while the bubbles are "obvious", when they will burst is not. Hence the trader's adage "the markets climb the wall of worry"[7].

Figure 1-1   Dow Jones index

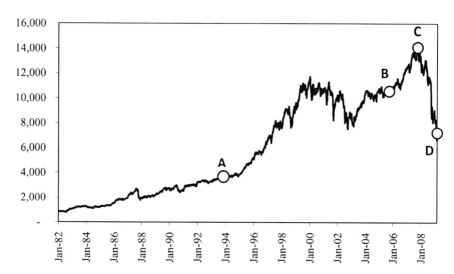

Yet conventional measure of risk, VaR, does not account for this obvious asymmetry. Table 1-1 compares the 97.5% VaR[8] for the Dow Jones index at various points. Notice that A, B and C have about the same risks.

---

[7] This is supported by empirical evidence that put-call ratios tend to rise as stock market bubbles peak. This is the ratio of premium between equally out-of-money puts and calls, and is a well-studied indicator of "fears of a crash".

[8] The VaR is computed using a 250-day observation period, and expressed as a percentage loss of the index. VaR should always be understood as a loss; sometimes a negative sign is used to denote the loss.

Table 1-1   97.5% Value-at-risk for Dow Jones Index using historical simulation

Point in time	97.5% VAR (weekly)	VAR (mean adjusted)	Maximum weekly drawdown	Max weekly drawdown (St. Dev)
A	-2.3%	-2.5%	-3.4%	2.7
B	-3.3%	-3.4%	-3.6%	2.1
C	-3.2%	-3.5%	-4.3%	2.5
D	-6.4%	-5.8%	-20.0%	6.9

Only *after* the crash (at D) does VaR register any meaningful increase in risks. It's like a lighthouse that switches on upon contact with a ship! It seems VaR is reactive rather than preventive. What happened?

Figure 1-2   Crude oil price (in US dollars)

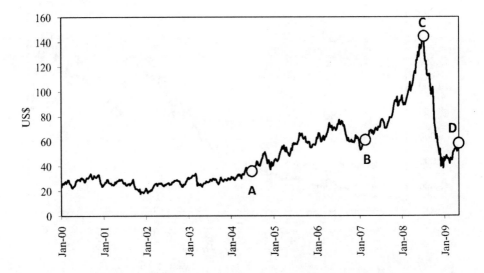

Table 1-2   97.5% Value at risk for Crude Oil Price

Point in time	97.5% VAR (weekly)	VAR (mean adjusted)	Maximum weekly drawdown	Max weekly drawdown (St. Dev)
A	-8.2%	-8.5%	-25.4%	6.0
B	-7.1%	-7.3%	-9.0%	2.5
C	-6.4%	-7.0%	-9.0%	2.5
D	-13.7%	-13.6%	-29.7%	4.4

The same situation can also be observed for Brent crude oil prices (Figure 1-2 and Table 1-2). Is VaR just a "peace-time" tool? The root cause can be traced back to model assumptions.

VaR and most risk models used by banks assume returns are *independent and identically distributed* (or i.i.d.), meaning that each return event is not affected by past returns, yet they are identical (in distribution)! As a result, the return time series is *stationary*. Here stationary means, if you take, say, a 250-day rolling window of daily returns, its distribution looks the same in terms of behavior whether you observe the rolling window today, a week ago, or at any date. In other words, the distribution is *time invariant*. Let's look at one such time series, the 1-day *returns* of the Dow Jones index (Figure 1-3). Compared to Figure 1-1, the trend has been removed completely (*de-trended* by taking the daily change); you are left with wiggles which look almost identical anywhere along the time scale (say at A, B or C) and almost *symmetrical* about zero. At D, risk is higher only because it wiggles more.

Figure 1-3   Daily price change of Dow Jones index

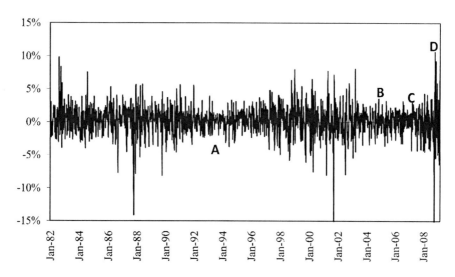

VaR models are built on statistics of only these de-trended wiggles. Information on price levels even if they contain telltale signs—such as the formation of bubbles, a price run-up, widening of spreads—are ignored (they do not meet the requirement of i.i.d.). VaR is truly nothing more than the science of wiggles. The i.i.d. assumption lends itself to a lot of mathematical tractability. It gives modelers a high degree of precision in their predictions[9]. Unfortunately precision does not equate to accuracy. To see the difference between precision and accuracy, look at the bull's eye diagrams in Figure 1-4. The right side diagram illustrates the "shot gun" approach to getting the correct answer—accurate but not precise. Accuracy is the degree of authenticity while precision is the degree of reproducibility.

In risk measurement, Keynes's dictum is spot on: "it is clearly better to be approximately right, than to be precisely wrong". The gross underestimation of risk by VaR during the credit crisis, a Black Swan event, is a painful objective lesson for banks and regulators. 2008 challenges the very foundation of VaR and is a wake-up call to consider exploring beyond the restrictive, albeit convenient, assumption of i.i.d. BuVaR is one such initiative.

Figure 1-4   Precision vs. accuracy

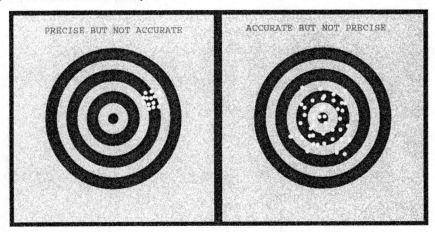

The Turner Review calls for the creation of countercyclical capital buffers on a global scale. It will be ideal if we have a VaR system which automatically penalizes the bank—by inflating—when positions are long during a "bubble" rally, and continues to penalize the bank during a crash. Then when the crash is over and the market overshoots on the downside, VaR penalizes the short side positions instead. As we shall learn, buVaR does this—it is an asymmetrical, preventive and countercyclical risk measure that discourages position taking in the direction of a bubble.

---

[9] By assuming i.i.d., the return time series becomes stationary. This allows the Law of large numbers to apply. This Law states that, as more data is collected, the sample mean will converge to a stable expected value. This gives the statistician the ability to predict (perform estimation) with a stated, often high, level of precision.

Figure 1-5 is a preview of buVaR versus VaR[10] for the Dow Jones index during the recent credit crisis. VaR is perpetually late during a crisis and does not differentiate between long and short positions. BuVaR peaks ahead of the crash (is countercyclical) and is always larger than VaR, to buffer against the risk of a crash on one side. It recognizes that the "crash" risk faced by long and short positions are unequal. Used for capital purposes, it will penalize positions which are chasing an asset bubble more than contrarian positions.

Figure 1-5 BuVaR and VaR comparison

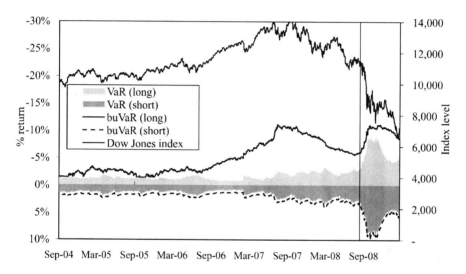

If implemented on a global scale, buVaR would have the effect of regulating and dampening the market cycle. Perhaps then, this new framework echoes the venerable philosophy of the FED:

"It's the job of the FED to take away the punch bowl just as the party gets going." (William McChesney Martin Jr. FED Chairman 1951-1970)

In order to internalize the idea of risk, this book takes the reader through the developmental path of VaR starting from its mathematical foundation to its advanced forms. In this journey, fault lines and weaknesses of this methodology are uncovered and discussed. This will set the stage for the new approach, buVaR.

---

[10] The VaR is computed by the Riskmetrics method using exponentially decaying weights.

Chapter 2 goes into the foundational mathematics of VaR with emphasis on intuition and concepts rather than mathematical rigor.

Chapter 3 introduces the basic building blocks used in VaR. The conventional VaR systems are then formalized in Chapter 4. At the end of the chapter, readers will be able to calculate VaR on a simple spreadsheet and experiment with the various nuances of VaR.

Chapter 5 discusses some advanced VaR models developed by the academia in the last decade. They are interesting and promising, and are selected to give the reader a flavor of current risk research.

Chapter 6 deals with the tools used by banks for VaR reporting. It also contains a prelude to the Basel Rules used to compute minimum capital.

Chapter 7 explores the phenomenology of risks. In particular, it details the inherent weaknesses of VaR and the dangers of extreme risks not captured by VaR.

Chapter 8 covers the statistical tests used to measure the goodness of a VaR model.

Chapter 9 discusses the weaknesses of VaR which are not of a theoretical nature. These are practical problems commonly encountered in VaR implementation.

Since this book deals primarily with market risk, Chapter 10 is a minor digression devoted to other (non-market) risk classes. A broad understanding is necessary for the reader to appreciate the academic quest (and industry's ambition) for a unified risk framework where all risks are modeled under one umbrella.

Chapter 11 gives a brief history of the Basel capital framework. It then proceeds to summarize the key regulatory reforms that were introduced in 2009 – 2010.

Chapter 12 discusses developments in measuring and detecting systemic risks. These are recent research initiatives by regulators who are concerned about global crisis contagion. Network models are introduced with as little math as possible. The aim is to give the reader a foretaste of this important direction of development.

The final part of this book, part IV—spanning 5 chapters in total—introduces various topics of bubble-VaR. Chapter 13 lays the conceptual framework for buVaR, formalized for market risk.

Chapter 14 shows that with a slight modification, the buVaR idea can be expanded to cover credit risks, including default risk.

Chapter 15 contains the results of various empirical tests of the effectiveness of buVaR.

Chapter 16 is a concluding chapter that covers miscellaneous topics for bu-VaR. In particular, it summarizes how buVaR is able to meet the ideals proposed by the Turner Review.

Lastly, Chapter 17 lists suggestions for future research. It is a wish-list for buVaR which is beyond the scope of this volume.

Chapter 2

Essential Mathematics

This chapter provides the statistical concepts essential for the understanding of risk management. There are many good textbooks on the topic, see Carol Alexander (2008). Here, we have chosen to adopt a *selective approach*. Our goal is to provide adequate math background to understand the rest of the book. It is fair to say that if you do not find it here, it is not needed later. As mentioned in the preface, this book tells a story. In fact, the math here is part of the plot. Therefore, we will include philosophy or principles of statistical thinking and other pertinent topics that will contribute to the development of the story. And we will not sidetrack the reader with unneeded theorems and lemmas.

Throughout this book, ideas are also formulated in the syntax of Excel functions so that the reader can easily implement examples in a spreadsheet. Important case studies and examples are included as Excel spreadsheets at the end of each chapter and can be downloaded from the companion website:

www.bubble-value-at-risk.com

Excel is an excellent platform to perform simulations and visualization—useful learning tools for a risk manager to develop practical intuition.

2.1 Frequentist Statistics

Two schools of thought have emerged from the history of statistics—frequentist and Bayesian schools of thought. Bayesians and frequentists hold very different philosophical views on what defines probability. From a frequentist perspective, probability is *objective* and can be inferred from the frequency of observation in a large number of trials. All parameters and unknowns that characterize an assumed distribution or regression relationship can be backed out from the sample data. Frequentists will base their interpretations on a limited sample; as we shall see, there is a limit to how much data they can collect without running into other practical difficulties. Frequentists will assume the true value of their estimate lies within the confidence interval that they set (typically at 95%). To qualify their estimate, they will perform hypothesis testing which will (or will not) reject their estimate, in which case they will assume the estimate as false (or true).

Bayesians, on the other hand, interpret the concept of probability as "a measure of a state of knowledge or personal belief" that can be updated on arrival of more information (i.e. incorporates learning). Bayesians embrace the universality of imperfect knowledge. Hence probability is *subjective*; beliefs and "expert judgment" are permissible inputs to the model and are also expressed in terms of probability distributions. As mentioned earlier, a frequentist hypothesis (or estimate) is either true or false but in Bayesian statistics the hypothesis is also assigned a probability.

VaR falls under the domain of frequentist statistics—inferences are backed out from data alone. The risk manager, by legacy of industry development, is a frequentist[1].

A random variable or *stochastic* variable (often just called variable) is a variable that has an uncertain value in the future. Contrast this to a *deterministic* variable in physics; for example the future position of a planet can be determined (calculated) to an exact value using Newton's laws. But in financial markets, the price of a stock tomorrow is unknown and can only be *estimated* using statistics.

Let X be a random variable. The observation of X (data point) obtained by the act of sampling is denoted with a lower case letter x_i as a convention, where the subscript $i=1,2,\ldots$, is a running index representing the number of observations. In general, X can be anything—price sequences, returns, heights of a group of people, a sample of dice tosses, income samples of a population, etc. In finance, variables are usually price (levels) or returns (changes in levels). We shall discuss the various types of returns later and their subtle differences. Unless mentioned otherwise, we shall talk about returns as daily percentage change in prices. In VaR, the data set we will be working with is primarily distributions of sample returns and distributions of profit and loss (PL).

Figure 2-1 is a plot of the frequency distribution (or *histogram*) of S&P 500 index returns using 500 days data (Jul 2007 – Jun 2009). One can think of this as a *probability* distribution of events—each day's return being a single event. So as we obtain more and more data (trials), we get closer to the correct estimate of the "true" distribution.

---

[1] "Plight of the fortune tellers: Why we need to manage financial risk differently" by Riccardo Rebonato (2007) challenges the frequentist paradigm and advocates the Bayesian alternative. The book introduces (without using equations) potential use of subjective probability and decision theory in risk management.

We posit that this distribution contains all available information about risks of a particular market. In so doing, we have implicitly assumed that the past is an accurate guide to future risks, at least for the next immediate time step. This is a necessary (though arguable) assumption, otherwise without an intelligent structure, forecasting would be no different from fortune telling.

Figure 2-1 S&P 500 Index frequency distribution

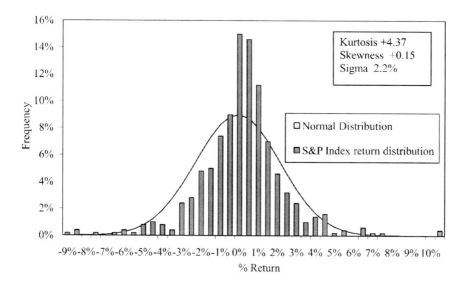

In risk management, we want to estimate four properties of the return distribution—the so-called first four moments—mean, variance, skewness and kurtosis. To be sure, higher moments exist mathematically but they are not intuitive and hence of lesser interest.

The mean of a random variable X is also called the *expectation* or *expected value*, written $\mu = E(X)$. The *mean* or *average* of a sample $x_1, \ldots, x_n$ is just the sum of all the data divided by the number of observations n. It is denoted by $\bar{x}$ or $\hat{\mu}$.

$$\bar{x} = \frac{1}{n}\sum_{i=1}^{n} x_i \tag{2.1}$$

The Excel function is AVERAGE(..). It measures the center location of a sample. A word on statistical notation—generally, when we consider the actual *parameter* in question μ (a theoretical idea), we want to measure this parameter using an *estimator* $\hat{\mu}$ (a formula). The outcome of this measurement is called an *estimate*, also denoted $\hat{\mu}$ (a value). Note the use of the ^ symbol henceforth.

The *k'th moment* of a sample $x_1, \ldots, x_n$ is defined and estimated as:

$$\frac{1}{(n-1)} \sum_{i=1}^{n} (x_i - \bar{x})^k \qquad (2.2)$$

The *variance* or second moment of a sample is defined as the average of the squared distances to the mean:

$$\hat{\sigma}^2 = \frac{1}{n-1} \sum_{i=1}^{n} (x_i - \bar{x})^2 \qquad (2.3)$$

The Excel function is VAR(..). It represents the dispersion from the mean. The square-root of variance is called the *standard deviation* or sigma σ. In risk management, *risk* is usually defined as uncertainty in returns, and is measured in terms of sigma. The Excel function is STDEV(..).

The *skewness* or third moment (divided by $\hat{\sigma}^3$) measures the degree of asymmetry about the mean of the sample distribution. A positive (negative) skew means the distribution slants to the right (left). The Excel function is SKEW(..).

$$skewness = \frac{1}{n-1} \sum_{i=1}^{n} (x_i - \bar{x})^3 \cdot \frac{1}{\hat{\sigma}^3} \qquad (2.4)$$

The *kurtosis* or fourth moment (divided by $\hat{\sigma}^4$) measures the "peakness" of the sample distribution and is given by:

$$kurtosis = \frac{1}{n-1} \sum_{i=1}^{n} (x_i - \bar{x})^4 \cdot \frac{1}{\hat{\sigma}^4} \qquad (2.5)$$

Since the total area under the probability distribution must sum up to a total probability of 1, a very peakish distribution will naturally have *fatter tails*. Such a behavior is called *leptokurtic*. Its Excel function is KURT(..). A normal distribution has a kurtosis of 3. For convenience, Excel shifts the KURT(..)

function such that a normal distribution gives an *excess kurtosis* of 0. We will follow this convention and simply call it kurtosis for brevity.

Back to Figure 2-1, the S&P distribution is overlaid with a normal distribution (of the same variance) for comparison. Notice the sharp central peak above the normal line, and the more frequent than normal observations in the left and right tails. The sample period (Jul 2007 – Jun 2009) corresponds to the credit crisis—as expected the distribution is fat tailed. Interestingly, the distribution is not symmetric—it is positively skewed! (We shall see why in Section 7.1.)

2.2 Just Assumptions

i.i.d. and Stationarity

This is a pillar assumption for most statistical modeling. A random sample $(y_1, \ldots, y_n)$ of size n is *independent and identically distributed* (or i.i.d.) if each observation in the sample belongs to the same probability distribution as all others, and all are mutually independent. Imagine yourself drawing random numbers from a distribution. Identical means each draw must come from the *same* distribution (it need not even be bell-shaped). Independent means you must *not meddle* with each draw, like making the next random draw a function of the previous draw. For example, a sample of coin tosses is i.i.d.

A *time series* is a sequence $X_1, \ldots, X_t$ of random variables indexed by time. A time series is *stationary* if the distribution of $(X_1, \ldots, X_t)$ is identical to that of $(X_{1+k}, \ldots, X_{t+k})$ for all t and all positive integer k. In other words, the distribution is invariant under time shift k. Since it is difficult to prove empirically, that two distributions are identical (in every aspect), in financial modeling, we content ourselves with just showing that the first two moments—mean and variance—are invariant under time shift[2]. This condition is called *weakly stationary* (often just called stationary) and is a common assumption.

A market price series is seldom stationary—trends and periodic components make the time series non-stationary. However, if we take the percentage change or take the *first difference*, this *price change* can be shown to be often stationary. This process is called *de-trending* (of *differencing*) a time series and is a common practice.

---

[2] To be precise, the mean does not depend on t and the autocovariance $COV(X_t, X_{t+k})$ is constant for any time lag k.

Figure 2-2 illustrates a dummy price series and its corresponding return series. We divide the 200-day period into two 100-day periods, and compute the
first two moments. For the price series, the mean moved from 4693 (first half) to
5109 (second half). Likewise, the standard deviation changed from 50 to 212.
Clearly the price series is non-stationary. The return series, on the other hand, is
stationary—its mean and standard deviation remained roughly unchanged at 0%
and 0.5% respectively in both periods. Visually a stationary time series always
look like "white noise".

Figure 2-2 Dummy price and return series

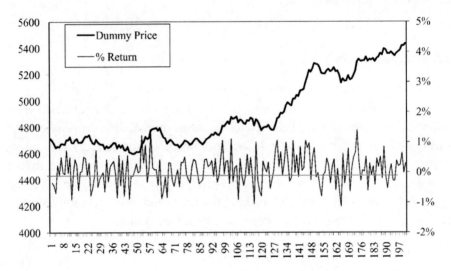

An i.i.d. process will be stationary for finite distributions[3]. The benefit of the
stationarity assumption is we can then invoke the *Law of Large Numbers* to
estimate properties such as mean and variance in a tractable way.

Law of Large Numbers

Expected values can be estimated by sampling. Let X be a random variable and
suppose we want to estimate the expected value of some function $g(X)$, where
the expected value is $\mu_g \equiv E(g(X))$. We sample for n observations x_i of X where
$i=1, \ldots, n$. The Law of Large Numbers states that if the sample is i.i.d. then:

---

[3] A finite distribution is one whereby its variance does not go to infinity.

$$\lim_{n \to \infty} \frac{1}{n} \sum g(x_i) = \mu_g \qquad (2.6)$$

For example, in equations (2.3) to (2.5) used to estimate the moments, as we take larger and larger samples, precision improves, our estimate converges to the ("true") expected value. We say our estimate is *consistent*. On the other hand, if the sample is not i.i.d., one cannot guarantee the estimate will always converge (it may or may not); the forecast is said to be inconsistent.

Let's look at some examples. We have a coin flip (head +1, tail -1), a *return* series of a standard normal $N(0,1)$ process and a *return* series of an autoregressive process called AR(1). The first two are known i.i.d. processes; the AR(1) is not i.i.d. (it depends on the previous random variable) and is generated using:

AR(1) process: $X_t = k_0 + k_1 X_{t-1} + \varepsilon_t$ (2.7)

where k_1 is a constant and ε_t, $t=1,2,..$ is a sequence of i.i.d. random variable with zero mean and a finite variance, also known as *white noise*. Under certain conditions (i.e. $|k_1|>1$), the AR(1) process becomes non-stationary.

Figure 2-3 Behavior of mean estimates as number of trials increase

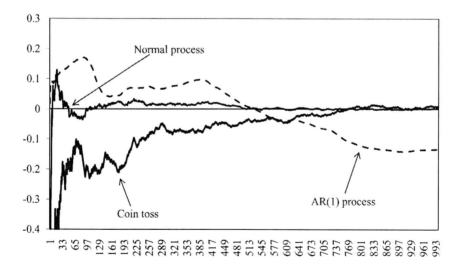

Figure 2-3 illustrates the estimation of the expected value of the 3 processes using 1000 simulations. For AR(1), we set $k_0=0$, $k_1=0.99$. The coin flip and

normal process both converge to zero (the expected value) as *n* increases, but the AR(1) does not. See Spreadsheet 2.1.

Figure 2-4 plots the return series for both the normal process and the AR(1) process. Notice there is some "non-stationary" pattern in the AR(1) plot, whereas the normal process shows characteristic "white noise".

Figure 2-4 Return time series for normal and AR(1) processes.

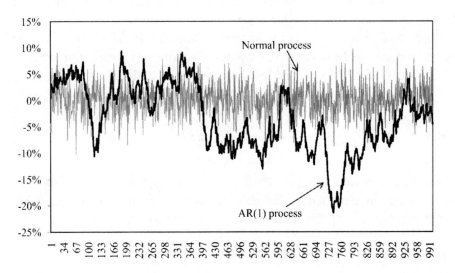

To "ensure" stationarity, risk modelers usually de-trend the price data and model changes instead. In contrast, *technical analysis* (TA) has always modeled *prices*. This is a well-accepted technique for speculative trading since the 1960's after the ticker tape machine became obsolete. Dealing with non-i.i.d. data does not make TA any less effective. It does, however, mean that the method is less consistent in a statistical sense. Thus, TA has always been regarded as unscientific by academia.

In fact, it would seem that the popular and persistent use of TA (such as in program trading) by the global trading community, has made its effectiveness self-fulfilling and the market returns more persistent (and less i.i.d.). Market momentum is a known fact. Ignoring it by de-trending and assuming returns are i.i.d. does not make risk measurement more scientific. There is no compelling reason why risk management cannot borrow some of the modelling techniques of TA such as that pertaining to momentum and cycles. From an epistemology perspective, such debate can be seen as a tacit choice between intuitive knowledge (heuristics) and mathematical correctness.

PDF and CDF

In practice, moments are computed using discrete data from an observed frequency distribution (like the histogram in Figure 2-1). However, it is intuitive and often necessary to think in terms of an abstract continuous distribution. In the continuous world, frequency distribution is replaced by *probability density function* (PDF). If $f(x)$ is a PDF of a random variable X, then the probability that X is between some numbers a and b is the area under the graph $f(x)$ between a and b. In other words,

$$P(a < X < b) = \int_a^b f(u)du \qquad (2.8)$$

where $f(.)$ is understood to be a function of x here. The probability density function $f(x)$ has the following intuitive properties:

$$f(x) \geq 0 \text{ ; for all x} \qquad (2.9)$$

$$\int_{-\infty}^{\infty} f(u)du = 1 \qquad (2.10)$$

The *cumulative distribution function* (CDF) is defined as:

$$F(x) = \int_{-\infty}^{x} f(u)du \qquad (2.11)$$

It is the probability of observing the variable having values at or below x, written $F(x)= \Pr[X \leq x]$. As shown in Figure 2-5, $F(x)$ is just the area under the graph $f(x)$ at a particular value x.

Normal Distribution

The most important continuous distribution is the *normal distribution* a.k.a. *Gaussian distribution*. Among many bell-shaped distributions, this famous one describes amazingly well physical characteristics of natural phenomena such as

Bubble Value-at-Risk

the biological growth of plants and animals, the so-called Brownian motion of gas, the outcome of casino games, etc. It seems logical to assume that a distribution that describes science so accurately should also be applicable in the human sphere of trading.

Figure 2-5 Density function and distribution function

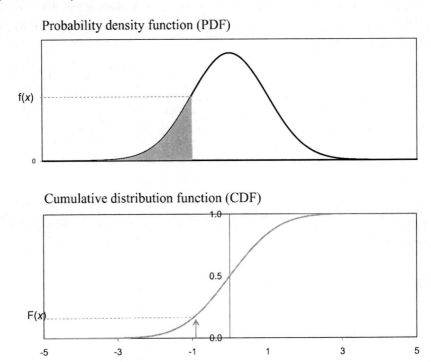

The normal distribution can be described fully by just two parameters—its mean μ and variance σ^2. Its PDF is given by:

$$f(x) = \frac{1}{\sqrt{2\pi\sigma^2}}\exp[-\frac{1}{2\sigma^2}(x-\mu)^2] \tag{2.12}$$

The normal distribution is written in shorthand as $X{\sim}N(\mu,\ \sigma^2)$. The *standard normal*, defined as a normal distribution with mean zero and variance 1, is a convenient simplification for modeling purposes. We denote a random variable ε as following a standard normal distribution by $\varepsilon{\sim}N(0,1)$.

Figure 2-6 plots the standard normal distribution. Note that it is symmetric about the mean; it has skewness 0 and kurtosis 3 (or 0 excess kurtosis in Excel convention).

How do we interpret the idea of one standard deviation σ for $N(\mu, \sigma^2)$? It means 68% of its observations (area under $f(x)$) lies in the interval $[-\sigma, +\sigma]$ and 95% of the observations lies within $[-2\sigma, +2\sigma]$. Under normal conditions, a stock's daily return will fluctuate between -2σ and 2σ roughly 95% of the time, or roughly 237 days out of 250 trading days per year, as a rule of thumb.

Figure 2-6 Standard normal probability density function

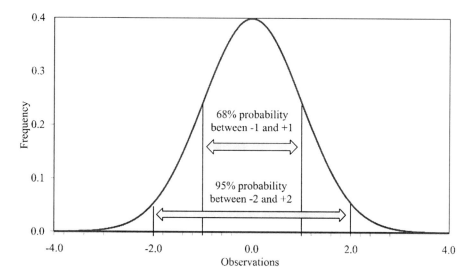

Central Limit Theorem

The *central limit theorem* (CLT) is a very fundamental result. It states that the mean of a sample of i.i.d. distributed random variables (regardless of distribution shape) will converge to the normal distribution as the number of samples becomes very large. Hence, the normal distribution is the limiting distribution for the mean. See Spreadsheet 2.2 for an illustration.

The CLT is a very useful result—it means that if you have a very large portfolio of assets, regardless of how each asset's returns is distributed (some may be fat-tailed, others may be skewed, yet another may be uniform) the average portfolio return behaves like a normal distribution. The only catch is that all the assets must be independent of each other (even though at times it is not).

We summarize the advantages of the normal distribution that make it widely used in financial models:
1. By CLT, it is the limiting distribution for large systems.
2. You can describe all its characteristics with just two parameters, μ and σ.
3. A linear combination (addition) of normally distributed random variables is also normally distributed. This makes standard deviation σ sub-additive which is a nice feature for risk measurement (see Section 2.8).
4. It is widely applicable in science, and financial markets are shown to be Gaussian under most (although not all) situations.

2.3 Quantiles, VaR and Tails

A *quantile* is a statistical way to divide ordered data into essentially equal-sized data subsets. For n data points and any q between [0,1], the q-th quantile is the number x such that qn of the data points are less than x and $(1-q)n$ of the data is greater than x. The *median* is just the special case of a quantile where q=0.5. Note that the median is not the same as the mean especially for a skewed distribution.

To obtain the quantile from the CDF (lower panel of Figure 2-5) follow the horizontal line from the vertical axis. When you reach the CDF, the value at the horizontal axis is the quantile. In other words, the quantile is just the inverse function of the CDF, or $F^{-1}(x)$. The Excel function is PERCENTILE($\{x\},q$).

VaR is a statistical measure of risk based on *loss* quantiles. It measures market risk on a total portfolio basis taking into account diversification and leverage. VaR of confidence level c% is defined[4] as:

$$\Pr(X \leq VaR) = q \qquad (2.13)$$

where q=1-c is the quantile and X is the return random variable.

There are three possible interpretations of VaR. Consider a 95% VaR of $1 million; it could mean:
1. 95% chance of losing up to $1 million in the next day (maximum loss).
2. 5% chance that the loss is at least $1 million in the next one day (minimum loss).
3. 5% chance that the loss is greater than $1 million in the next one day (loss beyond).

---

[4] Unless mentioned otherwise, in this book we will retain the negative sign for the VaR number to denote loss (or negative P&L), to follow the convention used in most banks.

Interestingly, all three mean the same thing mathematically but reflect the mental bias we have. See Figure 2-7. In light of the 2008 crisis and the criticism of VaR, it seems the more conservative interpretation (3) is appropriate. Regardless, VaR is certainly *not* the expected loss.

Figure 2-7 Different interpretations of VaR

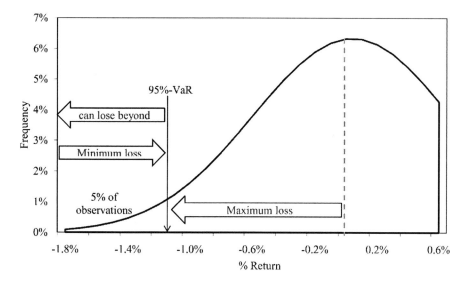

Since key decision-makers in banks are often not experts from the risk management department, knowledge gaps may exist. It was argued that the ignorance of what VaR truly represents encouraged a false sense of security that things were under control during the run-up and subsequent crash in the 2008 credit crisis. See Section 13.1.

The target horizon of concern for banks is usually the next one day. That means we need to work with daily returns. Regulators normally stipulate a 10-day horizon for the purpose of capital computation, so the daily VaR is scaled up to 10 days. For limits monitoring and regulatory capital, VaR is often reported in dollar amounts by portfolios. For risk comparison between individual markets, talking in units of sigma (σ) or percentage loss is often more intuitive.

As a convention, the VaR confidence level c is defined on the left tail of the distribution. Hence, 97.5%-VaR or $c = 0.975$ means the quantile of interest is $q = (1-0.975) = 0.025$.

Banks can choose the observation period (or *window length*) and confidence level c for their VaR. This is a balancing act. The window must be short enough to make VaR sensitive to market changes, yet long enough to be statistically meaningful. Likewise, if the confidence level is too high, there are too few observations in the left tail to give statistically meaningful inferences.

Figure 2-8 is an example of the return distribution of the S&P 500 taken over a 500-day window (Jan05 - Dec06). We overlay with a normal distribution line to show that the stock market behavior was reasonably Gaussian during non-crisis periods. From this data, we can calculate VaR in a few ways using Excel:

1. Assume the normal distribution. Then the 0.025 quantile is roughly two times σ. You can check this on Excel: NORMSINV(0.025) = -1.96. Thus, VaR is -1.96*STDEV(..) = 1.2% loss.
2. Take the 0.025 quantile. VaR is PERCENTILE(.,0.025) = -1.2% loss.
3. There are 0.025*500 =12.5 observations at the tail to the left of the VaR cutoff. So we can approximate VaR by the 13th largest loss computed using Excel function SMALL(.,13) = -1.3% loss.

Figure 2-8 Return distribution of S&P 500 Index (Jan05-Dec06)

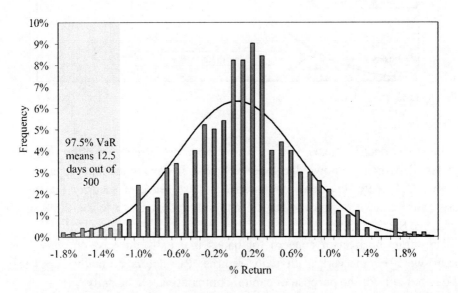

Note the 1.2% loss is the *daily* VaR. VaR, like volatility, is often quoted in annualized terms. Assuming a normal distribution and 250 business days for a typical trading year, the annual VaR is given by 1.2%*√250 = 19%. (Section 6.4 covers such time scaling.)

From experience, a window length of 250 days and a 97.5%-VaR can be a reasonable choice. Unless stated otherwise, we will use this choice throughout this book.

Note that VaR does not really model the behavior of the left tail of the distribution. It is a *point estimate*, a convenient proxy to represent our knowledge of the probability distribution for the purpose of decision-making. Because it is just a quantile cutoff, VaR is oblivious to observations to its left. These *exceedences* (nq =12 of them in the above example) can be distributed in any number of ways without having an impact on the VaR number. As we shall learn in Chapter 5, there are commendable efforts to model the left tail, but exceedences have so far remained elusive. This is the dangerous domain of extremistan.

2.4 Correlation and Autocorrelation

Correlation

Correlation measures the linear dependency between two variables. In financial applications, these are usually asset return time series. Understanding how one asset "co-varies" with another is key to understanding hedging between a pair of assets and risk diversification within a portfolio.

The *covariance* between two random variables X and Y is defined as:

$$Cov(x, y) = \sigma_{XY} = E(XY) - E(X)E(Y) \qquad (2.14)$$

Given two sets of observed samples $\{x_i\}$ and $\{y_i\}$ where i=1, . . ,n, we can estimate their covariance using:

$$\hat{\sigma}_{XY} = \frac{1}{n-1}\sum_{i=1}^{n}(x_i - \bar{x})(y_i - \bar{y}) \qquad (2.15)$$

where n is the number of observations, $\bar{x}$ and $\bar{y}$ are the sample means of X and Y respectively. The Excel function is COVAR(..).

Then *correlation* (sometimes called *Pearson's* or *linear correlation*) is just covariance standardized so that it is unitless and falls in the interval [-1, 1].

$$\rho(X,Y) = \frac{Cov(X,Y)}{\sigma_X \sigma_Y} \qquad (2.16)$$

A correlation of +1 means two assets move perfectly in tandem, whereas a correlation of -1 means that they move perfectly inversely relative to each other. A correlation of 0 means the two return variables are *independent*. Correlation in the data (i.e. association) does not imply causation, although causation will imply correlation. Correlation measures the sign (or direction) of asset movements but not the magnitudes. The Excel function is CORREL(..).

Linear correlation is a fundamental concept in Markowitz portfolio theory (see Section 2.8) and is widely used in portfolio risk management. But correlation is a minefield for the unaware. A very good paper by Embrechts et al. (1999) documented the pitfalls of correlation. Here we will go over the main points by looking at the bivariate case; the technical reader is recommended to read that paper.

For correlation to be problem-free, not only must X and Y be normally distributed, their *joint distributions* must also be normally distributed. More generally, the joint distribution must be an *elliptical* distribution, of which the multivariate normal is a special case. In our bivariate case, this means the contour line of its 2D plot traces out an ellipse[5]. See Figure 2-9. Both diagrams—one actual, one simulated—are generated using $N(0,1)$ with $\rho=0.7$.

Figure 2-9 An elliptical joint distribution

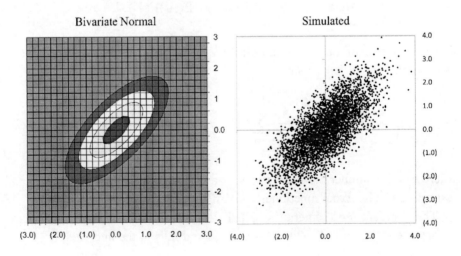

[5] For *N*-variate joint distribution, imagine an object of *N*-dimensions which when projected onto any two dimensional plane casts an elliptical shadow.

As long as the joint distribution is not elliptical, linear correlation will be a bad measure of dependency. It helps to remember that correlation only measures clustering around a straight line. Figure 2-10 shows two obviously non-elliptical distributions even though they show the same correlation (ρ=0.7) as Figure 2-9. Clearly correlation, as a scalar (single number) representation of dependency, tells us very little about the shape (and hence joint risk) of the joint distribution. Correlation is also very sensitive to extreme values or outliers. If we remove the few outliers (bottom right) in the right panel of Figure 2-10, the correlation increases drastically from 0.7 to 0.95.

Figure 2-11, left panel shows the actual joint distribution of Lehman 5-year CDS spread and Morgan Stanley 5-year CDS spread. During normal times (the shaded zone) the distribution is reasonably elliptical, but during times of stress the outliers show otherwise.

Figure 2-10 Non-elliptical joint distributions

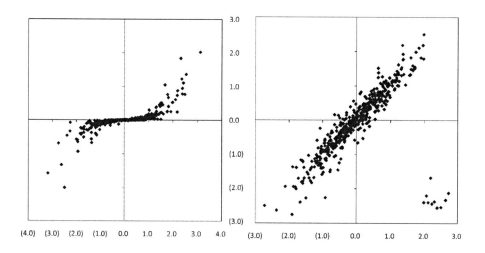

Let's summarize key weaknesses of linear correlation when used on non-elliptical distributions:

1 Correlation is a scalar measure. It tells us nothing about the shape (or structure) of the joint distribution.

2 Our interpretation of correlation on a scale from -1 to 1 becomes inconsistent. Perfect dependency does not necessarily show ρ=1 and perfect inverse dependency does not necessarily show ρ= -1.

3 Correlation of zero no longer implies that the two return variables are independent.

4   Correlation changes under transformation of risks. This means that if X and Y are correlated by ρ, it does not follow that functions $g(X)$ and $g(Y)$ are correlated by ρ. In practice, $g(.)$ could be a pricing formula.

5   Correlation is unsuitable for fat tail events because the variances can appear infinite. By (2.16), correlation is undefined. This is the extremistan zone.

An alternative measure of dependency, *rank correlation*, can solve problems 2, 4 and 5. Unfortunately, rank correlations cannot be applied to the Markowitz portfolio framework. They are still useful, though, as standalone correlation measures.

We introduce two rank correlations: Kendall's tau and Spearman's rho. Suppose we have n pairs of observations $\{x_1, y_1\}, \ldots, \{x_n, y_n\}$ of the random variables X and Y. The i'th pair and j'th pair are said to be *concordant* if $(x_i\text{-}x_j)(y_i\text{-}y_j)>0$, and *discordant* if $(x_i\text{-}x_j)(y_i\text{-}y_j)<0$. The sample estimate of Kendall's tau is computed by comparing all possible pairs of observations (where $i{\neq}j$), and there are $0.5n(n\text{-}1)$ pairs.

Kendall's tau: $$\hat{\tau} = \frac{c - d}{0.5n(n - 1)}$$ (2.17)

where c is the number of concordant pairs and d the number of discordant pairs.

The sample estimate of the Spearman's rho is calculated by applying the Pearson's (linear) correlation on the ranked paired data:

Spearman's rho: $$\hat{\rho}_s = Correlation(rank(x), rank(y))$$ (2.18)

where $rank(x)$ is a n-vector containing the ranks[6] of $\{x_i\}$ and similarly for $rank(y)$. This can be written in Excel function as: CORREL(RANK(x, x),RANK(y, y)).

Figure 2-11, right panel shows a bivariate distribution that has perfect correlation since all pairs are concordant. Kendall's tau is 1.0, Spearman's rho is 1.0 but linear correlation gives 0.9. This illustrates weakness (2). One can easily illustrate weakness (4) as well as shown in Spreadsheet 2.3.

A more correct but complicated measure of association is by using the *copula function* (not covered here). A copula is a function that links the marginal distributions (or standalone distribution) to form a joint distribution. If we can

---

[6] For example, $rank(0.5, 0.2, 0.34, -0.23, 0) = (1, 3, 2, 5, 4)$

fully specify the functional form of the N-dimensional joint distribution of N assets in a portfolio, and specify the marginal distributions of each asset, then we can use the copula function to tell us useful information about risk of this system. Clearly, this is a difficult task to say the least. In the absence of such perfect knowledge, a risk manager has to rely on linear and rank correlations. He has to be mindful of the limitations of these imperfect tools.

Figure 2-11 (Left panel) Joint return distribution of credit spreads. (Right panel) Perfect dependency shows 1.0 rank correlation.

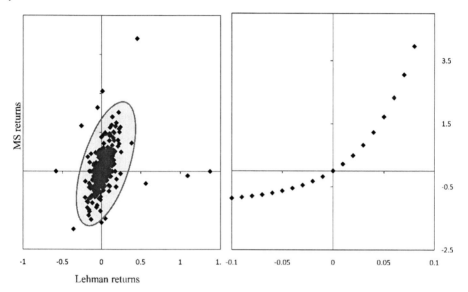

Autocorrelation

Autocorrelation is a useful extension of the correlation idea. For a time series variable Y_t the autocorrelation of lag k is defined as:

$$\rho(Y_t, Y_{t-k}) = \frac{Cov(Y_t, Y_{t-k})}{\sigma(Y_t)\sigma(Y_{t-k})} \tag{2.19}$$

In other words, it is just the correlation of a time series with itself but with a lag of k, hence the synonymous term *serial correlation*.

This autocorrelation can be estimated using equation (2.15) but on samples $(y_1, \ldots, y_T)$ and $(y_{1-k}, \ldots, y_{T-k})$ instead. The plot of autocorrelation for various lags is called the *autocorrelation function (ACF)* or *correlogram*. Figure 2-12 is an ACF plot of a $N(0,1)$ process and an AR(1) process described by equation (2.7) with $k_0=0$, $k_1=0.7$. We will discuss AR(p) processes next but for now, notice that the ACF plot shows significant autocorrelation for various k lags which tapers off as k increases. This compares to the Gaussian process which has no serial correlation—its ACF fluctuates near zero for all k. The ACF is a practical way to detect serial correlation for a time series. See Spreadsheet 2.4.

The *autoregressive model* AR(p) for time series variable X is described by:

$$X_t = k_0 + k_1 X_{t-1} + ... + k_p X_{t-p} + \varepsilon_t \qquad (2.20)$$

where p is a positive integer, k's are constant coefficients and ε_t is an i.i.d. random sequence. Clearly AR(p) models are non-i.i.d. (they are past dependent).

Figure 2-12 ACF plot for $N(0,1)$ process and AR(1) process, with up to 25 lags

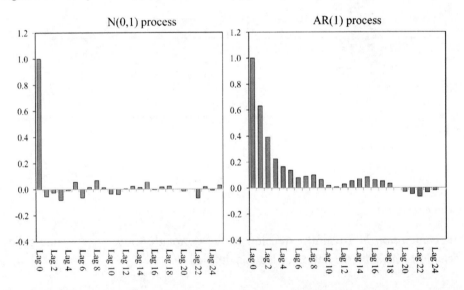

It is instructive to use the AR(1), equation (2.7), to clarify some important concepts learned previously:

1. The AR(1) process is non-i.i.d. although "driven" by an i.i.d. random variable ε_t.
2. An i.i.d. process will be stationary. That does not imply a non-i.i.d. process (like the AR(1)) is necessarily non-stationary. Indeed, it is stationary given certain conditions ($|k_1|<1$).

3. It is always serially correlated as shown by its ACF.

In short, i.i.d., stationarity and serial correlation are related yet distinct ideas. Only under certain conditions, does one lead to another.

2.5 Regression Models and Residual Errors

Regression is a basic tool in time series modeling to find and to *quantify relationships* between variables. This has many applications in finance for example, a trader may form his trading view from the analysis of relationships between stocks and bonds, an economist may need to find relationships between the dollar and various macroeconomic data, an interest rate hedger may need to find relationships between one section of the yield curve against another.

Figure 2-13 Price series of USD 5-year swap and 10-year swap

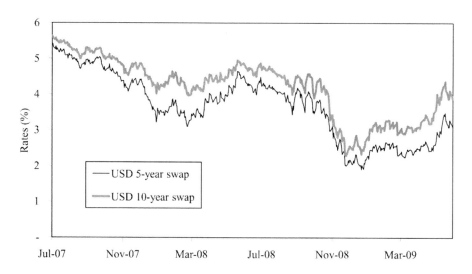

Source: Bloomberg Finance L.P.

The modeler starts by specifying (guessing) some relationship between the variables based on his knowledge of the markets or by visual study of chart patterns. For example, our interest rate hedger may look at Figure 2-13 and conclude that there is an obvious relationship between the USD 5-year swap rate and 10-year swap rate. A reasonable guess is to assume a linear relationship of the form:

$$Y_t = \alpha + \beta X_t + \varepsilon_t \qquad\qquad (2.21)$$

where Y_t and X_t are the two random variables representing 5-year and 10-year swap rates respectively. ε_t is a residual error term which captures all other (unknown) effects not explained by the chosen variables. α and β are constant parameters that need to be estimated from data. The method of estimation is called *ordinary least squares* (OLS). If ε_t is a white noise (i.i.d.) series then the OLS method produces consistent estimates. People often mistakenly model the level price rather than the change in prices. If one models the price, the residual error ε_t is often found to be serially correlated[7]. This means the OLS method will produce inconsistent (biased) estimates. To illustrate, we will do both regressions—one where data samples $\{y_i\}$, $\{x_i\}$ are levels, the other where they represent changes.

Figure 2-14 Scatter plots of prices and price changes

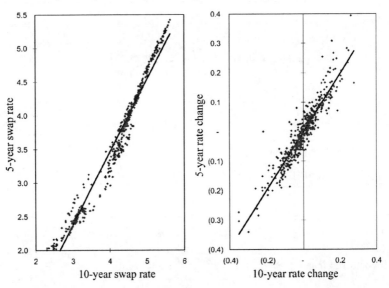

Start by drawing a scatter plot as in Figure 2-14—the more the data concentrate along a straight line, the stronger the regression relationship. Conceptually, OLS works by estimating the parameters α and β that will minimize the *residual sum squares* (RSS) given by:

[7] Possible exceptions are if the price itself is highly stationary such as the VIX index and implied volatilities observed in option markets.

$$RSS = \sum_i \left[y_i - (\alpha + \beta x_i) \right]^2 \qquad (2.22)$$

where x_i, y_i are the i'th observation. Intuitively, OLS is a fitting method which draws the best straight line which represents all data points by minimizing the residual distances (squared and summed) between the estimated line $\hat{y}_i = \hat{\alpha} + \hat{\beta} x_i$ and all the observed points y_i. Linear regression can easily be performed by Excel. From the toolbar, select: Tools ➔ Data Analysis ➔ Regression.

The estimated parameters are shown in Table 2-1. The β which represents the slope of the line is close to 1 for both cases. The α is the intercept of the line with the vertical axis. The R-square which ranges from 0 to 1 measures the goodness of fit. R-square of 0.9 means 90% of the variability in Y is explained linearly by X. The Excel functions are SLOPE(..), INTERCEPT(..) and RSQ(..) respectively.

Table 2-1 Linear regression results

	Using Price	Using Price change
Beta	1.079	0.987
Alpha	-0.858	-0.001
R -square	0.966	0.866

Figure 2-15 shows that if we model using level prices, the residual series does not behave like white noise, unlike the second case where we model using price changes. We can use an ACF plot on the residuals to prove that the first has serial autocorrelation and the second is stationary.

It is worth noting:

1. A noticeable correlation in the level price chart does not imply an authentic relationship. Most market prices have trends. In the presence of trends, you will likely get high correlation purely by chance (*spurious correlation*). Thus, correlation should be calculated on returns.

2. Always check the residuals for serial correlation. If we model non-stationary level prices then the OLS method may give inconsistent estimates due to serial correlation in residuals. (The only exception is when the price series are cointegrated. See Section 2.10.)

3. OLS regression can easily be extended to model multiple variables or to model time lagged variables.

4. Even when a good fit is obtained (high R-square), the result may not be useful for forecasting tomorrow's returns. Our simple regression measures contemporaneous relationships which can be useful for hedging. But for forecasting you will need a lead-lag relationship. Since markets

are mostly efficient, lead-lag relationships are hard to find. In our example, the trader can use the 5-year swap to hedge the 10-year swap, but he cannot use the 10-year swap movement as a signal to trade the 5-year swap.

Figure 2-15 Residual time series plots

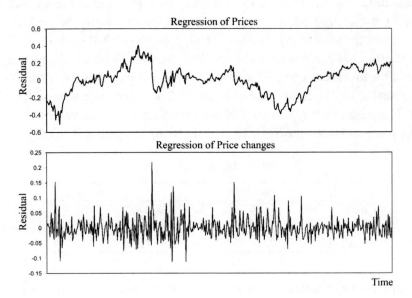

2.6 Significance Tests

We next look at how statisticians measure the *precision* of their models and express this in the form of statistical significance. So when we say a hypothesis (or whatever we defined to be measured) has a 95% confidence level that means we have chosen an error range around the expected value such that only 5% of observations fall outside this range. Clearly the tighter the range, the higher the precision.

How to compute t-ratio for regression

The *t-ratio* is the basic metric of significance for OLS regression. Consider again equation (2.21)—a simple two variable linear regression. First, we compute the *standard error* (SE) for the coefficient β defined by:

$$SE = \sqrt{\sum_i (y_i - \hat{y}_i)^2 / (n-2)} \Big/ \sqrt{\sum_i (x_i - \bar{x})^2} \qquad (2.23)$$

where $\hat{y}_i$ is the estimate of y at the i'th observation and $\bar{x}$ is the sample mean of x. Then the t-ratio is defined by:

$$t = \hat{\beta}\big/SE \qquad (2.24)$$

This measures how far away the slope is from showing no linear dependence ($\beta=0$) in units of standard error. Clearly, the larger the t-ratio the more significant is the linear relationship. The t-ratios can be calculated by the Excel regression tool.

Hypothesis testing

To determine how good the t-ratio is, we need to state the *null hypothesis* (H_0) and an *alternative hypothesis* (H_1).

H_0:	The slope of the regression line is equal to zero.
H_1:	The slope of the regression line is *not* equal to zero.

If the regression relationship is significant, the slope will *not* equal zero, i.e. we hope to reject H_0. We assume the t-ratio is distributed like the *student-t distribution* centered about H_0. The student-t is fatter than the normal distribution. But for large samples, the student-t approaches the standard normal $N(0,1)$ distribution and we assume this case. We need to see if the estimated t-ratio is larger than some *critical value* (CV) defined on a chosen confidence level p of the distribution. In Excel, the CV is given by NORMSINV(p).

For example, suppose we choose 95% confidence level for a *two tail test*, then at the left side tail, the CV= NORMSINV(0.025) = -1.96. Suppose the t-ratio of our regression works out to be -7.0 i.e. falls in the critical region (see Figure 2-16) then we can reject the null hypothesis H_0 and our regression is significant. On the other hand, if the t-ratio is -1.3, then we cannot reject H_0 and we have to think of another model.

Note that statisticians will never say *accept* the null hypothesis. A null hypothesis is never proven by such methods, as the absence of evidence against the null hypothesis does not confirm it. As an example, consider a series of 5 coin flips. If the outcome turns out to be 5 heads, an observer will be tempted to form the opinion (the null hypothesis) that the coin is an unfair two-headed coin. Statistically, we can say we cannot reject the null hypothesis. We cannot accept the null hypothesis since a series of 5 heads can occur from random chance alone. So likewise if we model financial time series using a chosen fat tail distributions (say the Laplace distribution) we cannot say we accept that distribution as the true distribution, even if the statistical test is highly significant. Perhaps there may be other distributions that fit the data better.

Figure 2-16 Rejecting and not rejecting the null hypothesis

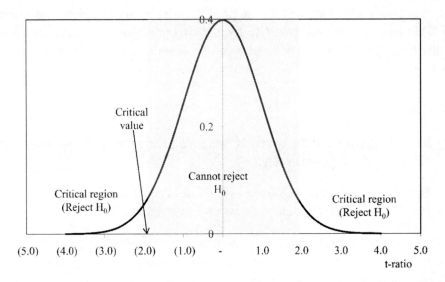

Stationarity tests

In statistics literature, there are many significance tests of stationarity, also called *unit root tests*. Here, we will only discuss the *augmented Dickey-Fuller test*, or ADF(q) test developed by Dickey and Fuller (1981). This test is based on the regression equation:

$$\Delta X_t = \alpha + \beta X_{t-1} + \delta_1 \Delta X_{t-1} ... + \delta_q \Delta X_{t-q} + \varepsilon_t \qquad (2.25)$$

where ΔX is the first difference of X, q is the number of lags, ε_t is the residual, and α, β, δ's are coefficients. The test statistic is the t-ratio for the coefficient β. The null hypothesis is for $\beta=0$ vs. a one-sided alternative hypothesis $\beta<0$. If the null hypothesis is rejected, then X is stationary. The critical values depend on q and are shown in Table 2-2 for a sample size between 500 and 600.

Equation (2.25) can easily be implemented in Excel for up to 16 lags if needed. We shall see an example of ADF test in Section 2.10.

Table 2-2 Critical values of ADF test

Number of lags, q	Significance level	
	1%	5%
1	-3.43	-2.86
2	-3.90	-3.34
3	-4.30	-3.74
4	-4.65	-4.10

2.7 Measuring Volatility

In modern risk management the basic unit of risk is measured as volatility. Risk measures such as notional, sensitivity, and others (see Section 1.1) fall short because they cannot be compared consistently across all products. It is instructive to compare four well-known models of volatility—standard deviation, EWMA, ARCH and GARCH.

Assuming we have a rolling window of n days with price data $p_1, \ldots, p_n$. If volatility is constant or varying slowly, we can estimate the n-th day volatility by:

St. Dev. model:
$$\hat{\sigma}_n^2 = \frac{1}{n} \sum_{i=1}^{n} r_i^2 \qquad (2.26)$$

where r_i is the observed percentage return $(p_i - p_{i-1})/p_{i-1}$ or log return $\ln(p_i/p_{i-1})$. Note that equation (2.26) is just the variance equation (2.3) but with zero mean. Therefore, volatility $\hat{\sigma}$ (normally written without the subscript n) is simply the standard deviation of returns. In Excel function, $\hat{\sigma}$ is given by STDEV(..).

But in financial markets, volatility is known to change with time, often rapidly. The first time-varying model, the *Autoregressive Conditional Heteroscedasticity* (ARCH) model was pioneered by Engle (1982).

$$\text{ARCH(n) model:} \qquad \hat{\sigma}_n^2 = \alpha\theta^2 + (1-\alpha)\frac{1}{n}\sum_{i=1}^{n} r_i^2 \qquad\qquad (2.27)$$

In some sense, equation (2.27) is an extension of equation (2.26) which incorporates mean reversion about a constant long-run volatility θ where α is the weight assigned to this long-run volatility term. Unfortunately, these first two models have an undesirable "plateau" effect as a result of giving equal weights $1/n$ to each observation. This effect kicks in whenever a large return observation drops off the rolling window as the window moves forward in time, as shown in Figure 2-18.

To overcome this problem, different weights should be assigned to each observation; logically, more recent observations (being more representative of the present) should be weighted more. Such models are called *conditional variance* since volatility is now conditional on information at past times. The time ordering of the returns matters in the calculation. In contrast, for the standard deviation model, the return distribution is assumed to be static. Hence, its variance is constant or unconditional, and equal weights can be used for every observation. A common scheme is the so-called *exponentially weighted moving average* (EWMA) method promoted by JP Morgan's Riskmetrics (1994).

$$\text{EWMA model:} \qquad \hat{\sigma}_n^2 = (1-\lambda)\sum_{i=1}^{\infty} \lambda^{i-1} r_{n-i+1}^2 \qquad\qquad (2.28)$$

The decay factor λ (an input parameter) must be larger than 0 and less than 1. Equation (2.28) can be simplified to an iterative formula which can be easily implemented in Excel:

$$\hat{\sigma}_n^2 = \lambda\hat{\sigma}_{n-1}^2 + (1-\lambda)r_n^2 \qquad\qquad (2.29)$$

Figure 2-17 shows the EWMA weights for past observations. The larger the λ, the slower the weights decay. Gradually falling weights solve the plateau problem because any (large) return that is exiting the rolling window will have a very tiny weight assigned to it. For a 1-day forecast horizon, Riskmetrics proposed a decay factor of 0.94.

Figure 2-17 EWMA weights of past observations

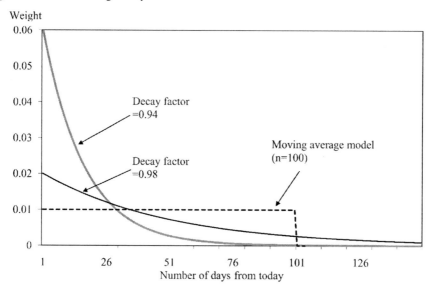

Bollerslev (1986) proposed a useful extension of ARCH called *Generalized Autoregressive Conditional Heteroscedasticity* (GARCH). There is a whole class of models under GARCH, and one simple example of a GARCH model is:

$$\text{Simple GARCH: } \hat{\sigma}_n^2 = \alpha\theta^2 + (1 - \alpha)\left(\lambda\hat{\sigma}_{n-1}^2 + (1 - \lambda)r_n^2\right) \tag{2.30}$$

Compared to equation (2.29) it looks like an extension of the EWMA model to include mean reversion about a constant long-term mean volatility θ which needs to be estimated separately. In fact, the EWMA is the simplest example of a GARCH model with only one parameter. When the weight $\alpha=0$, GARCH becomes the EWMA model.

Figure 2-18 graphs all four models for the same simulated time series. We set $\alpha=0.4$, $\lambda=0.99$ and $\sigma_L=0.02$. We simulated a 10% (large) return on a particular day, halfway in the time series. We can see this caused the artificial plateau effect for the standard deviation and ARCH models. There is no plateau effect for the EWMA and GARCH models. This implementation is in Spreadsheet 2.5.

The main advantage of GARCH is it can account for *volatility clustering* observed in financial markets. This phenomenon refers to the observation, as noted by Mandelbrot (1963), that "large changes tend to be followed by large changes, of either sign, and small changes tend to be followed by small changes." A quantitative manifestation of this is that *absolute* returns show a positive and slowly decaying ACF even though returns themselves are not autocorrelated. Figure 2-19 shows volatility clustering observed in the S&P 500 index during the credit crisis. The upper panel shows that the price return bunches together during late 2008. This is captured by GARCH and EWMA which showed a peak in volatility that tapers off thereafter (lower panel). The standard deviation and ARCH models registered the rise in risk but not the clustering.

Figure 2-18 Behavior of four volatility models and the plateau effect

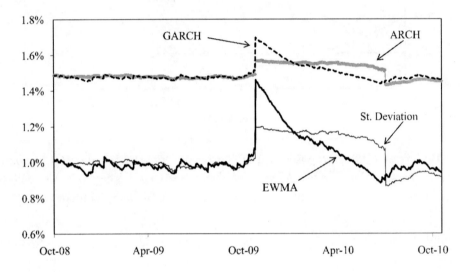

Another good feature is that ARCH and GARCH can produce fatter tails than the normal distribution. Unfortunately, they cannot explain the *leverage effect* (asymmetry) observed in the market, where volatility tends to be higher during a selloff compared to that during a rally. The *exponential GARCH* model (EGARCH) by Nelson (1991) allows for this asymmetric effect between positive and negative asset returns.

Note that what we have calculated so far is the volatility for today (the *n*-th day). In risk management, we are actually interested in forecasting the next day's volatility. It can be shown that for standard deviation and the EWMA model, the expected future variance is the same as today's. Taking expectations of equation (2.29).

$$E(\sigma_{n+1}^2) = \lambda E(\sigma_n^2) + (1 - \lambda)E(R_{n+1}^2) \text{ where } E(R_{n+1}^2) = E(\sigma_{n+1}^2)$$

$$\rightarrow \mathrm{E}(\sigma^2_{n+1}) = \mathrm{E}(\sigma^2_n) \qquad (2.31)$$

This is not strictly true for the ARCH and GARCH models because of the presence of mean-reversion towards the long-term volatility. Depending on whether the current volatility is above or below the long-term volatility, tomorrow's volatility will fall or rise slightly. However, for a 1-day forecast the effect is so tiny that equation (2.31) can still be applied.

Figure 2-19 Modeling volatility clustering for the S&P500 index

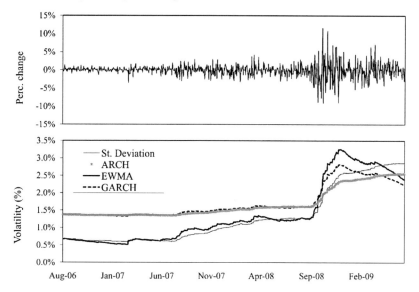

The key lesson from this section is that a different choice of method and parameters will produce materially different risk measurements (see Figure 2-18). This is unnerving. What then is the "true" volatility (risk)? Does it really exist? Some believe the *implied volatility* backed out from option markets can represent real volatility but this runs into its own set of problems. Firstly, not all assets have tradable options, which naturally limit risk management coverage. Secondly, there is the volatility "smile" where one asset has different volatilities depending on the strike of its options (so which one?). Mathematically, this reflects the fact that asset returns are not normally distributed, which gives rise to the third problem—such implied volatility cannot be used in the Markowitz portfolio framework (explained in the next section).

The current best practice in banks is to use standard deviation or EWMA volatility because of its practical simplicity. These measures are well understood and commonly used in various trades and industries.

2.8 Markowitz Portfolio Theory

Modern portfolio theory was founded by Harry Markowitz (see Markowitz, 1952). The Nobel Prize for Economics was eventually awarded in 1990 for this seminal work. The theory served as the foundation for the research and practice of portfolio optimization, diversification and risk management.

Its basic assumption is that investors are risk-averse (assumption 1)—given two assets, A and B with the same returns, investors will prefer the asset with lower risk. Equally, investors will take on more risk only for higher return. So what is the portfolio composition that will give the best risk-return tradeoff? This is an optimization problem. To answer that question, Markowitz further assumed that investors will only consider the first two moments—mean (expected return) and variance—for their decision making (assumption 2), and the distributions of returns are jointly normal (assumption 3). Investors are indifferent to other characteristics of the distribution such as skew and kurtosis. The Markowitz *mean-variance* framework makes use of linear correlation to account for dependency, valid for normal distributions.

However, behavioral finance has found evidence that investors are not always rational i.e. not risk-averse. Assumption 2 is challenged by the observation that skew is often priced into the market as evident in the so-called "volatility smile" of option markets. So investors do consider skewness. There is also empirical evidence that asset prices do not follow the normal distribution during stressful periods. Moreover, distributions are seldom normal for credit markets or when there are options in the portfolio. Despite the weak assumptions, the mean-variance framework is well-accepted because of its practical simplicity.

In the mean-variance framework, the expected return of a portfolio μ_p is given by the weighted sum of the expected returns of individual assets μ_i.

$$\mu_p = \sum_i \omega_i \mu_i \tag{2.32}$$

where the weights are the asset allocations such that $\sum \omega_i = 1$. The portfolio variance is given by:

$$\sigma_p^2 = \sum_i \sum_j \omega_i \omega_j \sigma_i \sigma_j \rho_{ij} \tag{2.33}$$

where the correlation $\rho_{ij}=1$ when $i=j$. If there are n assets then $i, j=1, . . ,n$.

The incorporation of correlation into equation (2.33) leads to the idea of diversification. An investor can reduce portfolio risk simply by holding combinations of assets which are not perfectly positively correlated. To see the effects of diversification, consider a portfolio with just two assets a, b. Equation (2.33) then becomes:

$$\sigma_p^2 = \omega_a^2 \sigma_a^2 + \omega_b^2 \sigma_b^2 + 2\omega_a \omega_b \sigma_a \sigma_b \rho_{ab} \tag{2.34}$$

As long as the assets are not perfectly correlated ($\rho_{ab}<1$) then:

$$\sigma_p < \omega_a \sigma_a + \omega_b \sigma_b \tag{2.35}$$

The risk (volatility) of the portfolio is always less than the sum of the risk of its components. Merging portfolios should not increase risks (conversely splitting portfolios should not decrease risk). This desirable property called *subadditivity* is generally true for *standard deviation* (regardless of distribution).

For the purpose of mathematical manipulation, it is convenient to write the list of correlation pairs in the form of a matrix, the *correlation matrix*. Then basic matrix algebra can be applied to solve equations efficiently. Excel has a simple tool that generates the correlation matrix (Tools➔Data analysis➔Correlation) and some functions to do matrix algebra.

The problem of finding the optimal asset allocation is called the *Markowitz problem*. The optimization problem can be stated in matrix form:

$$\min_w(w^T \Sigma w) \text{ subject to } \sum_i \omega_i = 1 \text{ and } w^T \mu = r_T \tag{2.36}$$

where w is the column vector of weights ω_i, μ is the vector of investor's expected returns μ_i, r_T the targeted portfolio return, Σ the covariance matrix derived using equation (2.15). We need to find the weights w that minimize the portfolio variance subject to constraints on expected returns and portfolio target return.

Spreadsheet 2.6 is an example of portfolio optimization with four assets per-formed using Excel Solver.

The key weakness of the classical Markowitz problem is that the expected returns and target are all assumed inputs (guesswork)—they are not random variables which are amenable to statistical estimation. The only concrete input is the covariance matrix which can be statistically estimated from time series. It is found that the optimization result (weights) is unstable and very sensitive to return assumptions. This could lead to slippage losses when the portfolio is rebalanced too frequently. The Markowitz theory has evolved over the years to handle weaknesses in the original version, but that is outside the scope of this book.

Imagine a universe of stocks available for investment and we have to select a portfolio of stocks by choosing different weights for each stock. Each combina-tion of assets will have its own risk-return characteristics and can be represented as a point in the risk/return space (see Figure 2-20). It can be shown that if we use equation (2.36) to determine our choice of assets, these optimal portfolios will lie on a hyperbola. The upper half of this hyperbola is preferable to the rest of the curve and is called the *efficient frontier*. Along this frontier *risky* portfolios have the lowest risk for a given level of return. The heart of portfolio management is to rebalance the weights dynamically so that a portfolio is always located on the efficient frontier.

Figure 2-20 The efficient frontier

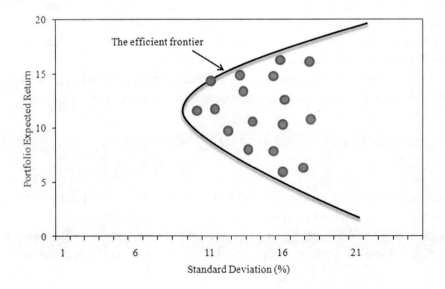

It is also convenient to express the risk of an individual asset relative to its market benchmark index. This is called the *beta approach,* commonly used for equities. It is reasonable to assume a linear relationship given by the regression:

$$R_i(t) = \alpha_i + \beta_i R_M(t) + \varepsilon_i(t) \tag{2.37}$$

where R_i is the return variable for asset-*i* and R_M is the return of the market index at time *t*, α_i is a constant drift for asset-*i*. $\varepsilon_i(t)$ is an i.i.d. residual random variable specific to the *i*'th asset; this idiosyncratic risk is assumed to be uncorrelated to the index. The *beta* β_i also called the *hedge ratio*, is the sensitivity of the asset to a unit change in the market index. Thus, in the beta model, an asset return is broken down into a systematic component and an idiosyncratic component. The parameters can be estimated using the Excel regression tool.

2.9 Maximum Likelihood Method

Maximum likelihood estimation (MLE) is a popular statistical method used for fitting a statistical model to data and estimating the model's parameters. Suppose we have a sample of observations $x_1, x_2, \ldots, x_n$ which are assumed to be drawn from a known distribution with PDF given by $f_\theta(x)$ with parameter θ (where θ can also be a vector). The question is: what is the model parameter θ such that we obtain the maximum likelihood (or probability) of drawing from the distribution, the *same sample* as the observed sample?

If we assume the draws are all i.i.d. then their probabilities $f_\theta(.)$ are multiplicative. Thus, we need to find θ that maximizes the *likelihood function*:

$$L(\theta) = \prod_{i=1}^{n} f_\theta(x_i) \tag{2.38}$$

Since the log function is a monotonic function (i.e. perpetually increasing), maximizing $L(\theta)$ is equivalent to maximizing $\ln(L(\theta))$. In fact, it is easier to maximize the *log-likelihood function*:

$$L^*(\theta) = \sum_{i=1}^{n} \ln[f_\theta(x_i)] \tag{2.39}$$

because it is easier to deal with a summation series than a multiplicative series.

As an example, we will use MLE to estimate the decay factor λ of the EWMA volatility model (see Section 2.7). We assume the PDF $f_0(x)$ is normal as given by equation (2.12). Then, the likelihood function is given by:

$$L(\lambda) = \prod_{i=1}^{n} \left[\frac{1}{\sqrt{2\pi v_i}} \exp\left(\frac{-x_i^2}{2v_i} \right) \right] \tag{2.40}$$

where the variance $v_i = v_i(\lambda)$ is calculated using the EWMA model. Taking logs we can simplify to the following log-likelihood function (ignoring the constant term and multiplicative factor):

$$L^*(\lambda) = \sum_{i=1}^{n} \left[-\ln(v_i) - \frac{x_i^2}{v_i} \right] \tag{2.41}$$

The conditional variance $v_i(\lambda)=\sigma_i^2$ on day i is estimated iteratively using equation (2.29). After that, the objective $L^*(\lambda)$ can be maximized using Excel Solver to solve for parameter λ. Spreadsheet 2.7 illustrates how this can be done for Dow Jones index data. The optimal decay factor works out to be $\hat{\lambda}=0.94$ as was estimated and proposed by Riskmetrics.

2.10 Cointegration

Cointegration analysis tests if there is a long-run equilibrium relationship between two time series. Hence, if two stocks are cointegrated they have the tendency to gravitate toward a common equilibrium path in the *long-run* i.e. short-term deviation will be corrected. Hence, cointegration has found popular application in the area of pair trading (statistical arbitrage) where a trader will buy one security and short another security, betting that the securities will mean revert towards each other. This idea is also used by index-tracking funds where a portfolio of stocks is designed to track the performance of a chosen index.

Cointegration and correlation are very different ideas. Correlated stocks rise and fall in synchrony, whereas cointegrated stocks will not wander off from each other for very long without reverting back to some long-term spread. Figure 2-21 shows the difference between the two ideas.

Figure 2-21 Cointegration and correlation

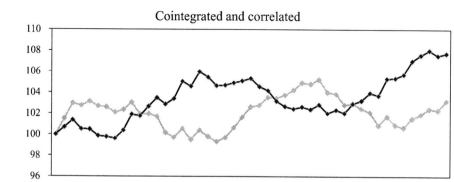

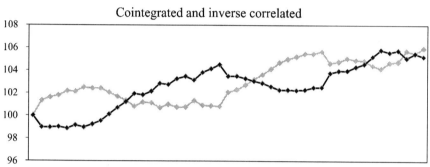

In the 1980's many economists simply used regression on level prices, which ran into the problem of serial correlation of residuals. This means the OLS estimation is not consistent and the correlation relationship may be spurious. Engle and Granger (1987) formalized the cointegration approach and spelled out the necessary conditions for OLS regression to be applied to *level prices* (non-stationary data).

A time series is said to be *integrated* of order p written $I(p)$ if we can obtain a stationary series by differencing p times (but no less). Most financial market time series are found to be $I(1)$. A stationary time series is a special case of $I(0)$. Suppose $X_1, X_2, .., X_n$ are integrated prices (or log prices) then these variables are *cointegrated* if a linear combination of them produces a stationary time series. This can be formalized using the *Engle-Granger regression*:

$$X_1(t) = a_1 + a_2 X_2(t) + ... + a_n X_n(t) + \varepsilon(t) \qquad (2.42)$$

The Engle-Granger test is for the residuals $\varepsilon(t)$ to be stationary or I(0). If affirmative, then $X_1, X_2, .., X_n$ are said to be cointegrated. Only in this situation, OLS regression can be applied to these random variables.

The coefficients $a_1, .., a_n$ can be estimated using the OLS method. The problem with the Engle-Granger regression is that the coefficients obviously depend on which variable you choose as the dependent variable (i.e. as X_1). Hence, the estimates are not unique—there can be n-1 sets of coefficients. This is not a problem for $n=2$ which is mostly our case.

Figure 2-22 Dow Jones vs. Nasdaq (in log scale)

A more advanced cointegration test that does not have such weakness is the Johansen method (1988). Once a cointegration relationship has been established, various models can be used to determine the degree of deviation from equilibrium and the strength of subsequent corrections. For further reading, read Alexander (2008).

There are many examples of securities in the market that show highly visible correlation when plotted, but no cointegration when tested. Figure 2-22 shows the chart of Dow Jones index vs. Nasdaq index—both I(1) time series. The correlation of their log returns over the period Jan 1990 – Jun 2009 is 0.86. Using the Engle-Granger regression test, we can show that the two indices are *not* cointegrated. The worked out example in Spreadsheet 2.8 also shows how the augmented Dickey-Fuller stationarity test can be performed in Excel.

On the other hand, empirical research has found that different points on the same yield curve are often cointegrated. Pair trading, for example, thrives on searching for cointegrated pairs of stocks, typically from the same industry sector. Cointegrated systems are almost always tied together by common underlying dynamics.

2.11 Monte Carlo Method

Monte Carlo (MC) simulation is a numerical algorithm that is used extensively in finance for derivatives pricing and VaR calculation. The method involves the generation of large samples of random numbers repeatedly drawn from some known distribution. With the advent of powerful computers this method of "brute force" became popular because of its intuitive and flexible nature. Furthermore, the simulation method is a useful visualization device for the modeler to gain a deeper understanding of the behavior of the model. In actual implementation, the MC simulation is generally coded in more efficient languages such as C++ and R. But for reasons of pedagogy, examples here will be implemented in Excel.

In simulating a path for a time series X_t where $t=1, . . . ,n,$ a random variable ε_t needs to be generated by the computer to represent the stochastic change element. This change is then used to evolve the price (or return) X_t to its value X_{t+1} in the next time step. This is repeated n times until the whole path is generated. The stochastic element represents the price impact due to the arrival of new information to the market. If the market is efficient, it is reasonable to assume ε_t is an i.i.d. white noise.

Excel has a random generator RAND() that draws a real number between 0 and 1 with equal probability. This is called the *uniform distribution*. The i.i.d. random variable is typically modeled using the standard normal $N(0,1)$ for convenience. We can get this number easily from the following *inverse transformation* NORMSINV(RAND()). This is the inverse function of the normal CDF. Essentially Excel goes to the CDF (see Figure 2-5), reference the probability as chosen by RAND() on the vertical axis, and finds the corresponding horizontal axis value. Pressing the F9 (calculate) button in Excel will regenerate all the random numbers given by RAND().

In general, there are two classes of time series processes that are fundamentally different—*stochastic trend* processes and *deterministic trend* processes. A stochastic trend process is one where the trend itself is also random. In other words $(X_t - X_{t-1})$ shows a stationary randomness. One example is the so-called *random walk with drift process* given by:

Random walk: $$X_t = \mu + X_{t-1} + \varepsilon_t \qquad (2.43)$$

where the constant μ is the drift, ε_t is i.i.d. Clearly this is an I(1) process as the first difference will produce $\mu + \varepsilon_t$ which is an I(0) stationary process. We call such a process stochastic trend. Another example is the *geometric Brownian motion* (GBM) process[8]:

GBM: $$\frac{\Delta X_t}{X_t} = \mu\Delta t + \sigma\sqrt{\Delta t}\,\varepsilon_t \qquad (2.44)$$

where the constant μ is the annualized drift, σ the annualized volatility, $\varepsilon_t \sim N(0,1)$ and $\Delta X_t = X_t - X_{t-1}$. The time step is in unit of years, so for one day step, $\Delta t = 1/250$. Hence, in GBM, we simulate the percentage changes in price; we can then construct the price series itself iteratively.

The GBM process is commonly used for derivatives pricing and VaR calculation because it describes the motion of stock prices quite well. In particular, negative prices are not allowed because the resulting prices are lognormally distributed. A random variable X_t is said to follow a *lognormal distribution* if its log return, $\ln(X_t / X_{t-1})$ is normally distributed. Figure 2-23 shows simulated GBM paths using $\sigma = 10\%$, $\mu = 5\%$. The larger μ is, the larger the upward drift, the larger σ is, the larger the dispersion of paths.

The other process is the *deterministic trend process*, where the trend is fixed, only the fluctuations are random. It is an "I(0)+trend" process and one simple form is:

Deterministic Trend: $$X_t = \alpha + \mu t + \varepsilon_t \qquad (2.45)$$

where α is a constant, μ is the drift and ε_t is i.i.d. $(\alpha + \varepsilon_t)$ is I(0) and μt is the trend.

Figure 2-24 shows a comparison of the three processes generated using -30% drift and 50% volatility. Although not obvious from the chart, the I(1) and

---

[8] The Brownian motion is originally used in physics to describe the random motion of gas particles.

I(0)+trend processes are fundamentally different and this will determine the correct method used to de-trend them (see next section). It is instructive to experiment with the processes in Excel (see Spreadsheet 2.9).

Figure 2-23 Geometric Brownian motion of 50 simulated paths

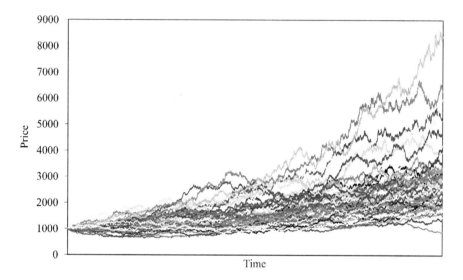

As we shall see in Monte Carlo simulation VaR (Chapter 4), we will need to simulate returns for many assets that are correlated. The dependence structure of the portfolio of assets is contained in the correlation matrix. To generate random numbers which are correlated, the correlation matrix Σ needs to be decomposed into the *Cholesky* matrix L. L is a lower triangular matrix (i.e. entries above the diagonal are all zero) with positive diagonal entries, such that $LL^T=\Sigma$ where L^T is the transpose of L.

We coded this function as *cholesky(..)* in Excel, i.e. $L=cholesky(\Sigma)$. The code is explained in the reference book by Wilmott (2007). Let's say we have n assets; first, we compute L (n-by-n matrix). Secondly, an n-vector of random numbers $\{\varepsilon_1(t), \ldots, \varepsilon_n(t)\}$ is sampled from an i.i.d. $N(0,1)$ distribution. This column vector is denoted $\varepsilon(t)$. Finally, the n-column-vector of correlated random numbers $r(t)$ can be computed by simple matrix multiplication: $r(t) = L\varepsilon(t)$. For example, to generate n correlated time series of T days, perform the above calculations for $t=1,2,\ldots,T$. In Excel function notation, this is written as: r=MMULT(L,ε). If the vectors are rows instead, the Excel function is written in a transposed form: r=TRANSPOSE(MMULT(L,TRANSPOSE(ε))). Correlated random numbers are generated in Spreadsheet 2.10.

Figure 2-24 Stochastic trend vs. deterministic trend processes

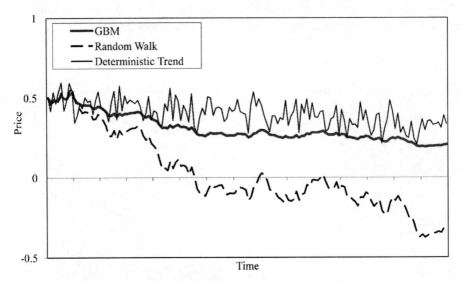

2.12 The Classical Decomposition

The study of financial market cycles is of paramount importance to policy makers, economists and the trading community. Clearly being able to forecast where we are in the business cycle, can bring great fortunes to a trader or allow the regulator to legislate preemptive policies to cool a bubbling economy. It is the million dollar question. This area of research is far from established as endeavors of such economic impact are, by nature, often elusive.

Actual time series observed in markets are seldom stationary—they exhibit trends and cycles. The problem is statistical estimation methods are mostly designed to handle stationary data. Hence, in time series analysis, we need to decompose the data so that we obtain something stationary to work with. Figure 2-25 illustrates a stylized time series decomposition. The *classical decomposition* breaks an observed price series x_t (t=1,2, ..) into three additive components:

$$x_t = l_t + s_t + z_t \qquad (2.46)$$

where l_t is the long-term trend, s_t the cycle (or seasonality) and z_t the noise (or irregular) component. Of the three components, z_t is assumed to be stationary and i.i.d. There is an abundant of research in this area of seasonal decomposition; for a reference book, read Ghysels and Osborn (2001).

Figure 2-25 Stylized classical decomposition

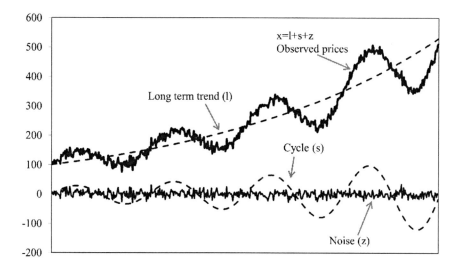

A general approach to time series analysis follows these steps:
1. Plot the time series x_t to visually check for trend and seasonality.
2. De-trend data into a stationary time series z_t.
3. Chose a model (for example AR(p), GARCH, etc.) and try to fit z_t.
4. Run diagnostic tests (such as residual analysis). If the model is unacceptable go back to step 3.
5. Generate the forecasted distribution (say for a one-day horizon).
6. Invert the transformation in step 2 to bring the forecasted distribution back to the price level.

This is illustrated in Figure 2-26.

There are many ways to de-trend the data in step 2. If the times series is a stochastic trend process then the correct approach is to take differences. There is considerable evidence that suggests most financial market prices are I(1) stochastic trend processes.

On the other hand, if the data is a deterministic trend "I(0)+trend" process then the correct approach is to take the deviation from a fitted trend line (the decomposition approach). Note that if we do this to an I(1) process, the resulting deviation from trend line may not be stationary. Nevertheless, this is a common practice among forecasters and it remains an open debate. Beveridge and Nelson

(1981) found that if the trend is defined as the long-run forecast, then decomposition of a I(1) process can lead to a stationary deviation.

Figure 2-26 Time series forecast approach

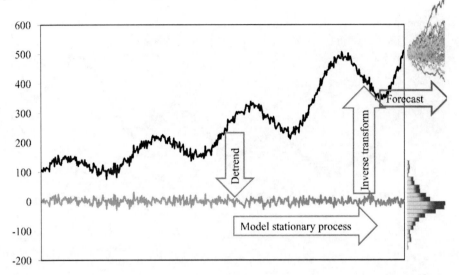

As a typical example, the *Berlin procedure*, developed by the Federal Statistical Office of Germany, models the long-term trend as a polynomial and the cycle as a Fourier series. It assumes the stochastic trend follows a highly auto-correlated process such that the realizations will be smooth enough to be approximated using a low order polynomial (of order *p*):

$$l_t = \sum_{i=0}^{p} \alpha_i t^i \tag{2.47}$$

The cycle component is assumed to be weakly stationary and changes slowly with time, so that it can be approximated using a finite *Fourier series*:

$$s_t = \sum_{i=0}^{k} \left[\beta_i Cos \lambda_i t + \gamma_i Sin \lambda_i t \right] \tag{2.48}$$

We are dealing with 250 daily observations per year, so $\lambda_1 = 2\pi/250$ and $\lambda_i = i\lambda_1$ with $i = 1, 2, \dots, k$ are the harmonic waves for λ_1. We can use least square minimization[9] to estimate the coefficients α_i, β_i and γ_i. Spreadsheet 2.11 shows the decomposition of S&P500 index daily closing prices using a cubic polynomial ($p=3$) and Fourier series ($k=12$). The result is shown in Figure 2-27.

Figure 2-27 Classical decomposition of S&P500 index

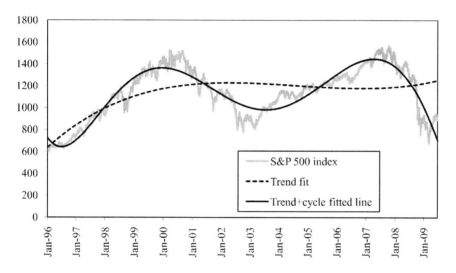

When statisticians speak of "forecast", they mean estimating the most statistically likely *distribution* the next day. While a risk manager will be interested in the four moments of such a distribution and its quantile (the VaR), such forecast of uncertainty (or risk) is of lesser importance to traders who are more concerned about the trend, cycle and direction of the market. There is a fundamental difference between forecasting distribution and forecasting direction. Statistics is good for distributional forecasts but poor for directional forecasts. The problem is estimation methods are mostly designed to handle stationary data. During the de-trending process, valuable information on trend (or anything other than noise) is lost.

Many analysts and researchers still perform analysis on direction, trends and cycles using technical analysis and component models, but things become murky once we deal with non-stationary data. We no longer have the law of large numbers on our side, precision is lost, and we can no longer state our results with

---

[9] The actual estimation in the Berlin procedure is more sophisticated than what is described here. For more information, the avid reader can refer to the procedural manual and free application software downloadable from its website http://www.destatis.de/.

a high confidence level. Furthermore, the model is not *identifiable*—for example there are many ways to decompose a time series into its three components.

Table 2-3 compares the two schools of forecasting. In Chapter 13 we will propose a *new interpretation of decomposition* that will incorporate directional elements into VaR forecasts.

Table 2-3 Distributional forecast vs. directional forecast.

Type	Distributional forecast	Directional forecast
Forecast	Distributions, moments,risks, quantiles	Trend, cycles, direction
Nature of time series	Stationary	Non-stationary
Results	High precision subject to model error	Non unique solutions
Users	Risk managers, statisticians	Traders, economist, analyst, policy makers

2.13 Quantile Regression Model

Aside from OLS and MLE methods, another statistical estimation method that is increasingly useful in risk management is the quantile regression model (QRM) introduced by Koenker and Bassett (1978).

The beauty of QRM is that it is "model free" in the sense that it does not impose any distributional assumptions. The only requirement is i.i.d. In contrast, for OLS estimation, the variables must be jointly normal, otherwise the estimate is biased. Furthermore, OLS only produces an estimate of mean or *location* of the regression line for the whole sample. It assumes the regression model used is appropriate for *all* data, and thus ignores the possibility of a different degree of skewness and kurtosis at different levels of the independent variable (such as at extreme data points).

But what if there is an internal structure in the population data? For example, the mean salary of the population (as a function of say, age) contains trivial information because there may be some structure in the data which is omitted, such as segmentation into certain salary quantiles based on differences in industry type and income tax bracket. QRM can be used to study these internal structures.

The intuition of QRM is easy to understand if we view quantiles as a solution to an optimization problem. Just as we can define the mean as the solution of the optimization problem of minimizing the sum of residual squares (RSS), the median (or 0.5-quantile) is the solution to minimizing the sum of *absolute* residuals. Referring to the linear regression equation (2.21), taking its expectation and noting that $E(\varepsilon_t)=0$, gives equation (2.49), the *conditional* mean (i.e. conditional on X):

Conditional mean: $\qquad E(Y \mid X) = \alpha + \beta X_t$ $\qquad\qquad\qquad$ (2.49)

Given a sample, the OLS solution $\hat{\beta}, \hat{\alpha}$ will provide an estimate $\hat{E}(Y|X)$ shown as the thin (middle) line in Figure 2-28. This "best fit" line is drawn such that the sum of residual *squares* above and below the line offset. Likewise, to estimate median, we draw a line such that the sum of *absolute* residuals above and below the line offset. We can extend this idea to estimate the q-quantile by imposing *different weights* to the residuals above and below the line. Suppose $q=0.05$. We will draw the line such that the 0.05 weighted absolute residuals above the line offset the 0.95 weighted absolute residuals below the line. These are shown in Figure 2-28 for $q=0.05, 0.95$.

Mathematically, the quantile regression line (for a chosen q) can be found by minimizing the weighted equation (2.50) and estimating α and β.

$$\min_{\alpha,\beta} \sum_{t=1}^{T} (q - I_{Y_t \le \alpha + \beta X_t})(Y_t - (\alpha + \beta X_t)) \qquad\qquad (2.50)$$

where the indicator function I(.) is given by:

$$I_{Y_t \le \alpha + \beta X_t} = \begin{cases} 1 & if \ Y_t \le \alpha + \beta X_t, \\ 0 & otherwise \end{cases}$$

The newly estimated coefficients $\hat{\beta}, \hat{\alpha}$ depend on the choice of q (a different q leads to a line with a different slope β and intercept α). Note that they are not parameter estimates for the linear regression (2.21) but rather for the (linear) *quantile regression model*:

Conditional quantile: $F^{-1}(q \mid X) = \alpha + \beta X + F_\varepsilon^{-1}(q \mid X)$ $\qquad$ (2.51)

where $F^{-1}(.)$ represents the quantile function; recall a quantile is just the inverse CDF (see Section 2.3). So the conditional q-quantile $F^{-1}(q|X)$ is derived by taking the inverse of $F(Y|X)$ i.e. you can get equation (2.51) simply by taking the quantile function of equation (2.21). The last term is non zero because the i.i.d. error ε_t does not have zero quantile (even though it has zero mean).

Figure 2-28 Quantile regression lines

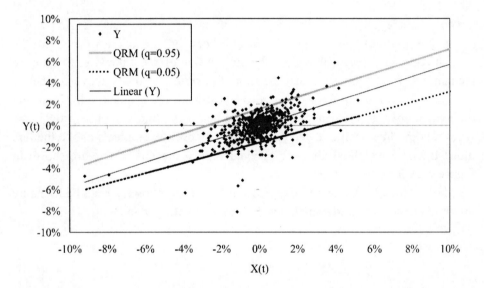

Now, since VaR is nothing but the quantile, then (2.51) basically gives the VaR of *Y conditional on another variable X*, which could be anything such as GDP, market indices, etc. or even a function of variables. This *conditional VaR* is a powerful result and will be exploited in Section 5.3 and Section 12.3. However, QRM is not "model free" in the sense that we still need to assume (2.51) is linear and specify what X is.

Spreadsheet 2.12 is a worked out example of QRM estimation using the Excel Solver. Here, we assume Y are returns of a portfolio, X is the change in some risk sentiment index[10]. Hence, the estimated $\hat{F}^{-1}(q \mid X)$ is the $c\%$ confidence level VaR conditional on X (where $q=1-c$ by convention). In other words,

---

[10] Risk sentiment (or risk appetite) indices are created by institutions for market timing and are typically made of some average function of VIX, FX option implied volatilities, bond-swap spreads, Treasury yields, etc. The indicator is supposed to gauge "fear" or risk perception.

we assume there is some relationship between our portfolio's VaR and variable X (perhaps we have used X as a market timing tool for the portfolio) and would like to study the tail loss behavior. We then use QRM to estimate the quantile loss (or VaR) at different q for different changes in X.

The result is shown in Figure 2-29. Negative return denotes loss. Notice the higher the VaR confidence level, the larger the loss obviously for the same line (i.e. same change in index). But the plot revealed an interesting structure in the tail loss—losses tend to be even higher when the risk sentiment index shows large positive changes (large X). It shows that the index is doing what it is supposed to do—predicting risky sentiment.

Figure 2-29 Structure of quantile loss conditional on X

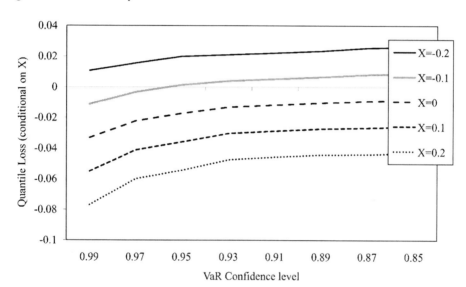

2.14 Spreadsheet

2.1 The Law of Large Numbers (LLN) is useful because it states that as more measurements N are taken, statistics will converge to "true" value, provided the random variable is i.i.d. Aim: illustrate LLN on three processes including a non-i.i.d. AR(1) process as N increases to 1000. Action: check the convergence of mean of AR(1) by modifying equation (2.7) for cases: $|k_1|<1$, $|k_1|>1$ and $k_1=0.999$.

2.2 The Central Limit Theorem (CLT) is useful because it states that as more samples are taken from various i.i.d. distributions, the means of those samples will be normally distributed. Aim: illustrates CLT by sampling from a uniform distribution 500 times. The distribution of the means of those samples is plotted. Action: extend the number of samples to 5000 to show that the histogram approaches a normal distribution.

2.3 Linear correlation is known to have weaknesses when the relationship between variables is non-linear. Rank correlation provides an alternative. Aim: illustrates the computation of rank correlations. Action: modify the spreadsheet to show that rank correlation is invariant under non-linear transformation of risk. Tip: first generate sample returns x, y using NORMSINV(RAND())*0.1, then do the transformation (for example to x^3, y^3) but keep the signs (directions) of x, y are unchanged.

2.4 An autocorrelation function (ACF) plot is useful in visually identifying serial correlation. Aim: illustrates the computation of ACF plots of N(0,1) and AR(1) processes. Action: experiment with the AR(1) process by modifying equation (2.7) for cases: $|k_1|<1$, $|k_1|>1$ and $k_1=0.999$.

2.5 Standard deviation, EWMA, ARCH, GARCH are four different ways to model the volatility (hence risks) of a financial variable. Aim: illustrates the implementation of the four volatility models. Note the behavior of the four graphs as the parameter α goes to 0, GARCH becomes the EWMA model. As α goes to 1.0, the volatility of ARCH and GARCH converges to the long-term (constant) volatility θ.

2.6 Markowitz modern portfolio theory was a breakthrough in modern understanding of risk/reward of investments and pioneered the use of variance as a measure of risks. Aim: illustrates the classical Markowitz portfolio optimization for a portfolio of four assets. Action: set a different target return for the portfolio and rerun the Excel Solver. Modify the expected return inputs for each asset and check how the optimal weights respond. Tip: if the target return is unreasonably high, the Solver cannot find an optimum solution.

2.7 Maximum likelihood method (MLE) is a popular statistical method to estimate the parameters of models given a sample of data. Aim: illustrates the use of MLE to estimate the decay parameter λ of the EWMA volatility model.

2.8 Cointegration measures the tendency for two time series to drift towards a common long term equilibrium path. It is a required behavior for pair trading. A pair of correlated variables is not necessarily cointegrated. Aim: illustrates how to check for cointegration using the Engle-Granger regression method. Note: the two I(1) time series are logs of Dow Jones index and S&P500 index. The residuals of the regression are tested for I(0) stationarity using the augmented Dickey-Fuller test.

2.9 Deterministic trend and stochastic trend processes are fundamentally different. The time series of the former wanders around a fixed trend, in the latter the trend itself wanders around. Aim: illustrates the two processes using three examples: random walk, geometric Brownian motion and a deterministic trend process. Note: First, the GBM process can never go below zero because it is a lognormal process. Second, the deterministic trend process tends to have a rather stable trend which is just the fixed line $\mu+\beta t$. On the other hand, the trend for the other two processes wanders around.

2.10 In Monte Carlo simulation it is crucial to be able to generate correlated variables because most financial assets that are modeled in the banking industry move in correlated fashion. Aim: illustrates the generation of correlated random variables using Cholesky decomposition. Note: the function *cholesky*(.) is written in Visual Basic (VB) code. Using a given correlation matrix, the example generated 50 sets of correlated random numbers for four assets.

2.11 The *classical decomposition* breaks down a time series into three theoretical components—the trend, the cycle, and the noise—for analysis. Aim: Illustrate the classical decomposition using cubic polynomial for the trend and Fourier series for the cycle. Note: the polynomial fit is done by OLS regression. The resulting deviation from trend is then fitted to a Fourier series. The Excel solver is used to estimate parameters β_i and γ_i in equation (2.48) by minimizing the sum of squared deviations of observation points from the fitted line.

2.12 Quantile regression model (QRM) is a statistical method to estimate parameters of a model given a sample of data. It is increasingly popular in VaR modeling because researchers are considering models that are conditional on external variables. Aim: illustrates QRM estimation using Excel Solver. Action: solve for the parameters using different choices of quantiles q. Then use $\hat{\alpha}$'s and $\hat{\beta}$'s to calculate the conditional quantile as per equation (2.51) for various X. Plot the results to produce the Figure 2-29.

PART *II*

VALUE-AT-RISK
METHODOLOGY

Chapter 3

Preprocessing

Before we explore the different VaR methodologies in Chapter 4, we need to introduce the building blocks used by VaR calculation. In particular, how positions in a portfolio are mapped to a set of *risk factors* and the generation of scenarios from these risk factor data. This "preprocessing step" represents the data aspect of VaR and forms the crucial first half of any VaR system.

3.1 System Architecture

To gain a perspective of how banks build and maintain their risk management systems, it helps to look at a typical risk management architecture. A good design incorporates the so-called "front-to-back" architecture within a single system. Unfortunately because of the merger mania in the late 1990's, many banks inherited legacy systems that were then interfaced together (loosely) by their in-house risk IT. In addition, the outsourcing mania in recent years may have moved the risk IT support to a different continent. Such a disconnect creates many weak links in the information chain. Some of the resulting problems could be incomplete position capture, incompatible rates and risk factors across systems, lack of risk aggregation tools, etc. In the extreme case, risk information becomes opaque and questionable, which could lead to problems in hedging activities and risk monitoring.

Figure 3-1 shows a stylized system architecture. The upper part represents the risk management system while the lower part represents the trade booking system. Both systems call on the pricing engine which consists of pricing libraries (models and codes) used to revalue a derivative product. Think of it as the "brain" that computes the fair price of each deal as you pass it through the engine.

The front-office (FO) booking interface lets the trader price and book deals. It invokes the pricing engine to get real-time pricing, risk and hedging information.

To value a product, the pricing engine requires rates information from the rates engine and deal information from the booking interface (see the bent arrows).

Once the trade is booked, the position is stored in portfolios (hierarchical database). Typically each trading desk has multiple portfolios. A cluster of portfolios gets rolled up into a "book" for that trading desk.

Figure 3-1 Stylized system architecture

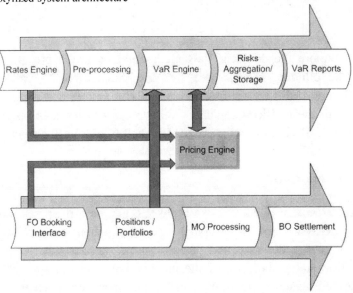

Deal information such as profit-loss (PL) and cashflows are passed to middle office (MO) for processing. Some of these *support functions* include a *product control* team which performs daily mark-to-market of trades, price testing and PL attribution. The verified PL is then passed on to the finance team that does management accounting. Finally, the back-office (BO) processing team performs deal verification, post-trade documentation and cash settlement with the bank's counter parties.

The rates engine takes in real-time market data feeds from sources such as Reuters and Bloomberg and stores the data at end-of-day (EOD *data snapping*). In the preprocessing step, the universe of data is cleaned, bootstrapped (for yield curves) and deals are mapped to a set of risk factors. From the risk factors, the preprocessor will generate a set of scenario vectors (for historical simulation hsVaR) or a covariance matrix (for parametric pVaR).

Next, the risk engine (or VaR engine) calculates the PL vectors for all positions in the case of hsVaR. Here, the pricing engine is called to perform full revaluation of each deal (using positional and rates information). In the case of pVaR, the covariance matrix is multiplied with the sensitivity vector directly to obtain pVaR. Here, the sensitivity vector is computed by the pricing engine as well.

Once the output of the VaR engine—the PL vector or covariance matrix—is generated, these risk results need to be stored at a chosen level of granularity. Clearly, it is ideal to have information as granular as possible (the finest being risk per deal by risk factor) so that the risk controller can drill down with a fine comb for analysis. In practice, this is constrained by computational time and storage space. Hence, the results are often *aggregated* to a coarser level of granularity—for example, risk may be reported at the portfolio level, by currency, or by product type.

The "VaR reports" box is an interface (often called a GUI or *graphic user interface*) which the risk managers use for daily reporting or ad hoc investigations. This function also performs *risk decomposition*. Finer levels of decomposition depend critically on the system's ability to perform ad hoc VaR runs on targeted portfolios under investigation.

VaR can be very computationally intensive. As an extreme example, suppose we want to compute hsVaR at the finest possible granularity, and there are 10,000 deals, 10,000 risk factors, 250 scenarios per risk factor (these are very conservative estimates). The system will need to perform full revaluation up to 25 billion times and may take a few days of computation time. If some of the deals require Monte Carlo simulation for their revaluation, the number can be even more staggering. In the fast-paced world of investment banking, any VaR system that takes more than a fraction of a day to calculate will become useless. The risk numbers will be obsolete by the time the VaR report reaches its audience.

In practice, most deals only depend on a very small subset of risk factors (for example a vanilla interest rate swap will only depend on a single currency yield curve), which could be used to considerable advantage through efficient portfolio construction and an intelligent VaR engine design. For example, such a VaR engine will not bother shocking risk factors that the deal/portfolio does not depend on, and thus reduces the time taken for VaR computation.

A less creative solution, given present-day technology, is to judiciously select the granularity level for meaningful risk control and to invest in system hardware. Thus, many banks are resorting to parallel computing to achieve higher computational power.

3.2 Risk Factor Mapping

Rationale for risk factor mapping

To understand why risk factor mapping is necessary, we reflect that VaR is a portfolio risk measure. In the Markowitz portfolio theory, risk can be diversified (lowered) when aggregated. The property of subadditivity allows the portfolio total risk to be lower than the sum of risks of individual deals.

Well, we can calculate the risk of each deal (say by looking at its price changes) and sub-add them using the Markowitz framework, but this is inconvenient and unintuitive. Since many products are driven by common risk factors it makes sense to map them to a set of risk factors and sub-add the risk factors instead.

This is natural. Risk managers typically perform risk decomposition (to analyze where the risk is coming from) based on risk factors, not based on deals. Dealing with risk factors is also computationally efficient because the number of deals can grow very large but the risk factor universe remains relatively fixed.

For example, a trader's portfolio may contain thousands of FX option deals and FX spot deals for hedging. The risk elements of each deal can be mapped to just a few risk factor classes—FX spot, interest rates and FX volatility—and they are naturally netted within each risk factor itself. The risk factors can then be sub-added to obtain portfolio risk.

Market risks and non-market risks

Before we classify the risk factor universe, we need to appreciate that only *market risks* can be measured by VaR *adequately* in a truly portfolio diversifiable sense. Market risks are tradable risks that have continuous price quotations. See Table 3-1. Hence, their time series, necessary basic building blocks of VaR, are available.

In contrast, *non-market risks* such as those listed in Table 3-2 are non-tradable. Without observed price series, this cannot be aggregated into portfolio VaR (in a fully diversifiable sense). The risk models in this area are still in their infancy and data is unreliable. There are many attempts to integrate all risks under the VaR umbrella, as seen in advances in *enterprise risk management*. It is an appealing school of thought but such "aggregation" is typically done as a simple VaR summation without considering the correlation.

Table 3-1 Types of market risks

Risk Type	Risk Dimension (representation)				
	Price	Yield curve	Implied volatility	Default risk	Implied correlation
Foreign exchange (FX)	Yes		Yes		Seldom
Interest rates		Yes	Yes		Seldom
Credit derivatives and Bonds		Yes	Yes	Yes	Seldom
Equities	Yes		Yes		Seldom
Commodities	Yes	Yes	Yes		Seldom

Sometimes the resulting VaR may not be meaningful. For example, market risk VaR is often expressed with a 10-day horizon for regulatory reporting. Can we really express operational risk over a 10-day horizon and what does it mean? Evidently, the industry is still far from a fully unified framework for risks. The challenges of unification are discussed in Chapter 10.

Table 3-2 Types of non-market risks

Risk Type	Example
Non-tradable credit risk	Counterparty risk, illiquid loans (credit cards, mortgages), Commercial loans
Operational risks	Rogue trader, deal errors, security breach, hardware breakdown, workplace hazard
Reputation risk (often considered Operational risk)	Law suits, fraud, misselling, violation of regulations, money laundering
Liquidity risks	Bid/offer cost, market disruption, enterprise funding risk, bank runs

Risk dimensions

The columns in Table 3-1 refer to the various possible *dimensions* of risk for a particular asset class. For example, options can be written on any asset class and that introduces an extra dimension of risk (on top of the common price risk), that of volatility. Likewise, the innovation of credit derivatives in the late 1990's created yet another dimension of risk, that of issuer default. Some asset classes by nature of their cost-of-carry, exhibit a term structure or yield curve. This means that each point (or pillar) on the yield curve is a single risk factor with its own bid/ask quotation. We consider the term structure a dimension of risk in its own right, because the curve features a unique *duration* risk. Lastly, the innovation of basket and spread products created a rather abstract dimension of risk to trade, that of correlation.

Crucially, to qualify as bona fide risk factors, the volatility and correlation dimensions have to be *implied* from market product prices as opposed to that derived from historical prices (of the underlying). For example, it is well-known that option implied volatility is often very different from historical volatility. In particular, it can exhibit a "volatility smile"—where options with strike prices away from at-the-money show progressively higher implied volatilities. Implied volatilities of differing strikes are distinct risk factors.

More subtly, implied correlation too is distinct from historical correlation. One cannot use historical correlation in place of implied correlation, any more than one can use historical volatility as an option's risk factor. Historical correlation is backward-looking (thus lagging) and provides the general construction for portfolio diversification of *any* assets i.e. it is already embedded in VaR.

In contrast, implied correlation exists *only* for exotic products that use correlation as a *pricing parameter*. Since this parameter is tradable and uncertain, there is (correlation) risk. Implied correlation is forward-looking and often responds instantly to market sentiment. Despite the obvious need, most banks do not include implied correlation risk into their VaR because this risk factor is difficult to handle. There is a wall of challenges in terms of modeling, technology and data scarcity. This issue is discussed in Section 4.5. Except in that section, implied correlation risk factors will not be considered.

Risk factor universe

To appreciate the size of the factor universe, let us look at a conservative illustration of the factors used by a typical bank. Table 3-3 shows the count of the number of factors for a combination of risk type and dimension. The last column is the product of each row. The sum of the last column (52,369) gives the size of the risk factor universe. Most banks will have a factor universe twice this size or larger because of finer gradation.

Let us briefly explain each risk type. The upper half of the table displays country specific risk types. For simplicity, we consider only G-20 countries; hence, there are 19 FX spot exchange rates (against the US dollar). Banks typically divide the maturity of deals into standard *tenor buckets* (or *pillars*) for risk-mapping, for example: {1d, 1w, 1m, 3m, 6m, 9m, 1y, 2y, 3y, 4y, 5y, 7y, 10y, 15y, 20y}.

If the bank trades in FX options, these can be in any of the 19 currencies. FX options are typically liquid from 1w to 5y maturity, so they fall into 10 tenor buckets. We also bucket the (implied) volatility risk into 5 strike levels (with delta of 10, 25, 50, 75, 90). Thus, the number of possible risk factors for FX options is 19*10*5 =950 combinations. The volatility plotted on a tenor vs. strike grid is called the *volatility surface*.

For interest rate risky assets, we assume the curves for each currency are quoted from 1d to 20y (15 buckets). At its simplest, there will be three types of rate curves—the swap curve, the government curve and the cross-currency basis curve (against USD). The basis curve is the rate curve implied from prices in the FX forward and currency swap markets. The basis curve reflects the demand-supply for the foreign currency versus the USD. Hence, for interest rate risk, we have 20*15*3=900 risk factors.

Table 3-3 An example of risk factor universe

Risk type	Currency/ asset name	Tenor buckets	Underlying tenor	Curve type	Strike levels	Number of risk factors
(Country specific)						
FX spot	19					19
FX volatility	19	10			5	950
Interest Rates	20	15		3		900
Cap/Floor	20	11			7	1,540
Swaption	20	11	7		7	10,780
						-
(Asset specific)						-
Equity spot	600					600
Equity volatility	600	5			10	30,000
Credit Trading	100	5		2		1,000
Credit swaption/ bond option	100	1			1	100
Commodity curve	24	30				720
Commodity option	24	12			20	5,760
					Total	52,369

Two *vanilla* (or basic) options for rates derivatives are *cap/floor* and *swaption*. They constitute the most liquid instruments available for volatility price discovery. A cap/floor is a basket of options to deliver a *forward rate agreement*

(FRA). A FRA is a forward (or deferred) start loan; for example, a 6x9 FRA is a 3 month loan that starts 6 months from trade date. The typical volatility surface for cap/floor is defined on a grid of 11 tenors vs. 7 strikes.

A swaption is an option contract to enter into a swap. Since the option maturity is distinct from the underlying swap maturity, the swaption volatility surface is actually 3 dimensional. For example, in the Table 3-3 we have 11 swaption maturities vs. 7 swap maturities vs. 7 strikes. This is sometimes called the "vol cube". With 20 vol cubes, one for each currency, the number of risk factors swells to 10,780.

The lower half of Table 3-3 displays risk factors belonging to specific named asset such as that linked to a company, a debt issuer or a specific commodity. Since there are many specific tradable assets in the world, the factor universe is even more nebulous and banks will limit the size of the set sufficient to cover the markets they actually trade in.

In Table 3-3, we simplistically assume the bank trades an average of 30 stocks in each of the 20 countries. Hence, there will be 600 equity names. For stock options, most listed options are quoted from 1m to 1y (5 tenors) and have 10 strike levels defined. Thus, we have 30,000 risk factors here.

The vanilla products in credit trading are risky bonds and *credit default swaps* (CDS). The universe of issuers (or *obligors*) is large but there are probably just around 100 liquid names traded before the 2008 crisis. Hence, 100 is a reasonable estimate for a small bank. For risk management purposes, it is important to distinguish between two curve types (for the same issuer)—the CDS curve and the asset swap curve—because of the basis risk between the two[1]. The credit curve typically contains 5 tenors (1y to 5y) although the reliable (liquid) point is really just the 5-year. Options on CDS and risky bonds are typically illiquid—the volatility surface is not observable and most banks will just estimate a single point volatility (5-year, at-the-money strike) as the risk factor.

For commodity factors, we note that the Goldman Sachs commodity index (a popular benchmark) has 24 components. These 24 commodities represent broadly the commodity world. For most commodity futures, there are typically 30 contract months (hence, 30 monthly tenors) in the forward curve. Thus, we estimated 24*30= 720 factors. As for listed commodity options, they are less liquid than futures and are commonly quoted up to 1 year (12 monthly tenors)

---

[1] The basis exists because of structural and liquidity differences between the two products. The asset swap curve is derived from risky bond yields, whereas CDS spreads are like an insurance premium on that issuer and are traded in a separate market.

with 20 defined strike levels. Thus, commodity options can contribute a huge number of factors—5760 in this case.

Each element in the risk factor universe has its own time series data that is collected daily. A bank needs to maintain this data set in order to operate its VaR engine.

In VaR application, each deal may be mapped to multiple risk factors that it is exposed to. For example, assuming the base currency for reporting VaR is USD, a 5-year risky bond denominated in EUR is mapped to the following factors: EUR interest rate curve (up to 5y), EUR/USD spot exchange rate, the credit curve of the issuer (up to 5y)—a total of 17 factors from Table 3-3. We will see more examples in Chapter 4.

3.3 Risk Factor Proxies

A *proxy risk factor* is a surrogate risk factor that is used when data history for the actual held asset is not available. Proxies are often used in emerging markets where the markets are illiquid and data history is sparse. Some asset classes such as corporate bonds and credit derivatives are by nature illiquid. These are issuer specific securities that at times fall out of popularity with investors. Hence, some parts of its price history may be stale or not updated. Under these circumstances, a suitable proxy is required.

The handling of proxies requires much subjectivity. Under what circumstances should a proxy be considered? What makes a good proxy and must the proxy be scaled?

If prices for an asset exist but are not well-behaved ("bad data") you are better off using a proxy. Remember that in practice we are interested in the portfolio level VaR i.e. how this single additional asset affects the overall VaR. If the bad data series has many erroneous spikes, the portfolio VaR will be overstated. On the other hand, if the bad data series has many stale points, the portfolio VaR will be understated.

The idea that small errors from a single asset may be diversified away in a large portfolio is dangerous. Small, unaccountable errors can build up in a VaR engine over time and it will be increasingly difficult to explain the drivers of a bank's VaR. Since early 2008, there has been a policy push by regulators in favour of including issuer specific or idiosyncratic risk into VaR. Because many of the data series in this space are bad, it is questionable whether the risk manager is including useful information or "garbage" into his VaR system. The guide to staying on the right path is to always remember that VaR *is only as good as the input data*. So how good is this particular data?

As an example, consider the data series of Lebanon 5-year CDS spread in Figure 3-2 for the period May 2007 to Apr 2008. During half of that time the data set was illiquid and hence stale; therefore a proxy is called for. The logical choice, based on geopolitical similarity will be the 5-year Israel CDS spread which has better data history. On closer inspection, one will be surprised to find the correlation of returns of the non-stale days to be near zero. This seems to be a general observation in the credit trading market and is due to illiquidity (compared to other asset classes). *Returns* are uncorrelated even for issuers within the same industry and even though the spread *levels* are themselves correlated. This poses less of a problem for VaR since we are actually interested in correlation in the tail or quantile—as long as large spikes in spreads are in sync between Israel and Lebanon, the VaR will be correlated. Taking only the largest 7 and smallest 7 scenarios and computing correlation again, we find a correlation of 0.5—a more intuitive result (that supports our choice).

Figure 3-2 Five-year CDS spreads for Lebanon and Israel

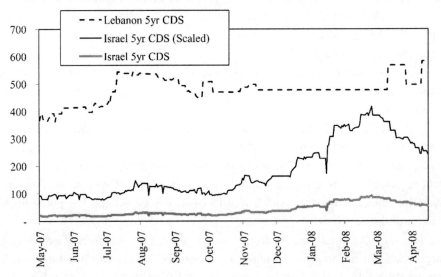

Source: Bloomberg Finance L.P.

Now, we just cannot replace the Lebanon time series with the Israel time series in the VaR system—their volatilities are vastly different—the standard deviations are 12bp vs. 2.8bp respectively. We need to scale up the Israel time series in the system by 4.5 times and rename it *Lebanon proxy*.

Using proxies introduces basis risk into VaR (addressed in Section 4.6). This is still more preferable than leaving bad actual data in the VaR system whose impact it is impossible to quantify. The basis risk between Israel and Lebanon CDS spreads should be conservatively estimated (even if only roughly) and provisioned for using a *reserve*[2].

3.4 Scenario Generation

In Section 3.2 we looked at how a risk factor universe is selected to represent all tradable assets relevant for a bank. Each risk factor comes in the form of a daily time series of level prices (or rates). But VaR uses *returns* as inputs since it is the quantile of a return distribution of an observation period. Hence, the returns series (or *scenarios*) need to be generated. In this book, we chose a 250-business day rolling observation period (or window) representing one calendar year. So the return series is represented by a scenario vector (of length 250). The scenarios are indexed 1 to 250; by convention, scenario-1 is the daily return at today's close-of-business (COB) date, scenario-250 is the return 250 days in the past from COB.

Once we have derived the scenarios, we can use a scenario to shift the current price level (or *base level*) to the *shifted level*. Each deal in a portfolio is then revalued at the current level and the shifted level. The difference between the two valuations is the profit & loss (PL) for that scenario. Do this for all 250 scenarios and we get a *PL vector*, which is actually a distribution with 250 data points. We shall see in the next chapter that VaR is just the quantile taken on the PL vector.

Different returns

There are three common ways to generate a return series from a price series:

Absolute: $$return(i) = rate(i) - rate(i+1) \qquad (3.1)$$

---

[2] A provision or a reserve is money set aside to cushion against any risks which are not well captured or understood. In this case it is the risk of "not knowing the difference in risk between the two risk factors".

$$shiftedlevel(i) = baselevel + return(i) \qquad\qquad (3.2)$$

Relative: $$return(i) = rate(i)/rate(i+1) - 1 \qquad\qquad (3.3)$$

$$shiftedlevel(i) = baselevel.[1 + return(i)] \qquad\qquad (3.4)$$

Log: $$return(i) = \ln[rate(i)/rate(i+1)] \qquad\qquad (3.5)$$

$$shiftedlevel(i) = baselevel.\exp[return(i)] \qquad\qquad (3.6)$$

where i=1, . . ,250 is the time index (in reverse chronological order). Here the terms *rate* and *price* are used interchangeably.

Absolute return is suitable for interest rate risk factors because it can handle low and negative rates. A daily change from +0.02% to +0.06% (a mere +4bp absolute change) would imply a 200% relative change. In the 2008 crisis, short-term overnight rates were set ultra low by central banks to counter the liquidity crunch. When the market recovers, rates may rise to a much higher base level even though the scenario vector remains largely unchanged. Thus, by equation (3.4) the PL vector (and hence VaR) will be overstated.

Sometimes rates can go negative momentarily. A change from -0.05% to -0.04% (+1bp *rise*) is reflected as a 20% *fall* by (3.3). Hence, relative return gives the wrong sign when rates are negative.

For all other risk factors (that never go to low/ negative prices) relative or log return is preferred because it takes into account the base level. For example, a gain of +$1 from $1 to $2 is a lot riskier (100% increase) compared to that of $100 to $101 (a 1% increase).

Negative rates

Negative rates do occur for *non-deliverable forwards* (NDF). For some semi-convertible currencies, government restrictions create a dislocation that makes arbitrage difficult between onshore and offshore forward markets. Without a corrective mechanism, the implied forward rates of offshore NDF can go negative momentarily.

These negative implied rates are not fictitious—they do represent real MTM PL should the position be liquidated. Nevertheless, for the purpose of VaR, there are a few good reasons why we should floor these rates at a small positive number (say at +0.05%). Firstly, the rate normally goes negative for very short periods and is corrected in a matter of days. Secondly, the negative rates typically happen at the very short end of the curve (say less than 1 week tenor) where the duration risk is tiny. Thirdly, even though vanilla product pricing can admit negative rates, many pricing models for complex products cannot. Since most banks run exotic books hedged with vanilla products, the overall risk of the portfolio can be misrepresented if negative rates are permitted.

3.5 Basic VaR Specification

Simplistically VaR is just the loss quantile of the PL distribution over the chosen observation period. In the industry, different banks use different specifications for their VaR system. Often a firm-wide VaR number is reported to the public or the regulator. In order to attribute any meaning to the understanding or comparison of VaR numbers, it is important to first specify the VaR system. A succinct way to do this is to use the format in Table 3-4.

Table 3-4 VaR system specification format

Item	Possible choice
Valuation method	Linear approximation, full revaluation, delta-gamma approx.
Weighting	Equal weight/ exponential weight in volatility/ correlation
VaR model	Parametric, historical simulation, Monte-Carlo
Observation period	250 days, 500 days, 1000 days
Confidence level	95%, 97.5%, 99%
Return definition[3]	Relative, absolute, log
Return period	Daily, weekly
Mean adjustment	Yes/no
Scaling (if any)	Scaled to 10-days, scaled to 99% confidence level

As a prelude, let's describe a reasonable VaR system specification which is workable in my opinion and which we shall use as a base case throughout the book. See Table 3-5.

The advantages of a full revaluation and historical simulation model will be covered in Chapter 4. A rolling window of 250 days (1-year) is short enough to be sensitive to structural changes (*innovation*) in the market. Had we chosen a

---

[3] Different return definitions may be more suitable for different risk factors. Hence a real world VaR system may contain a mixture of return definitions.

1000-day (4-year) window, the VaR will hardly move even when faced with a regime change. This is undesirable.

Table 3-5 VaR system specification example

Item	Selection
Valuation method	Full revaluation
Weighting	Equal weight
VaR model	Historical simulation
Observation period	250 days
Confidence level	97.5%
Return definition	Log return
Return period	Daily
Mean adjustment	Yes
Scaling (if any)	Scaled to 10-day holding period and 99% confidence level

At 97.5% confidence, the number of exceedences in the left tail is 6-7 data points. At higher confidence (say 99%), the number of exceedences becomes too few to be statistically meaningful (2-3 points). And at lower confidence, the quantile may not be representative of tail risk; we may be measuring "peace-time" returns instead.

Log returns with flooring of rates (no negative rates allowed) have the advantages mentioned in Section 3.4. Daily data is used because it is the most granular information[4] and will be more responsive than say weekly data. The specified scaling is a regulatory requirement. For the bank's internal risk monitoring, the scaling is often omitted.

The case for mean adjustment

Mean-adjustment is the process of deducting the average of the PL vector from the VaR quantile. Then, the PL distribution which may be skewed to one side becomes centered (see Figure 3-3). Some banks report VaR based on a mean-adjusted basis, other don't. This book adopts the former approach.

---

[4] Intraday data is seldom considered because price gaps which occur during opening and session breaks often make the data non-stationary.

Figure 3-3 Mean adjustment applied to PL distribution

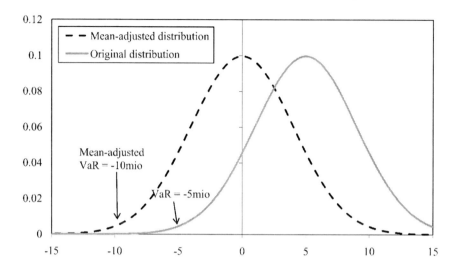

Mean adjustment is necessary to make the VaR measure consistent. Let's see why.

1. In mathematical finance we have chosen to define risk in terms of uncertainty of *returns*. (We could have chosen a different metric such as leverage, duration, etc. but that is a different starting point.). As long as there is a distribution there is uncertainty of returns, hence risk. Since we measure this uncertainty as *dispersion from the mean* (or expected value), it follows that mean adjustment is necessary.

2. Suppose you have a return distribution for a "super bullish" stock which is so right skewed such that all return observations are positive i.e. it went up (if only slightly) every day for the last 250 days. Without mean adjustment your VaR will be zero since by its definition, VaR is the quantile of *loss*. It is not meaningful to say that the holder of this stock runs no risks, since clearly a stock is a risky asset.

When implementing mean adjustment, it is important to deduct the mean at the level of the dollar PL vector, not at the return scenario vector. In practice, this means the adjustment is done *after* product revaluation. For linear products it doesn't matter—mean adjustment done at the scenario vector (return distribution) or done at the PL vector (PL distribution), produces the same VaR. However, in the presence of options, they are generally unequal.

To see why it matters for options, suppose the underlying stock has a return distribution with a mean (say -0.1%) skewed very slightly to the left. If the portfolio contains call options, the *portfolio's* PL distribution (after revaluation) can be skewed to the right (say with mean +0.5%) as a result of the loss protection provided by the options. So we mean-adjust the PL distribution to the left. But had we performed mean adjustment in the *return* distribution instead, we would have mistakenly adjusted to the right resulting in a very different VaR outcome.

For the sake of simplicity, in this book, we will often mean-adjust the *return* distribution unless the example involves an actual dollar PL distribution.

Chapter 4

Conventional VaR Methods

VaR is simplistically the loss quantile of the PL distribution. There are many ways to generate the distribution and to compute the quantile. By far the three most common methods used by banks are the parametric VaR, historical simulation VaR and Monte Carlo VaR. Their popular use stems from the practical balance between simplicity and validity.

A VaR system must be simple enough to be intuitively understood by top management, regulators and operators of the system. Abstract models that require specialized domain knowledge to comprehend seldom make it to conventional use. This is because risk management is a huge team effort—there are often hundreds of staff managing different aspects of the risk architecture and in different geographic locations. A simple model provides a common language in the chain of command.

The validity of a VaR model must be tested against the market. Until recently, VaR models have been generally accepted (for lack of a better alternative) on the grounds that the market behavior generally falls within the prediction of VaR. Statistically speaking, almost all (say 99%) of the time, the system is predictive. But the 2008 crisis has highlighted that this "peace time" tool breaks down during times of crisis, just when it is needed most.

The best way to learn about VaR is to implement it on an Excel spreadsheet. We will illustrate all three VaR methods using the same test portfolio comprising a stock index, an option and a bond. This test set will let us illustrate all the nuances of VaR in Section 4.4. Some basic product knowledge is assumed; the absolute beginner is referred to the excellent textbook by Hull (2008).

The formal definition of VaR, equation (2.13) can also be expressed as:

$$VaR_q = F^{-1}(q) \qquad (4.1)$$

where F^{-1}, the *quantile function* is defined as the inverse of the CDF of the return variable X. The $c\%$ confidence level VaR is then just the $q=(1-c)$ quantile. The final step of any VaR method will involve "taking the quantile" as per (4.1).

4.1 Parametric VaR

Parametric VaR (pVaR) or *variance-covariance* (VCV) VaR was popularized by JP Morgan's Riskmetrics©. The original methodology was published in 1994 and evolved over the years as it took hold as the industry standard. Strictly speaking, Riskmetrics proposed the modeling of VaR using the normal distribution and the EWMA volatility measure[1]. For simplicity, we will model the volatility using standard deviation of returns (i.e. using equal weights) and combine the risks using a variance-covariance method. The model specification is per Table 4-1.

Table 4-1 pVaR model specification

Parameter	Selection
Valuation method	Linear approximation
Weighting	Equal weight
VaR model	Parametric
Observation period	250 days
Confidence level	97.50%
Return definition	Relative
Return period	Daily
Mean adjustment	N.A.
Scaling (if any)	No

The valuation method of pVaR is by the *sensitivity approach*. This means that to derive the PL of each scenario, we do *not* reprice a deal using its pricing formula (such as the Black-Scholes equation for an option deal); instead, we get an approximation of the PL by multiplying the deal's risk factor *sensitivity* with the risk factor's return scenario.

Risk sensitivities or *Greeks* are the bread and butter of risk management. Risk managers look at Greek reports across portfolios and product types every day.

---

[1] To get a precise definition of Riskmetrics and how it has evolved, refer: Riskmetrics, 2001, "Return to Riskmetrics: The evolution of a standard"

Sensitivities measure the change in valuation (i.e. the PL) of a deal due to a unit change in the risk factor that the deal is exposed to. The number of Greeks and their mathematical intricacy have expanded in recent years because of product innovation. Here we will consider only the basic sensitivities which are relevant for pVaR as listed in Table 4-2.

Table 4-2 Basic risk sensitivities

Basic Sensitivity	Definition	Application
Delta	PL due to 1 unit change in price	Price based products and their options
Gamma	PL due to 1 unit change in Delta i.e. second order sensitivity to price	Options
Vega	PL due to 1% change in volatility	Options
PV01	PL due to +1bp change in rates	Interest rate products
Convexity	Second order PL adjustment due to +1bp change in rates	Interest rate products
Credit01	PL due to +1bp change in credit spread	Credit risky products

The logic of pVaR can be understood in terms of a *Taylor series expansion* of a product's price P around its initial price P_0. P is a function of risk factor Y.

$$P - P_0 = f'(Y_0)\Delta Y + 0.5 f''(Y_0)(\Delta Y)^2 + .. \qquad (4.2)$$

where $f'(.) = dP/dY$ is the first derivative and $f''(.) = d^2P/dY^2$ the second derivative of the pricing function $f(.)$ evaluated at the starting point Y_0. $\Delta Y = Y - Y_0$ represents a shift (or perturbation) away from Y_0. Note the following:
1. If the product is linear (such as a stock) the second and higher order terms do not exist (are zero).
2. $f'(.)$ gives the first order or delta sensitivity. Depending on the risk factors involved, it is called delta, PV01, vega or Credit01 (see Table 4-2). For example, for a stock option, $f(.)$ is the Black-Scholes formula. If Y is the spot (share price) risk factor, then $f'(.)$ is called the *delta*. If Y is the volatility risk factor, then $f'(.)$ is called the *vega*.

3. For yield curve sensitive products (such as a bond) if ΔY represents a one basis point (1bp=0.01%) parallel shift of the *entire* yield curve then $f'(.)$ is called the PV01 or *present value per basis point*. We can make finer gradations by shifting individually the t-year points on the curve to calculate the so-called *bucketed* PV01s. These are needed for pVaR.
4. For non-linear products, the second order derivative $f''(.)$ is called the *gamma* for an option and *convexity* for a yield curve product.
5. The higher order terms are progressively smaller for a small change ΔY and are often neglected. PVaR quite often just uses the first (linear) term to approximate the PL ($= P - P_0$); this is called the *linear approximation* or delta approach. One can improve accuracy by also including the second order term; this is called the *delta-gamma* approach.

The test portfolio is shown in Table 4-3. To calculate pVaR, we need each deal's sensitivities to all the relevant risk factors. The sensitivities in Table 4-3 are calculated using *discrete differences*. For example, to calculate vega for deal-2, we reprice the option twice using the Black-Scholes formula—once using the current parameters, and once with the volatility bumped up by 1%. The vega is just the dollar change in valuation due to this bumping. The sensitivity numbers of the test deals are worked out in Spreadsheet 4.1.

Table 4-3 Test portfolio

Deal 1	Equity	Deal 2	Put option	Deal 3	Bond
Risk feature	Linear	Risk feature	Non-linear	Risk feature	Convexity
Asset	Dow Jones index	Asset	Dow Jones option	Asset	2-year T-bond
Notional	$ 1,000,000	Notional	$ 1,000,000	Notional	$ 1,000,000
Index level	10,718	Maturity	1 year	Maturity	2 years
		Strike	10,718	Coupon (p.a.)	5%
		Volatility	12.07%	1-yr rate	4.836%
				2-yr rate	4.8295%
(Valuation)					
Valuation	$ 1,000,000	Premium	491.7	Price	100.1
		Valuation	$ 45,875	Valuation	$ 1,000,964
(Sensitivity)					
Delta	$ 93.3	Delta	(0.45)	PV01 (1y)	$ (4.8)
		Delta ($)	$ (42.3)	PV01 (2y)	$ (190.6)
		Vega ($)	$ 3,794		
		PV01 (1y)	$ (4.6)		

Each risk factor (more precisely its scenario vector) is assumed to be normally distributed. For large portfolios this assumption is justified by the Central Limit Theorem. There are four risk factors affecting our portfolio: 1-year rate, 2-year rate, index price (spot) and index volatility[2]. The volatility of each risk factor, σ_i (where i=1, . . ,4), is computed using the standard deviation of 250 days return data. To account for the dependence structure, a 4x4 correlation matrix is computed from the four scenario vectors[3].

To aggregate the risk, we apply Markowitz portfolio theory, similar to equation (2.36). The portfolio variance is given by:

$$\sigma^2 = w^T \Sigma w \qquad (4.3)$$

where Σ is the correlation matrix, and w the vector of *standalone* VaR given by:

$$w_i = \alpha \delta_i \sigma_i \qquad (4.4)$$

where δ_i is the linear sensitivity to risk factor-i and σ_i is the volatility of risk factor-i. The constant α is the *standard normal deviate* related to the confidence level c. In Excel function syntax α = NORMSINV(1-c). So for 97.5% VaR, α = -1.96.

Multiplying by -1.96 is just a way to "take the quantile". This goes back to the theoretical meaning of VaR—a 97.5% VaR is defined as a 0.025-quantile; under the normal distribution, this roughly corresponds to a loss of 2 sigma. This is a handy rule-of-thumb since sigma can easily be estimated.

The portfolio pVaR is then the square-root of equation (4.3). The pVaR implementation for the test portfolio is shown in Spreadsheet 4.1.

Weakness of pVaR

Firstly, the assumption of normality is a major model weakness of pVaR. As such—fat-tailness and skewness—two important behaviors of price returns during market crises are ignored (see Chapter 7).

---

[2] The index volatility is an example of *implied* volatility that is observed from the market (it's traded); this is different from the volatility σ which is a statistic on returns.
[3] A more advanced pVaR system may involve exponentially weighting the volatility or correlation or both.

Secondly, the sensitivity approach (without doing full re-pricing of deals) gives only a first order approximation of the PL. In other words, pVaR is a *local* risk measure—the sensitivity $f'(Y_0)$ is computed for and true only at the *current* level Y_0. This is okay for small shifts, but when the shift ΔY is large, the second and higher order terms which we have ignored become significant. This means that non-linear risks such as optionality and convexity are ignored by pVaR.

Thirdly, when the correlation matrix gets too large, it runs into non positive semi-definite problems (or becomes corrupted). This problem is insidious and warrants some explanation.

An n-by-n square matrix Σ is *positive semi-definite* if all its *eigenvalues* are non-negative. Eigenvalues λ_i are the elements of the diagonal matrix M given by the "Eigen decomposition":

$$\Sigma = e^T M e \tag{4.5}$$

where:

$$M = \begin{pmatrix} \lambda_1 & 0 & .. & 0 \\ 0 & \lambda_2 & .. & 0 \\ .. & .. & .. & .. \\ 0 & 0 & .. & \lambda_n \end{pmatrix}$$

and e is a matrix whose rows are called *eigenvectors* and e^T is the transpose of e.

As a working definition, a non positive semi-definite matrix is one whereby its Cholesky matrix (see Section 2.11) is undefined. For example, consider a correlation matrix of 3 assets: A, B and C. Suppose the correlation of (A,B) and (A,C) are both +0.9, and correlation (B,C) is -0.9, then the Cholesky decomposition will fail because the relationship is logically impossible[4]. The requirement of positive semi-definiteness is a relational constraint to ensure that the correlation matrix is logical.

What happens to portfolio VaR when the correlation becomes illogical? Try replacing the correlation matrix in Spreadsheet 4.1 with the upper matrix in Table 4-4. You can check that the Cholesky matrix is undefined. The computed

---

[4] An analogy: Suppose there is a room with 2 exits (directions). There is a fire and three persons exit the room, but all three claimed that they exited the room from a different direction from another. This is logically impossible.

portfolio VaR is suspect and worse still—there is no obvious warning that something is amiss. Next, replace the correlation with the lower matrix in Table 4-4, and change the sign of the standalone VaR for Index volatility (a vulnerable situation where risk factors are almost perfectly correlated and positions are offsetting). The portfolio variance becomes negative, a meaningless number.

Table 4-4 Non-positive semi-definite matrix

	Dow Jones	USD 1y swap	USD 2y swap	Index vol
Dow Jones	1.000	0.008	(0.900)	0.900
USD 1y swap	0.008	1.000	0.749	0.020
USD 2y swap	(0.900)	0.749	1.000	(0.055)
Index vol	0.900	0.020	(0.055)	1.000

	Dow Jones	USD 1y swap	USD 2y swap	Index vol
Dow Jones	1.000	0.528	0.682	0.999
USD 1y swap	0.528	1.000	0.454	0.080
USD 2y swap	0.682	0.454	1.000	0.493
Index vol	0.999	0.080	0.493	1.000

When do correlation matrices become ill-behaved? When the dimension of the matrix grows too large relative to the length of the time series, the relational constraints among its elements become increasingly restrictive. The integrity of the matrix becomes vulnerable to corruption. At some point, the positive semi-definite condition may break down under certain situations such as:
1. When time series data is tampered with, for example, backfilled during a holiday, or interpolated over missing points.
2. When correlation elements are calculated using time series of different length, or when correlation elements are rounded off.
3. When the correlation matrix is estimated by traders subjectively (as opposed to being calculated statistically).
4. When the correlation is calibrated from prices of traded instruments.
5. When the correlation matrix is perturbed (i.e. shifted) for the purpose of a stress test.
6. When a correlation number is close to +0.99 and there is a long-short offsetting position, the integrity of the matrix becomes vulnerable.
7. When decay weights are used for correlation estimation, making the effective time series period even smaller compared to the matrix dimension.

As a solution, researchers have proposed adjustment schemes which slightly modify the matrix elements to ensure that the correlation matrix remains positive semi-definite. For example, see Finger (1997) and Rebonato (1999). This is a critical check for any VaR systems that explicitly use correlation matrices.

4.2 Monte Carlo VaR

We have seen that the pVaR method can only handle a normal distribution. However, it is well-known that markets are fat-tailed (not normal) during stressful times. If we know the exact functional form of the distribution, we can use Monte Carlo simulation to generate scenarios from this known distribution and compute Monte Carlo VaR (mcVaR).

Table 4-5 shows a simple mcVaR model specification that we will use in this section. Our mcVaR example uses the same test portfolio as per Table 4-3 and is also implemented in Spreadsheet 4.1.

Table 4-5 McVaR model specification

Parameter	Selection
Valuation method	Full revaluation
Weighting	N.A.
VaR model	Monte Carlo
Observation period	2000 paths
Confidence level	97.50%
Return definition	Relative
Return period	Daily
Mean adjustment	N.A.
Scaling (if any)	N.A.
Distribution model	Normal
Process model	Geometric Brownian motion

Referring to the spreadsheet, let's trace the following general steps in the mcVaR calculation:
1. The correlation matrix Σ and volatilities σ_i are computed from the risk factors' historical returns. The factors are indexed $i=1,2,3,4$.
2. Compute the Cholesky matrix of Σ and use it to generate correlated random number draws ε_t from a normal distribution $N(0,1)$ (see Section 2.11). In the example, we draw 2,000 paths ($t = 1, . . ,2000$).

3. Use ε_t to simulate the return scenarios for the risk factors, $R_t = (dX/X)_t$. We need to specify a model for this stochastic *process*.
4. Calculate the shifted level $X_t = (1+R_t)X_0$ where X_0 is the *current* level for the risk factor. Do this for all i risk factors.
5. The PL for scenario-t is just the present value of the deal re-priced at the shifted levels minus the present value of the deal re-priced at current levels. Do this for all t to arrive at the PL vector (it is a 1x2000 vector). Calculate the PL vector for each deal.
6. Sum the PL vectors for all deals *by scenario* to derive the portfolio PL vector. We take the 0.025-quantile for this PL vector to give the 97.5%-VaR.

In step (2), the larger the number of simulations, the more precise the mcVaR will be. Typically banks may simulate more than 10,000 paths. To model fat-tails, we will need to draw from a specified fat-tailed distribution. This is discussed in Section 4.4.

In step (3), we have chosen geometric Brownian motion (GBM) to model the process as per equation (2.44). Since our target horizon for VaR is 1 day, $\Delta t=1/365$. If a 10-day VaR is required for regulatory reporting, we just set $\Delta t=10/365$ i.e. no time scaling is required. For short horizons one can assume the drift μ is zero, and since σ is calculated directly from daily data (i.e. not annualized) there is no need for the factor $\sqrt{\Delta t}$ in the second term. With this simplification, equation (2.44) becomes (4.6). This is implemented in the spreadsheet.

Zero drift GBM: $$\frac{\Delta X_t}{X_t} = \sigma \varepsilon_t \tag{4.6}$$

Although the GBM model is suitable for stocks, it is less appropriate for interest rates, which exhibit mean reversion. *Short rate models* are required[5]. One class of short rate models is called the *one-factor model*, in that there is only one stochastic variable ε_t. There are many specific models under this class; $\gamma=0.5$ gives the popular *Cox-Ingersoll-Ross* (CIR) model (1985), $\gamma=0$ gives *Vasicek model*, $\gamma=1$ gives the *lognormal model*.

One-factor model: $$\Delta r_t = k(\theta - r_t)\Delta t + \sigma r_t^{\gamma} \varepsilon_t \tag{4.7}$$

---

[5] Likewise, to model the evolution of volatility risk factors, *stochastic volatility* models are required. A popular model is the *Heston model* (1993).

where r_t is the short rate, σ is the constant volatility, k and θ are parameters to be estimated. The first term controls drift and mean reversion while the second term controls volatility. The challenge in modeling complicated stochastic processes is that the parameters need to be calibrated using numerical methods such as *moments matching*. A computer algorithm is used to find the best values for the parameters that will match the moments of the simulated process with its theoretical moments. Unfortunately calibration is a highly unstable and error-prone exercise; for example, a slightly different way of coding the same theory can result in different results.

In step (5), *full revaluation* is applied using the pricing formulas for each product. In the spreadsheet we used the Black-Scholes equation to price the option and cash-flow discounting to price the bond. With exact solutions (unlike that in pVaR) mcVaR will account for non-linear risks of derivatives.

Often, all the risk factors are simulated *together* for *each* scenario re-pricing, this means that the final VaR can be broken down (for analysis) by deals but not by individual risk factors. Hence, risk decomposition is limited in scope, unless the bank takes the huge task of running mcVaR separately for each risk factor.

Weakness of mcVaR

The major difficulties in mcVaR are the risk of model misspecification and technological dependency.

The return distribution needs to be modeled. While we are sure the normal distribution is too idealistic to hold, we are less certain which fat-tailed distributions, of the many in the academia, is a good choice. Should it be based on extreme value theory, mixed normal distribution or skew-normal distributions, etc.? Evidence suggests that empirical distributions evolve over time and different markets show different distributions. How do we account for such variations?

In addition, the evolutional (stochastic) process of the risk factor needs to be modeled. There are many classes and sub-classes of models that attempt to describe observed market dynamics. With the exception of GBM, most models will require calibration to determine their parameters. Unfortunately, the parameters themselves are seldom constant so re-calibration is periodically required. Do we really know if an adopted model is the right one?

Monte Carlo simulation is also computationally intensive because full revaluation of all deals is performed. This is especially so for portfolios with many deals, non-linear products and exotic derivatives. In the latter case, if the re-pricing of products itself requires Monte Carlo simulation, we have a situation called *nested* Monte Carlo simulation—a simulation (inner step) within a simulation (outer step). The outer step generates the scenarios. For every outer step, many inner step paths are generated to price the product. Hence, it often takes a long time and many simulated paths for the portfolio VaR to converge to a stable result. Banks normally resort to parallel computing and numerical short-cuts—such as antithetic variable technique, control variates technique and importance sampling technique—to speed up computation.

Monte Carlo simulation uses *pseudo* random numbers generated by the computer. The RAND() function in Excel does this. These are not truly random numbers but a sequence that looks as i.i.d. random as possible. The sequence is deterministic and reproducible since it is generated using a known algorithm by the computer. Figure 4-1 illustrates a problem with such random numbers—notice some points tend to "clump" together to form patches, leaving out large areas. (You can easily check this by plotting two series of RAND() in a scatter plot in Excel). This *clumping effect* is caused by random sampling with replacement—after a point is drawn it is replaced back into the distribution (to ensure i.i.d.) so that the same point has equal chance to be picked again. (That increases the odds of a patch forming at locations that had been previously picked). The clumping effect is undesirable since it will take a much longer time to fill up the whole region evenly.

Figure 4-1 Clumping effect of random numbers

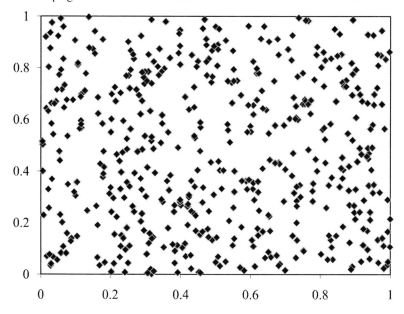

This is overcome by using a *quasi-random* number generator which is designed to select random numbers away from the last drawn number. It is also called a *low-discrepancy* sequence or *Sobol sequence*. Quasi-Monte Carlo converges much faster but one drawback is that it is no longer i.i.d.

As seen above, mcVaR faces many technological challenges. We list down the major ones:

1. Error correction algorithm to ensure that the correlation matrix is positive semi-definite.
2. Calibration of the model parameters is prone to numerical errors and instability.
3. Sobol sequence to generate random numbers and their inverse transformation to generate the specified distribution.
4. Numerical techniques to speed up Monte Carlo computation.
5. Exotic derivatives in the portfolio may require a nested Monte Carlo simulation approach.

Consequently, a huge investment overhead is required to get the technology right. The biggest danger comes from the accumulation of errors from the various moving parts of the mcVaR system. If not designed carefully, the estimation error in the final VaR could become a function of technology and model selection, and this is often opaque.

4.3 Historical Simulation VaR

Historical simulation VaR (hsVaR) is a popular method used by banks and is potentially the most accurate. Pérignon and Smith (2010) found that 73% of banks that disclose their VaR method report using historical simulation. It can be seen as a Monte Carlo simulation method that uses historical (rather than random) samples for its scenarios. It overcomes many of the problems encountered by pVaR and mcVaR. Let's look at the salient features of hsVaR.

First, it uses an empirical distribution (historical data) which bypasses the need to assume any distribution models. This takes care of fat-tails and skewness because we let the data dictate the shape of the distribution. Note that there will be one distribution for every risk factor.

Second, hsVaR computes the PL of each deal by full revaluation (unlike pVaR). This will capture the non-linear risk posed by the presence of non-linear derivatives. Given the complexity of today's derivatives, most portfolios are non-linear. Re-pricing deals avoids the error arising from delta approximation.

Third, risk aggregation is done by summation of PL *across scenarios* to form the portfolio VaR. The dependence structure is accounted for in this way. Hence, there is no need to maintain a large correlation matrix or to deal with positive semi-definite issues. This simple "cross summation" is easy to understand intuitively and allows for easy risk decomposition for the purpose of reporting.

Table 4-6 shows a simple hsVaR model specification that we shall use in this section. Our example uses the same test portfolio as per Table 4-3 and the same Spreadsheet 4.1.

Table 4-6 hsVaR model specification

Parameter	Selection
Valuation method	Full revaluation
Weighting	Equal weight
VaR model	Historical simulation
Observation period	250 days
Confidence level	97.50%
Return definition	Relative
Return period	Daily
Mean adjustment	Yes
Scaling (if any)	No

Let's summarize the steps in computing hsVaR as illustrated in the spreadsheet:

1. A 250-day scenario (i.e. return) vector is derived from the risk factor's historical prices $(x_1, \ldots, x_{251})$. Hence, the returns are $r_t = (x_t / x_{t+1}) - 1$ where $t = 1, \ldots, 250$ is the time index in reverse chronological order.

2. For each risk factor, calculate the shifted level of scenario-t, $x'_t = (1+r_t)x_1$ where x_1 is the *current* level for that risk factor.

3. For a deal, the PL for scenario-t is just the present value of the deal revalued at the shifted level x'_t minus the present value of the deal revalued at the current level x_1. Do this for all t scenarios to derive the PL vector for that deal (a vector of 1x250). Repeat this for all deals. In practice, a product's pricing formula $g(.)$ may be a function of multiple risk factors say x_t, y_t, z_t. In this case, the deal needs to be revalued at shifted levels, i.e. $g(x'_t, y'_t, z'_t)$.

4. Sum the PL vectors for all deals *by scenario* to derive the PL vector for the entire portfolio, which is actually a PL distribution with 250 points. We take the 0.025-quantile of this distribution and perform mean-adjustment to derive the 97.5%-VaR.

Note that in step (2) we always apply the historical shifts to *current* price levels and *current* positions. This is like replaying the tape of history on today's position to see what the daily PL would have looked like. This, in essence, is what hsVaR is about.

For additional accuracy, a bank may also account for the *theta* effect or time decay in hsVaR. By definition, VaR is the risk of loss moving 1 day into the future. Derivatives and cash-flow products will be affected by time decay since their maturity will be shortened by 1 day. This is accounted for by simply rolling the pricing engine's date 1 day forward (to COB+1) during full-revaluation in step (3) such that: PL = PV_{COB+1}(*shifted state*) - PV_{COB}(*current state*).

The final step (4) can easily be implemented using the Excel function: PERCENTILE(.,.)-AVERAGE(..) which gives the portfolio VaR after mean-adjustment (see Section 3.5).

The hsVaR method of "cross summation" (by scenario) allows for very flexible risk decomposition and diagnosis. For example, if we are interested in knowing the risk due to FX spot alone, we can shift *only* the FX spot risk factor and repeat the above steps. If we are interested in VaR breakdown by portfolio, we can do the PL vector summation for each portfolio separately. If we are interested in the impact of a single deal, we can exclude the PL vector of that deal from the summation, and see the difference which is known as the incremental VaR. We can even answer complicated questions such as: what will be the impact on overall portfolio VaR contributed by volatility alone if we put on a particular option deal to hedge the portfolio, assuming the FX spot level is 20% higher than the current level?

Weaknesses of hsVaR

HsVaR is subject to a few subtle weaknesses below. Note that (1) and (2) are also true for VaR in general.

1. VaR assumes returns are i.i.d. In other words, the distribution of the last 250 days can be projected 1 day into the future—past risk is a good predictor of future risk (if only for a day). The problem with this assumption is that it breaks down when there is a regime shift such as at the onset of a crisis. By definition, a regime shift marks the arrival of (breaking) new information absent from past data. Hence, VaR will always lag major price shocks and is only a good tool during "peacetime" when changes are gradual and representative of the past.

2. VaR is only a point estimate. It is a single number chosen to represent risk for the entire distribution and contains no information on the shape of the tail to the left of the loss quantile. The extreme quantile itself is notoriously hard to estimate with so few data points in the tail.

3. The aggregation of PL vectors "by scenario" is affected by data quality. The price series must not be unusually quiet (or stale) and must not be too choppy (has spikes). Otherwise, the portfolio VaR becomes unstable. This is because the tail of an empirical distribution is not as smooth as a theoretical one as used in pVaR and mcVaR. This problem is more pronounced for short observation period, high confidence level or small portfolio size. Thus, the sampling error (precision) of hsVaR is generally poorer.

4.4 Issue: Convexity, Optionality and Fat tails

An important topic increasingly emphasized by regulators is the so-called "risks not in VaR" (or RNIV). It is accepted by regulators and banks that, in practice, not all market risk can be captured in VaR. As a compensating control, regulators normally require banks to quantify and report these missing risks, and hold capital (reserves) against them. The rest of this chapter will explore some of these issues.

Convexity

Convexity is a residual second order risk that affects products which are predominantly made of cash-flows. It is interesting to trace the origin of convexity. Because the pricing of these products involves cost-of-carry (or equally cash-flow discounting) the yield (y) appears in the denominator of the pricing formula. Consider the pricing formula for a simple fixed coupon bond:

$$P(y) = \frac{100}{(1+y)^n} + \sum_{i=1}^{n} \frac{c}{(1+y)^i} \qquad (4.8)$$

where $P(y)$ is the price, c is the coupon, $i = 1, \ldots, n$ is the remaining time to each cash-flow in fractional years.

Because y is in the denominator, the profile of the price-yield relationship is necessarily convex (like the shape of the $P=1/y$ graph). The actual plot of (4.8) for a 20-year bond with a coupon of 5% is shown as the dotted line in Figure 4-2. Convexity is a measure of the dispersion of cash-flows (coupons) across time. So the 20-year bond, having more dispersed coupons, is more convex than a 5-year bond. See Figure 4-2.

HsVaR and mcVaR use (4.8) for full revaluation of bond deals so the convexity risk is already included. However, pVaR uses an approximation based on the Taylor expansion. Inserting equation (4.8) into (4.2) keeping only the first two terms, we obtain:

$$\frac{P(y) - P(y_0)}{P(y_0)} = -D(y - y_0) + 0.5\gamma(y - y_0)^2 \tag{4.9}$$

$$P(y) - P(y_0) = (PV01)(y - y_0)10000 + 0.5P(y_0)\gamma(y - y_0)^2 \tag{4.10}$$

where D the *modified duration* and γ the convexity (also called *gamma*) are measures of first order (linear) and second order (quadratic) sensitivities.

Figure 4-2 Convexity of the price-yield relationship of a bond

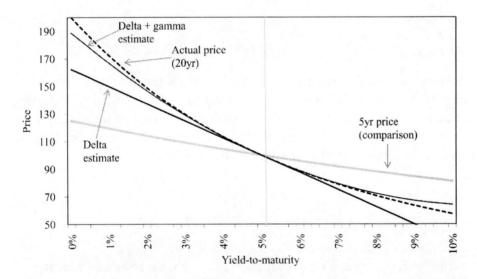

Equations (4.9) and (4.10) show that duration is really just another way to express PV01 risk. Duration is measured in unit of years and can be thought of as the *average weighted time* of the bond (weighted by discounted cash-flows). The reader can refer to Hull (2008) for further study. Here, it suffices to know that modified duration D can be calculated by the Excel function MDURATION(..) and convexity is given by:

$$\gamma = \frac{1}{P}\left[\sum_{i=1}^{n}\frac{i(i+1)c}{(1+y)^{i+2}}+\frac{n(n+1)100}{(1+y)^{n+2}}\right]$$ (4.11)

These formulas are used in Spreadsheet 4.2 to generate Figure 4-2. HsVaR and mcVaR refer to shifts along the dotted line to derive its PL vector. Such PL occurs when the yield y moves away from the current yield y_0 (this base case is marked by the vertical line). In contrast, pVaR refers to shifts along the linear line (marked "delta estimate") to estimate its PL vector. The error between full revaluation and linear approximation (deviation between the dotted and linear lines) becomes apparent for large shifts away from y_0. One way to mitigate the error is to use the delta-gamma approximation, which also takes into account the second order convexity term. As seen in the figure, the deviation between the delta-gamma line and dotted line is much smaller.

Note that convexity (curvature) *benefits the bond holder* (long position). For an adverse shift in yield (to the right), actual loss is smaller than the straight line. On the other hand, for a yield shift to the left, actual gains are larger than the straight line. This can also be seen in equation (4.9)—the convexity term is always positive owing to the square. Conversely, convexity hurts the short sellers.

Spreadsheet 4.2 investigates the VaR impact. Our test portfolio contains only a 20-year *zero coupon* bond. First note that pVaR and mcVaR are roughly the same under normal distribution. We then multiply the volatility of the 20-year rate risk factor by a factor of 10 to exaggerate the scenario shifts and hence convexity. As a result, pVaR overstates the risk as compared to mcVaR for a long position because pVaR (delta approach) ignores the effect of convexity. For short bonds, pVaR understates the true risk because it does not get hurt by short convexity. This can be tested in the spreadsheet by changing the sign of the bond notional to negative.

In a nutshell, our investigation shows that convexity is a tiny residual risk except for long dated bonds and under extreme movements. This risk will be omitted if pVaR is used.

Optionality

An option allows the buyer the right, but not the obligation, to buy (call option) or sell (put option) an asset at a predetermined price (the *strike*). All options have the benefit of flooring the downside loss for the buyer (but not for seller). In return for that benefit, the seller is paid a premium. The present value or "price" of an option refers to this premium. Options are very common in the financial markets, sometimes embedded in bonds, deposits, swaps and other derivatives.

The flooring of risk has two effects—the risk profile becomes non-linear (curved) and the PL distribution becomes skewed to the positive side (which is good for the buyer).

Figure 4-3 shows the payoff diagram for a put option where both strike (K) and spot (S) are at 750 or *at-the-money*[6]. The dotted line shows the actual PL profile of the put *prior* to maturity calculated using Black-Scholes formula, while the straight line is the linear estimate of the PL profile estimated from delta. The tangent point where they touch is the current spot price. As we move away (shift) from the spot, there is a significant deviation between the two lines. Thus, a linear estimate is only good when shifts are not large i.e. it's a *local* risk measure.

McVaR and hsVaR use the actual profile, while pVaR uses the linear approximation. By the same reasoning as before, pVaR will overstate the risk for long options (does not benefit from curvature) and understate the risk for short options (does not get hurt by short curvature).

Figure 4-3 Non-linearity of an at-the-money vanilla put option

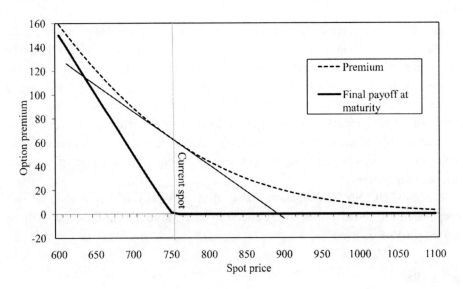

[6] When $S=K$, an option is termed at-the-money (ATM). When an option is profitable ($S>K$ for calls, $S<K$ for puts) it is in-the-money (ITM). When an option is at a loss ($S<K$ for calls, $S>K$ for puts) it is called out-of-the-money (OTM).

Spreadsheet 4.3 is used to derive Figure 4-3. The spot is at 750. If we change the strike to 1000 (ITM) the deviation between the two lines becomes negligible. At a strike of 600 (OTM), the deviation between the two lines becomes exaggerated. This shows that the risk of a deep-ITM option is very much like the underlying; it's linear. Whereas, when the option goes OTM, optionality risk becomes more important.

Spreadsheet 4.3 also contains a test portfolio of one put option with a strike of 10,718 (ATM). If we change the strike to 30,000 (ITM), pVaR and mcVaR are roughly the same. At 9,000 strike (OTM), pVaR overstates mcVaR by more than 20%.

Figure 4-4 illustrates the benefit of loss protection offered by the option. The distributions are generated using mcVaR from the spreadsheet. The left panel shows the ATM case; the distribution is largely symmetric. The right panel shows the OTM case where optionality becomes an important effect—the PL distribution becomes skewed to the right and the loss side is buffered.

Figure 4-4 Skewness of PL distribution for put option

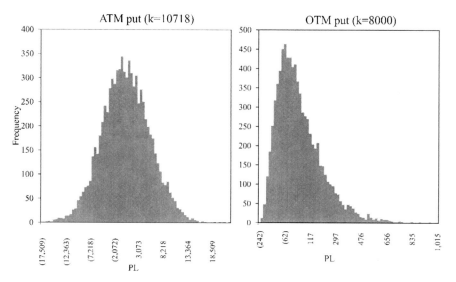

Optionality is a serious challenge to the VaR metric. Its effects are significant and often skew the distribution in a way that threatens the basic assumptions of normality and subadditivity. The curvature effect (gamma) is substantial when we deal with exotic options and consider the volatility smile. This gives rise to non-local risk features (located away from the current state) in a complex way not well-captured by a point estimate such as VaR.

Fat-tails

The 2008 crisis has shown that the danger of fat-tails cannot be underestimated. Spreadsheet 4.4 illustrates a VaR implementation similar to Spreadsheet 4.1, except that the "peacetime" data of 2005 has been replaced by the "crisis" data of 2008. To focus solely on the effects of a fat-tail, we consider only a linear portfolio of stocks. In the mcVaR sheet there is a choice of using the normal distribution or a fat-tailed (mixed-normal) distribution.

Under the normal distribution, pVaR is roughly the same as mcVaR. HsVaR is larger than both because in 2008 the stock market returns were generally fat-tailed and skewed. This will hurt the long stock position and is manifested as a higher hsVaR. As expected, pVaR and mcVaR failed to capture these higher moments because of the normal assumption.

McVaR can account for fat-tails if a suitable distribution is applied. One simple way to generate random numbers with zero mean, unit variance but with a high degree of kurtosis is to use a *mixture of normal* model. The idea is that a fat-tail "bell shaped" distribution can be created by randomly mixing variables from two normal distributions with different variances.

To do this, draw a random outcome y of either 1 or 0, with probability p and $(1-p)$. Draw a sample z from the standard normal $N(0,1)$ distribution. Designate σ_1 and σ_2 as the standard deviations for the two normal distributions. To independently mix them, if $y=1$ then let $x= \sigma_1 z$; if $y=0$ then let $x= \sigma_2 z$. To normalize the mixed distribution of X such that its variance is 1, we set:

$$Var(X) = p\sigma_1^2 + (1-p)\sigma_2^2 = 1 \quad \rightarrow \quad \sigma_2 = \sqrt{\frac{1-p\sigma_1^2}{1-p}} \qquad (4.12)$$

Thus, we can choose p and σ_1 to achieve the desired level of kurtosis given by:

$$Kurt(X) = 3(p\sigma_1^4 + (1-p)\sigma_2^4) \qquad (4.13)$$

This is implemented in Spreadsheet 4.4 for all four risk factors. The two parameters are chosen such that the theoretical kurtosis matches the observed kurtosis from the market. Figure 4-5 shows conceptually how the mixed-normal (the bar chart) is created using two normals with different sigmas. One distribution dominates the peak and a second distribution dominates the two tails. The resulting distribution has a peak and tails that are thicker than normal. It is symmetric and fat-tailed. If the mixed-normal model is chosen, mcVaR will be larger than pVaR. For a more methodical application of normal-mixture in mcVaR, the astute reader can refer to Zangari (1996).

Figure 4-5 Mixture of normal distributions

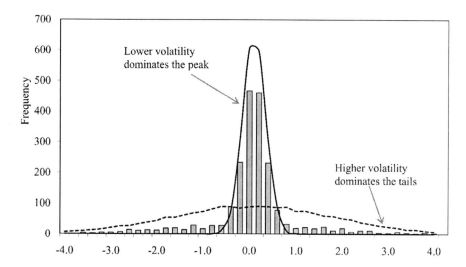

4.5 Issue: Hidden Correlation

It is common knowledge that correlation or the dependence structure is inherent in Markowitz portfolio theory. The correlation allows for subadditivity, which acts to reduce (diversify away) portfolio risk. But there is another type of correlation which is less known, that is, the *implied* correlation used as a parameter to price *correlation products*. Unlike the former, this is actually a risk factor. (See Section 3.2—risk dimensions.)

For these bespoke products, price series are seldom observed and banks typically exclude this risk factor from VaR and simply assume implied correlation as a constant.

An alternative is to replace the unobservable implied correlation with the historical correlation. We can calculate the latter using a short observation window (such as 50 days) to reduce its lag and to make it more sensitive to regime changes.

We illustrate this in Spreadsheet 4.5 using a *spread option* example. A spread option has a payoff that depends on the difference (or spread) between two underlying assets, F_1 and F_2, and can be priced analytically by modifying the Black-Scholes equation to include correlation ρ. We consider a call spread option with payoff MAX(F_1-F_2-K,0) where K is the spread strike. The hsVaR is computed for the case where implied correlation is stochastic (proxied here using a 50-day historical correlation) versus a case where the correlation is assumed to be constant. To focus solely on the effects of correlation, we kept the other parameters—such as maturity, rate and volatility—constant. In a realistic situation, all parameters are variable.

We want to test the responsiveness of VaR when a regime switch is encountered. To do so, we simulate random paths which are highly correlated (ρ=0.5) then switch the direction of the correlation abruptly (to ρ= -0.5) at half way through the time series. Figure 4-6 illustrates the generated time series and the resulting VaRs. The VaR is extremely responsive to the regime break if the correlation parameter is stochastic. VaR rises rapidly once the break is encountered.

Figure 4-6 HsVaR of spread option- constant vs. stochastic correlation

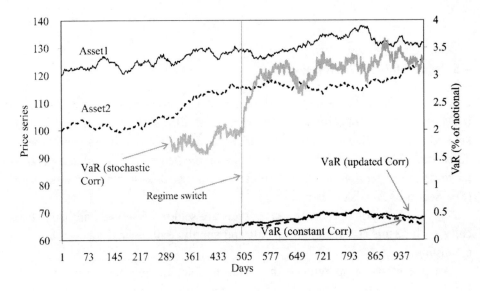

Figure 4-6 also shows VaR for two other cases where correlation is *not included* as a risk factor. One of them, the implied correlation, is updated (marked) daily and the other, the correlation is kept constant. In practice the correlation is

updated infrequently as and when prices are observed. The dangers of excluding implied correlation as a risk factor are apparent—the VaR will be significantly understated and regime breaks when they occur will not be detected. Fortunately the problem is confined to correlation products.

Most banks do not have a systematic way to handle implied correlation risk factors, especially if correlation trading is not their core business. Implied correlations are quoted by traders based on consensus "gut feel" and hence will often violate positive semi-definiteness. The storage of these "implieds" can be a technological nightmare because the matrix size will grow rapidly[7] as new correlation products are traded. When this happens, data that was not previously collected will need to be back-filled for VaR. This can be an impossible task.

A good trade-off is to use *historical* correlation as a proxy risk factor and compute the required correlation pairs "on-the-fly" during deal revaluation. This bypasses the need for storage of correlation matrices.

4.6 Issue: Missing Basis and Beta Approach

Basis risks

The term "basis" generally refers to the difference between two related markets and basis risk is the uncertainty of this basis. Usually the trader goes long one market and shorts another in the so-called "arbitrage", spread or basis trading. Some examples are the spot vs. futures basis, the CDS vs. assetswap basis, the basis between two points on the yield curve, cross-currency basis between two curves of different currency denominations, the basis between one security vs. another, the basis between a stock and its benchmark index, etc. Can VaR account for such diverse basis risks?

The answer depends on how we map risks. To the extent that the risk factor mapping differentiates the two markets constituting the basis, basis risk will be captured. Sometimes data limitations cannot afford us this level of granularity. This is particularly serious for emerging markets. Also, certain securities are naturally illiquid and continuous price quotation is not available, such as in credit trading, where securities are issue-specific. For example, an *off-the-run* (old

---

[7] In fact, the number of matrix elements will grow quadratically. For example a bank sells equity spread options and basket options to customers. Suppose the bank can quote on 30 Hong Kong stocks at the moment and wishes to expand by an additional 3 stocks. This increases the number of pairwise correlations by 93 (from 435 to 528), i.e. a 21% increase and each one is a time series.

issue of a) corporate bond often falls out of favor with investors and its price becomes "stale", but an *on-the-run* (newly issued) bond is often more liquid. This gives rise to a basis between the two bonds that is not well-captured. In fact, most banks will risk-map (or benchmark) the bonds of the same issuer and roughly of same maturity to the on-the-run bond, effectively ignoring such basis risk.

Not surprisingly, there is a push from regulators for banks to quantify the magnitude of missing basis risks for prudential supervision. This is a somewhat self-contradictory (but necessary) proposition. For how can one quantify a risk that has little or no data? Some banks estimate this by assuming worst case scenarios (stress test) or by looking at other similar securities that do have the basis data (proxying).

Beta approach

Certain markets have a vast number of risk factors, so risk managers often benchmark them to a manageable subset using the beta approach (see Section 2.8). This is a common practice for *name specific* instruments such as equities and, to some extent, for credit default swaps. In fact the *Revision to Basel II Market Risk Framework* (2009) prescribed that "Positions in individual securities or in sector indices could be expressed in "beta-equivalents" relative to this market-wide index".

Equation (2.37) relates the return for security-i to the return of the market index by way of a beta coefficient. Assets with higher betas are more sensitive to the general market. Sharpe (1964) proved that under equilibrium conditions of capital markets, $\alpha_i = R_f(1-\beta_i)$ where R_f is the risk free rate. In this case, (2.37) becomes:

$$E(R_i) - R_f = \beta_i \left(E(R_M) - R_f \right) + E(\varepsilon_i) \qquad (4.14)$$

where E(.) stands for expectation and the time subscript has been dropped for brevity. This relationship is the famous *Capital Asset Pricing Model* (CAPM) which states that the return (over the risk free rate) of an asset consists of two *uncorrelated* components—a systematic component (first term) and a name-specific component (second term). The risk decomposition for asset-i is given by the variance formula:

$$Var(R_i) = \beta_i^2 Var(R_M) + Var(\varepsilon_i) \qquad (4.15)$$

Specific risk can be diversified away if a portfolio P is very large i.e. $Var(\varepsilon_P)=0$. When the portfolio is small, $Var(\varepsilon_P)>0$, hence the risk calculated using the beta approach will always *understate* the true risk. This is illustrated by taking the square-root of (4.15) with $i=P$:

$$\sigma(R_P) > \beta_P \sigma(R_M) \qquad (4.16)$$

Spreadsheet 4.6 is an illustration of pVaR and hsVaR of a portfolio of two stocks calculated using the beta approach. It can be shown that regardless of the portfolio composition (you can even include short sales) the beta approach understates true VaR. The lesson is that when using the beta approach, the risk manager needs to be mindful of missing basis risks when the portfolio is small or not well diversified.

4.7 Issue: The Real Risk of Premiums

Consider what happens when a trader purchases an out-of-the-money option of notional $1 million. Suppose the pricing formula tells him the premium is -$3,600 and he books this deal which the risk system values at +$3,600. However, he needs to pay -$3,600 cash (premium) upfront, hence, on a net basis his inception PL is zero. (A fairly priced derivative gives zero PL at inception.) If the market remains unchanged during the life of the option, the option value will decay from +$3,600 to 0 at expiry (an option value cannot go below 0). His maximum loss will be floored at -$3,600 PL.

Now suppose the trader is willing to write-off this maximum loss by recognizing this loss upfront as -$3,600 PL and providing (paid) for this loss[8]. Is there any risk left in his position?

Firstly, let's verify that one can never lose more than the premium (on a long position). Figure 4-7 shows two PL distributions for the option deal. The distributions are right-skewed because of the downside protection. As we increase the simulated volatility to an extreme (say 200%) the skew become

---

[8] In practice, this may happen if a small bank does not have the proper risk system to book the option and is long only. One way is to record only the premium part (-$3,600) and at expiry, the final value of the option (which can only be ≥ 0).

larger but the left tail can never go below -\$3,600 no matter how extreme prices behave.

Secondly, we note that VaR satisfies a mathematical property called *translation invariance* (see Section 7.6):

$$VaR(X + k) = VaR(X) - k \qquad (4.17)$$

In other words, adding cash k to portfolio X will reduce the portfolio risk by k. This means that if we pay upfront the full potential loss k, the PL distribution gets shifted (translated) to the right by k. As a result, the entire distribution in Figure 4-7 will be in the positive territory regardless of market conditions.

Since VaR is defined as the *loss* quantile of the distribution, the VaR becomes zero. It really boils down to how you define risks. If risk is defined as uncertainty in PL, then yes, there is risk. But if risk is defined as a loss quantile, as required in VaR and risk capital, then there is no risk. In this case, one can argue that deals that are fully written down can be managed outside the VaR regime. This example forces us to think deeply about what risk really is. See *Knightian uncertainty* in Section 11.2.

Figure 4-7 Simulated PL distribution of OTM option

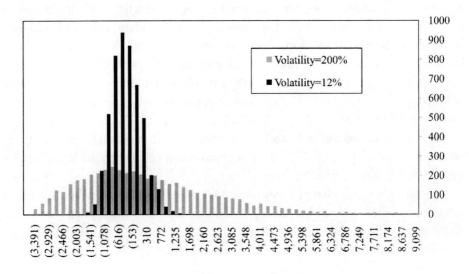

4.8 Spreadsheet

4.1 Historical simulation, Monte Carlo and parametric VaRs are the three most basic VaR models. More advanced models are often just variants of these basic models. Aim: illustrates the hsVaR, mcVaR and pVaR for a test portfolio of three deals—a stock, an option and a bond. Note: the historical data used is for 2005, representing "peace time" market conditions. As expected, all three methods produced roughly the same VaR.

4.2 Convexity is a (second order) curvature risk peculiar to bonds and cashflow-based products. It is not captured by simple parametric VaR (delta approach). Aim: illustrates the convexity effect using a bond's price-yield relationship, and shows its impact on pVaR. Note: the test portfolio contains only a 20-year bond and the volatility of the 20-year rate has been multiplied by 10 to exaggerate the convexity effect. McVaR (which includes convexity) is smaller than pVaR.

4.3 Option non-linearity is not captured by pVaR because of the linear approximation used. Aim: illustrates the non-linearity of a put option's payoff, and the skew imposed on the PL distribution as a result of the option's downside protection. A VaR calculator, containing an option, illustrates its different impact on mcVaR and pVaR. Action: change the strike to investigate the effects of OTM and ITM options.

4.4 The three VaR methods—pVaR, mcVaR and hsVaR—have different abilities (or inability) to account for fat-tails. pVaR fails to account for fat-tails, mcVaR models them theoretically, while hsVaR uses empirical distributional over a short window. Aim: explore the impact of the crisis conditions of 2008 on the three VaR methods for a single stock (linear position). Note: the hsVaR is larger than the other two VaRs. If the fat-tail distribution is chosen for mcVaR, the mcVaR will also be larger than pVaR.

4.5 Implied correlations of multi-underlying derivatives are often assumed to be constant (or not used as risk factors) in the computation of VaR. This is often due to data and technological limitations. Aim: illustrates the impact on VaR when implied correlation is stochastic (not kept constant) by using an example of a spread call option. Note: Monte Carlo simulation is used to generate two price series and a regime break is introduced in the middle. The hsVaR is found to be extremely responsive in the case of stochastic correlation compared to the constant correlation case. Action: press the first button to regenerate the paths, the second button to recalculate the hsVaRs.

4.6 The beta approach of representing risk factors in VaR can be shown in theory to underestimate true risks. Aim: verify the understatement of risks by the beta approach of VaR using actual data. PVaR and hsVaR are computed for a portfolio of two stocks with and without the beta method. Action: change the weights of the two stocks or even short the stocks, and note that the beta VaR will always understate the true VaR.

Chapter 5

Advanced VaR Methods

In this chapter, we will explore some advanced VaR models; there are many others[1]. Academics were the first to systematically catalog the weaknesses of VaR and improve the basic VaR model in order to make it consistent with observed market behaviors. Unfortunately, the added layer of mathematical complexity makes implementation and common understanding difficult. As such, these models are slow in gaining industry acceptance.

One common trait of these models is the reliance on a strong mathematical foundation and its basic assumptions such as stationarity and i.i.d. We will introduce the main ideas of these models without delving into the mathematical details as far as possible. Our goal is to cover just enough ground to be able to illustrate a simple example on a spreadsheet.

5.1 Hybrid Historical Simulation VaR

It is important for hsVaR to use an observation period long enough for the shape of the return distribution to be well-captured. But, because hsVaR uses a rolling history of empirical data, it encounters a dilemma when estimating the quantile—with a long history the method becomes insensitive to market changes[2], while with a short history it encounters estimation problems—there are too few data points that define the quantile. The Riskmetrics version of pVaR on the other hand is very sensitive to market innovation, because of the use of exponentially declining weights on past data to estimate the volatility.

The *hybrid historical simulation* VaR approach proposed by Boudoukh, Richardson and Whitelaw (1998) combines the best of both worlds. It combines the exponentially-weighed-moving-average (EWMA) scheme of Riskmetrics

---

[1] The interested reader can check the resource at: www.gloriamundi.org.
[2] This is a well-known catch-22 for anyone who has ever used moving averages (MA). If the window is long, the MA is stable but lags, if the window is short, the MA is responsive but unstable.

with hsVaR, so that it can have the benefit of using a long history and yet achieve market responsiveness.

The hybrid VaR is implemented in three steps:

1. Let $r(t)$ be the realized return from time $(t-1)$ to t. To each of the recent K returns: $r(t)$, $r(t-1)$, .., $r(t-K+1)$ assign a weight $[(1-\lambda)/(1-\lambda^K)]\lambda^0$, $[(1-\lambda)/(1-\lambda^K)]\lambda^1$, .., $[(1-\lambda)/(1-\lambda^K)]\lambda^{K-1}$ respectively.

2. Rank the *weighted* returns in ascending order.

3. To obtain $p\%$ VaR, start from the lowest weighted return and cumulatively add the *weights* until $p\%$ percentile is reached. Linear interpolation is used when necessary to get the exact point of $p\%$ between two adjacent points. The *return* at this point is the VaR's return.

Spreadsheet 5.1 illustrates the implementation of hybrid VaR using $K=250$ and decay factor $\lambda=0.98$ (as in the original 1998 paper). We calculate the 97.5% confidence VaR for Dow Jones index for the period 2005 to 2008; hence $p=2.5\%$. Figure 5-1 shows the resulting hybrid VaR versus hsVaR.

Figure 5-1 Hybrid VaR vs. Historical simulation VaR ($\lambda=0.98$)

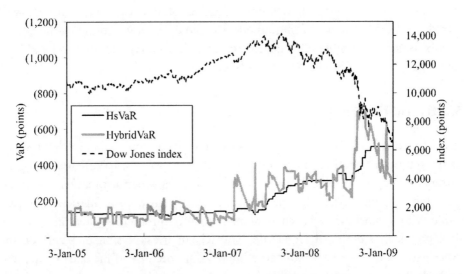

Hybrid VaR is more reactive than hsVaR to significant moves in market prices, but this unfortunately makes hybrid VaR very volatile as well. This key weakness of hybrid VaR can be a hindrance for the purpose of setting regulatory risk capital, where some degree of stability is desirable. Also, there is little room to fine tune λ for hybrid VaR. At $\lambda=0.98$ it becomes jagged, at lower values (say $\lambda=0.94$), it becomes saw-toothed. You can try this out in Spreadsheet 5.1.

The hybrid VaR is unsmooth because it effectively shortens the sampling period to capture the effects of stochastic (or changing) volatility. At λ=0.98, the most recent observation is weighted 2%—which means that a large incoming observation will skew the results i.e. make the VaR jump ranks.

5.2 Hull-White Volatility Updating VaR

Hull and White (1998) proposed a more natural and smoother way to capture stochastic volatility. Their insight was the observation that when a probability distribution is scaled by an estimate of its volatility, it is still approximately stationary. This suggests that historical simulation VaR can be scaled by a function of volatility without sacrificing stationarity. The basic idea is that VaR should be a stronger function of today's volatility than the volatility further in the past. This approach is similar to the hsVaR, except that each return observation in the past is scaled by the ratio of today's volatility to the volatility at the time of observation. To calculate the volatility, Hull-White uses the EWMA method with λ=0.94 as recommended by Riskmetrics.

The Hull-White VaR can be easily implemented in three steps:
1. Volatilities are estimated using the EWMA approach for the last 250 days, $\sigma_1, \sigma_2,\ldots, \sigma_{250}$ where the time index subscript represents the number of days into the past.
2. The historical percentage returns $r_1, r_{1,\ldots}, r_{250}$ are scaled as: $r_1(\sigma_1/\sigma_1)$, $r_2(\sigma_1/\sigma_2),\ldots, r_{250}(\sigma_1/\sigma_{250})$.
3. Take the quantile of the scaled returns to obtain the Hull-White VaR.

The 97.5% Hull-White VaR is implemented in Spreadsheet 5.2 using the same Dow Jones index data as before. Figure 5-2 shows that Hull-White VaR is more responsive than hsVaR which lagged the crash during the credit crisis (Jul 08 to Mar 09). Relative to hybrid VaR, it is reasonably continuous for the typical range of decay factor λ (0.94 to 0.99).

Note that mean-adjustment is not done in our examples for Hull-White VaR and hybrid VaR. For this small adjustment, the exercise is non-trivial especially if done at the portfolio level. The Hull-White VaR approach also performs well under statistical tests of goodness such as unbiasedness and reduced bunching (see Section 8.3). The interested reader is referred to the original paper for more details.

Figure 5-2 Hull-White VaR vs. Historical simulation VaR (λ=0.94)

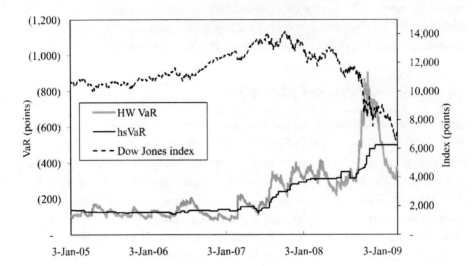

5.3 Conditional Autoregressive VaR (CAViaR)

VaR is just a loss quantile at the left tail, a point estimate. It tells us very little of the behavior of exceedences to the left of this cutoff point, nor is it accurately estimated, since there are too few observations in the left tail used to define the quantile. In the example of 97.5% VaR using 250 days data, only 6 to 7 data points in the left tail decide the VaR number.

Engle and Manganelli (2004) proposed the *conditional autoregressive value-at-risk* (CAViaR) model that could overcome these problems. It used the method of QRM estimation in Section 2.13. CAViaR proposes to model the *process* governing the quantile itself as a function of other variables. In QRM, data of the entire distribution is used for the estimation process; hence, the data scarcity problem is avoided. Moreover, the specification of the QRM regression explicitly models the tail behavior.

The starting point of CAViaR is the empirical observation of volatility clustering; in particular, extreme returns tend to be autocorrelated. Sharp price movements during a crash or mania tend to persist over a period as opposed to occurring randomly over time. As a result, large returns tend to cluster together temporally. Hence, VaR, being the tail quantile, must also exhibit properties of autocorrelation; an autoregressive specification is thus required.

In the most general form of CAViaR, today's VaR is modeled as a linear regression of previous VaRs, previous returns Y and some unknown parameters β's which need to be estimated. In the seminal CAViaR paper (2004), four specifications or models were proposed.

Adaptive Model: $\qquad VaR_t = VaR_{t-1} + \beta * hit$ $\qquad\qquad$ (5.1)

where

$$hit = I(Y_{t-1} < -VaR_{t-1}) - \theta$$

where I(.) is the indicator function, θ the chosen quantile for VaR, β's the parameter(s) to be estimated. The other three models were:

Symmetric Absolute Value:

$$VaR_t = \beta_1 + \beta_2 VaR_{t-1} + \beta_3 \mid Y_{t-1} \mid$$ $\qquad\qquad$ (5.2)

Asymmetric Slope:

$$VaR_t = \beta_1 + \beta_2 VaR_{t-1} + \beta_3 (Y_{t-1})^+ + \beta_4 (Y_{t-1})^-$$ $\qquad\qquad$ (5.3)

Indirect GARCH(1,1):

$$VaR_t = \left(\beta_1 + \beta_2 VaR_{t-1}^2 + \beta_3 Y_{t-1}^2 \right)^{1/2}$$ $\qquad\qquad$ (5.4)

where the short notation means: $(Y)^+ = \max(Y,0)$, $(Y)^- = -\min(Y,0)$.

For the purpose of illustration, we shall use the simple one-parameter adaptive model. Since (5.1) is an iterative equation, we need the VaR at the starting point $t=1$, which we simply take as: $VaR(1)= $ -NORMSINV(θ)*STDEV(..) i.e. the simple pVaR estimate. For 95%-VaR, $\theta=0.05$ and $VaR(1)=1.65\sigma$. Then $VaR(t)$ for subsequent days can be calculated iteratively.

$$VaR(t) = VaR(t-1) + \begin{cases} \beta(0.95) \ if \ I(.) = 1 \\ \beta(-0.05) \ if \ I(.) = 0 \end{cases} \tag{5.5}$$

Notice the behavior of the adaptive model: whenever the *loss* Y exceeds VaR we should immediately increase VaR (by 0.95β), but when Y does not exceed VaR, we should decrease it very slightly (by -0.05β). This model does not account for the magnitude of exceedence, only its frequency i.e. the increment/decrement is a constant regardless of the degree of exceedence.

The parameters β's of the CAViaR model are estimated using quantile regression (see Section 2.13). For the adaptive model, we estimate the β that minimizes the objective function:

$$\min_{\beta} \frac{1}{T} \sum_{t=1}^{T} [\theta - I(Y_t < VaR_t)][Y_t - VaR_t] \tag{5.6}$$

where T is the number of observations. The minimization problem for this simple example can easily be done using Excel Solver. Spreadsheet 5.3 illustrates this for the case of Dow Jones index for 5%-quantile. The resulting CAViaR is plotted against conventional hsVaR for comparison (see Figure 5-3).

Figure 5-3 CAViaR vs. Historical simulation VaR (θ=0.05)

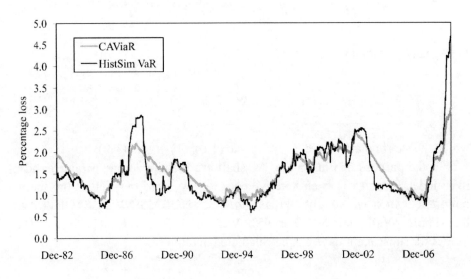

In a sense CAViaR has transformed the VaR problem of quantile determination (with data scarcity issues) to the problem of functional regression in the form of QRM. In this new form, one has to deal, instead, with the subjectivity of model specification (we have to presume we know the process for VaR) and parameterization. For example, in the adaptive model CAViaR shown in Figure 5-3, the shape of the downtrend is straighter than the uptrend. That is governed by the specification of the adaptive model and would be very different if we had chosen some other specification such as one of the other three models mentioned. But how do you choose and justify which models to use for different asset classes which clearly behave differently? Because of its generality and flexibility, CAViaR lacks the kind of standardization and simplicity that the risk industry favors.

5.4 Extreme Value Theory VaR

Extreme Value Theory (EVT) is a field of applied statistics traditionally used in the insurance industry and now increasingly applied in the area of operational risk. It provides estimation techniques to forecast extreme events with low probability of occurring.

The purpose of this section is to provide a brief foretaste of what EVT can do in the area of VaR. Entire books have been written on the subject; a good book is written by Embrechts et al. (1997). We will end with a simple Excel example of EVT VaR. As we shall see, EVT does not attempt to model the tail process, hence, one can think of it as a tool to fit the tail distribution in a *statistically correct* manner. The reasoning is that if the rare event lies outside the range of available observation, it seems essential to rely on well-founded methodology. The reason why EVT gained some acceptance in risk management is because return distributions in financial markets are heavily fat-tailed during times of stress.

Classical EVT

The fundamental model of EVT describes the behavior of the maxima or minima of a distribution. Consider a collection of n observed daily returns $\{x_1, \ldots, x_n\}$ where we will express losses as positive numbers. So consider the ranked loss $\{m_1, \ldots, m_n\}$ such that $m_n = \max\{x_1, \ldots, x_n\}$ is the worst-case loss in a sample and $m_1 = \min\{x_1, \ldots, x_n\}$ is the best-case gain. In VaR we are interested in modeling the extreme loss m_n.

We denote the cumulative distribution function (CDF) of variable X as $F(x)$. Assuming the maximas are i.i.d., the CDF of m_n i.e. $F_n(x)$ can be easily derived:

$$
\begin{aligned}
F_n(x) &= \Pr[m_n \leq x] \\
&= \Pr(m_1 \leq x, m_2 \leq x, \dots, m_n \leq x) \\
&= \prod_{i=1}^{n} \Pr(m_i \leq x) \\
&= \prod_{i=1}^{n} F(x) \\
&= [F(x)]^n
\end{aligned}
\tag{5.7}
$$

However, this result is *degenerate* i.e. the function becomes useless as n becomes very large. See Spreadsheet 5.4. We can avoid the degenerate result by modeling the *standardized maxima* instead:

$$
m^* = (m_n - b_n) / a_n
\tag{5.8}
$$

where $\{b_n\}$ and $\{a_n\}$ are sequences of real numbers and $a_n > 0$. The idea is to find $\{b_n\}$ and $\{a_n\}$ such that the distribution of m^* converges to a non-degenerate CDF as $n \rightarrow \infty$. This limiting distribution is called the extreme value distribution and is described by the *Fisher-Tippett theorem* (1928).

The resulting *generalized extreme value distribution* (GEV) has the following density function:

$$
H_\alpha(x) = \begin{cases} \exp\left(-(1+\alpha y)^{-1/\alpha}\right) & \alpha \neq 0 \\ \exp\left(-e^{-y}\right) & \alpha = 0 \end{cases}
\tag{5.9}
$$

where $y = (x-b)/a$ and $(1+\alpha y) > 0$. The parameters are called *shape* (α), *location* (b) and *scale* (a). The GEV encompasses three limiting families of distribution identified by Gnedenko (1943): the *Fréchet* family ($\alpha>0$), the *Gumbel* family ($\alpha=0$) and *Weibull* family ($\alpha<0$). The probability density functions $H_\alpha(x)$ for these families are plotted in Figure 5-4. Note that this is a distribution of the standardized maxima m^*, not m_n or the observed returns x_i. The Fréchet family is fat-tailed and is most useful for financial risk modeling.

Figure 5-4 Three families of extreme value distributions (scale=1, location=1)

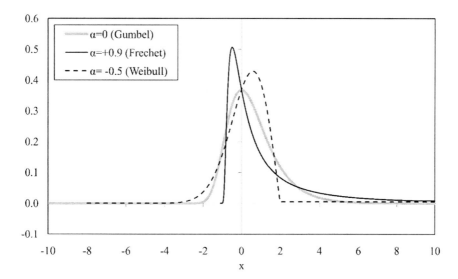

Gnedenko (1943) has established the necessary and sufficient conditions such that any probability distribution will have its *tail behavior* belonging to one of the three families. For example, the normal and lognormal distributions lead to a Gumbel distribution for their tails; the Student's T and Pareto stable distributions' tails follow a Fréchet distribution, the uniform distribution's tail belongs to a Weibull distribution.

The extreme value theorem is the cousin of the better known central limit theorem, which states that the *mean* of a sufficiently large number of i.i.d. random variables with finite mean and variance (regardless of individual distributional shapes) will be approximately normally distributed. In the same way, EVT tells us about the limiting distribution of *extreme values* (i.i.d. maximas or minimas) as the number of observations increases.

In this GEV form, the 3 parameters—shape, location, scale—are determined by the data itself. The parameters can be estimated using *block maxima* method. In this approach, the global sample set (with T data) is divided into g non-overlapping subsets with each subset having n observations, such that $T=gn$. The maxima of each subset is taken out $\{h_1, h_2, \ldots, h_g\}$ and they are used to fit the GEV distribution whose parameters need estimation. By assuming that h_i's are i.i.d., one can use the maximum likelihood method to estimate the parameters.

The block maxima approach is not efficient in data usage. For example, in a typical application, one would use yearly blocks of 250 days. Suppose we have

50 years of history, that will only afford 50 maxima points. And most markets will have a shorter history; hence estimated results will be statistically weak. The next approach is better able to exploit the data set.

Peaks-over-thresholds (POT) method

In POT, we model the *exceedence* (y) or excess above a certain threshold (u). We are interested in the conditional probability of the event $y = x$-u conditional on loss return x>u (losses are positively defined). It can be shown theoretically that if the maxima has a GEV distribution, then the exceedence y follows a *Generalized Pareto Distribution* (GPD) as shown by Pickands–Balkema–de Haan (1974/75). The GPD is a two parameter distribution with CDF given by:

$$G_{\alpha,\beta}(y) = \begin{cases} 1 - (1 + \alpha y / \beta)^{-1/\alpha} & \alpha \neq 0 \\ 1 - \exp(-y / \beta) & \alpha = 0 \end{cases} \tag{5.10}$$

where β>0, and where y≥0 when α≥0 and 0≤y≤ -β/α when α<0.

The first step in estimating the parameters β and α is to choose an appropriate threshold u. Clearly the threshold cannot be chosen too low, as this will mean that data beyond the threshold will deviate from GPD; GPD is really for data fitting in the tail, not suitable for the body of the sample distribution. If we choose a threshold that is too high, there will be too few data points to make meaningful statistical inferences. The appropriate choice of threshold can be chosen by first ordering the data sample $\{x_i\}$. Then for each chosen u, pick up the sample set where x_i>u i.e. the exceedences only. Calculate and plot the *mean excess function* $e(u)$ against u, as defined by:

$$e(u) = \frac{1}{N} \sum_{j=1}^{N} (x_j - u) \quad where \quad u < x \tag{5.11}$$

where $x_1, x_2, \ldots, x_N$ are N observations that exceeded u. Spreadsheet 5.4 illustrates the calculation of $e(u)$ for the left tail (losses) for Dow Jones index that is plotted in Figure 5-5.

Figure 5-5 Plot of mean excess function $e(u)$ vs. threshold (u) for the left tail

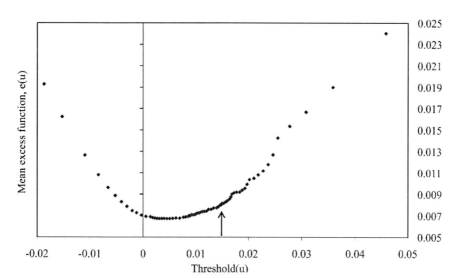

Since GPD is characterized by its linearity in $e(u)$ we identify from the plot, the point u above which the graph is approximately linear. Use this point (u=1.5% loss) as the threshold. In the Dow Jones example, data was taken from 1962 to 2009. Using the threshold, we have about 600 data points for the POT approach. In contrast, had we used the block minima approach, we would have only 47 data points to work with.

One way to estimate the parameters in equation (5.10) is to use the maximum likelihood method. It can be shown that the log-likelihood function for the GPD is given by:

$$L(\alpha,\beta) = \begin{cases} -N\ln(\beta)-(1+1/\alpha)\sum_{i=1}^{N}\ln(1+\alpha y_i/\beta) & \text{if } \alpha \neq 0 \\ -N\ln(\beta)-(1/\beta)\sum_{i=1}^{N}y_i & \text{if } \alpha = 0 \end{cases} \qquad (5.12)$$

In financial applications, the case of $\alpha \neq 0$ is of primary interest. We estimate α and β that maximize $L(.)$ for the sample defined by the N observations exceeding the chosen threshold u, where y_i are the exceedences. Spreadsheet 5.5 is a worked-out example using Excel Solver.

With the estimated parameters we can then compute VaR. First, we note that equation (5.10) can first be rewritten as a function of loss return x instead of y. From the definition of VaR in (4.1) inverting this CDF gives VaR:

$$VaR_q = u + \frac{\hat{\beta}}{\hat{\alpha}}\left(\left(\frac{n}{N}(1-q)\right)^{-\hat{\alpha}} - 1\right) \tag{5.13}$$

where N is the number of loss returns exceeding threshold (u), n is the total number of observations, q is the confidence level for VaR at ($1-q$) quantile. Equation (5.13) is plotted in Figure 5-6 along with pVaR for comparison. As can be seen, the EVT VaR grows faster than pVaR above a certain quantile because EVT fits the left tail data more appropriately than the normal distribution.

Figure 5-6 EVT VaR versus pVaR for different quantiles

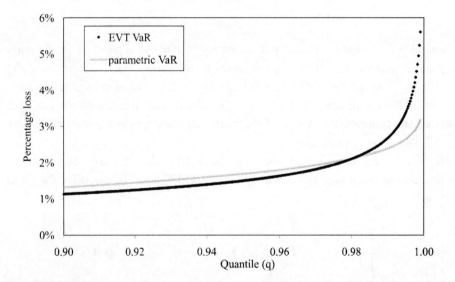

Many aspects of EVT application are still being researched. Some of the known limitations of EVT include:

1. In classical EVT one has to make assumptions on the tail model i.e. about the *shape*. One has to deal with data limitations in applying the block minima approach.

2. In the POT approach, the choice of threshold is too subjective even though one can get some graphical guidance from the mean excess plot. A slightly different u (and hence N) will give rise to a different VaR.

3. EVT VaR equation (5.13) does not depend on any recent returns (unless it happens to be an extreme event). It deals exclusively with exceedences and is oblivious to data outside the tail. For proper parameter estimation, we require at least 100 exceedences, hence a sizable history. Often, there are not enough exceedences to apply a rolling window like in conventional VaR. Thus, EVT VaR behaves more like a static measure that is not sensitive to market fluctuations. EVT has more promising application in areas where a rolling VaR is less required, such as in insurance and operational risks.

4. The existing literature usually focuses on EVT for a single variable. Practical portfolio risk management necessitates a multi-variate EVT, but this is only viable for a small number of dimensions. The major obstacle is the correlation measurement. There are just far too few observations of correlated extreme events for meaningful measurement—all the variables must take on extreme values *at the same time* to qualify—this is extremely rare. During crises, extreme correlations (calculated using only exceedences) and average correlations can be very different; so we cannot use the latter as a substitute.

5. EVT VaR is still a point estimate with a rather wide error range and this error gets uncomfortably big as we move to more extreme quantiles.

On a positive note, EVT is a useful tool that provides smooth extrapolation into the extreme tail zone (say <1% quantile) where there is no observable data. This is based on our knowledge of the functional distribution of the tail. Some argue that this is a dangerous practice; one has to have faith in the EVT theorem to do this, the same kind of faith you would have that the central limit theorem works in the real world. See Diebold et al. (1999) for a cautionary discussion of the potential misuse of EVT.

5.5 Spreadsheet

5.1 Hybrid historical simulation VaR is an approach that combines the exponential weighting scheme of Riskmetrics with hsVaR, so that it can have the benefit of using a long history and yet achieve market responsiveness. Aim: illustrates the implementation of hybrid VaR. Note: our VaR parameters $K=250$, $\lambda=0.98$, $p=0.025$. The hybrid VaR is choppy compared to hsVaR. Action: if VaR is too unstable, it will be unsuitable for minimum capital. Can you choose a suitable λ setting to reduce the jaggedness?

5.2 Hull-White introduced stochastic volatility into hsVaR by scaling the VaR scenarios with a ratio of changing volatilities. Aim: illustrates the implementation of Hull-White VaR. Note: we have set the decay factor to $\lambda=0.94$ as in Riskmetrics. Action: experiment with various values of λ to see if the

Hull-White approach is stable.

5.3 The CAViaR (conditional autoregressive value-at-risk) model uses the method of quantile regression to make VaR a function of other variables. It bypasses the problem of lack of tail data since the whole distribution is used in modeling, but the method requires us to presume (specify) the process for VaR. Aim: illustrates the implementation of the CAViaR model at 95% confidence (quantile of θ=0.05). Note: CAViaR tracks the level of the hsVaR generally, but it has its own peculiar pattern depending on the model specification. Action: choose a different quantile θ and rerun the Excel Solver. To help the Solver along, set the beta at a low number such as 0.001 before running Solver.

5.4 (a) The cumulative distribution function (CDF) of maximas is known to be degenerate. With a slight transformation this degeneracy can be avoided, which allows the modeling of extreme value theory. Aim: illustrates the concept of a degenerate function by plotting the CDF of the maximas. Action: pull the slider to make n large, and observe that the shape of the CDF becomes degenerate (or useless). (b) The *peaks-over-thresholds* (POT) method is a popular EVT approach. To use it, a suitable exceedence threshold u needs to be determined visually using a plot of the *mean excess function*. Aim: illustrates the calculation and plot of the *mean excess function* of the POT approach.

5.5 A popular EVT approach is to model the tail as a generalized Pareto distribution (GPD). To obtain the VaR, the parameters of the GPD need to be estimated statistically. Aim: illustrates the estimation of the parameters β and α for the GPD using maximum likelihood estimation. Action: this is done using the Excel Solver. To work within the Solver's limitation (it is not a sophisticated optimizer) we assume the case of $\alpha \neq 0$ in equation (5.12). We first constrain $\alpha>0$ and estimate the parameters to maximize the objective function $L(.)$. Then we constrain $\alpha<0$ and re-estimate to maximize $L(.)$. We take the parameters β and α that give the larger $L(.)$. EVT VaR is then computed using (5.13) for various quantiles. PVaR is also plotted with EVT VaR as a comparison.

Chapter 6

VaR Reporting

In this chapter, we shall study how VaR is aggregated "bottom up"—that is measured at the most elemental deal level and then progressively aggregated up into portfolios and then into business lines. Generally, if VaR is computed using scenarios or simulations, the aggregation is done by adding PL vectors *by scenarios*. In the parametric method, VaR is aggregated by variance-covariance matrix multiplication. In both cases, the correlation structure is inherent and manifested as a lower overall VaR (risk diversification).

VaR reporting usually includes explaining where the risk is coming from. This VaR *decomposition* involves slicing the VaR number into its component parts. Depending on the needs of the risk controller, the breakdown can be by portfolio, by risk factor dimension, by business line, by bank subsidiary, or even by deal at its most granular level.

6.1 VaR Aggregation and Limits

VaR reports are typically generated prior to the beginning of each trading day for position as of the end of the previous trading session. Normally reports are custom-made for various users—traders, risk controllers, top management, and regulators—and will show a relevant degree of detail and risk decomposition.

For illustration purposes, we shall use the hsVaR model as specified in Table 4.6. Six test deals (see Table 6-1) are booked into three portfolios. In practice, a large bank may deal in hundreds of thousands of deals booked in a vast array of portfolios. These portfolios are typically arranged in some logical hierarchy based on traders, business lines, branch location, currency or product type (as in our test case).

Table 6-1 Three portfolios containing 6 test deals

Portfolio/deal	Description
Equity Portfolio	
Deal 1	Long $1 million Dow Jones index
Deal 4	Short $200,000 Dow Jones index
Option Portfolio	
Deal 2	$1 million 1-year put option on Dow Jones (ATM strike 10718)
Deal 5	Short $5 million 1-year put option on Dow Jones (OTM strike 9000)
Bond Portfolio	
Deal 3	$1 million 2-year 5% bond
Deal 6	$1 million 20-year zero coupon bond

The PL vector for each deal is compiled[1] and aggregated to derive the portfolio level VaR. Spreadsheet 6.1 shows how the PL's are added *across scenarios*. A "high level" VaR report is shown in Table 6-2 along with some hypothetical *limits*. A limit is a ceiling set by risk managers to control the risk taking activities of traders. *It is the first line of defence for a bank.* A trader who breaches a limit will face disciplinary actions if the breach could not be justified. At times when VaR is very close to the limit, a big market movement may cause VaR to go above the limit, a "technical breach". In this case, a trader will often request a temporary limit extension (increase). If not approved by risk managers, the trader may be forced to unwind some positions to bring the VaR back under the limit.

Table 6-2 A simple VaR report with limits

Entity	VaR (97.5%)	Limits
Equity Portfolio	-$9,529	-$20,000
Option Portfolio	-$3,884	-$20,000
Bond Portfolio	-$9,512	-$20,000
Total Portfolio	-$14,244	-$35,000
Undiversified VaR	-$46,790	
Diversification ratio	30%	

---

[1] The PL vectors are actually computed using the previous calculator and data (Spreadsheet 4.1). The astute reader can use that spreadsheet to generate PL vectors for new test deals.

Thanks to diversification, the total VaR or *diversified VaR* is always smaller than the algebraic sum of its individual VaR components. This simple sum is called the *undiversified VaR*.

6.2 Diversification

Markowitz portfolio diversification is located at the heart of the VaR framework. The ratio between the diversified and undiversified VaR is called the *diversification ratio*—the smaller this number the larger the benefit of diversification. In our test portfolio, the ratio is 30% which implies 70% of the risk is diversified away. This is due to the long-short nature of the book; the hedging between long index and put option, and the negative correlation between stock index and bonds.

In general, diversification increases (and overall VaR reduces) when the number of securities in the portfolio increases. This is shown in Figure 6-1. The calculation is done in Spreadsheet 6-2 where we kept the portfolio's *undiversified* VaR fixed at $1 million, each security has equal risk, and each pair-wise correlation ρ is the same. As we increase the number of securities n, the *diversified* VaR falls exponentially. The smaller the correlation ρ, the more the portfolio benefits from diversification, the faster VaR falls with n. As a rule of thumb, the advantages of diversification tapers off once n is above 30.

Figure 6-1 Diversification and the number of securities

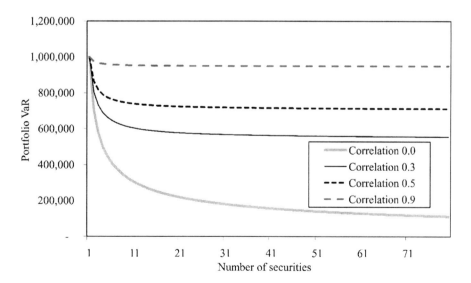

6.3 VaR Analytical Tools

The report in Table 6-2 gives a broad overview of portfolio risk and provides
risk managers a framework to set up limits monitoring. For risk control, it is
further necessary to determine the drivers of the VaR numbers and to see how
VaR evolves as the observation window moves forward in time. This is the
diagnostic aspect of VaR and some basic tools are available.

The tail profile

In hsVaR it is crucial to monitor the profile of the tail scenarios. To plot this,
rank the 250 P&L's of the PL vector, then plot the ranked PL (see Figure 6-2).
This "tangent shaped" profile is typical of all PL vectors, in particular, the points
on both ends (tails) space out very quickly. The tail loss (of 97.5% VaR) is
determined by the 7 extreme points on the left; if one holds the opposite position
to the test portfolio, the tail loss will be determined by the 7 extreme points on
the right. The tail profile evolves every day as new positions are traded and as
market data rolls in (and out) of the observation interval[2].

Figure 6-2 Profile of the ranked PL of the test portfolio

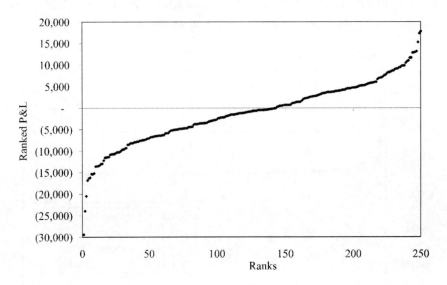

To zoom in on the tails, a horizontal bar chart is often plotted showing only the top ranking and bottom ranking P&L (see Figure 6-3 and Spreadsheet 6.1). The scenario number of each observation is labeled. The VaR is given approximately by the 7th largest loss i.e. $15.3k (scenario-71). Notice the 6th largest loss is $16.2k (scenario-165). Suppose a *new* loss scenario greater than $15.3k (say -$20k) comes into the PL vector, then scenario-71 will be "pushed out" of the quantile (now becomes rank 8), scenario-165 will be the new 7th largest loss, and the VaR will become $16.2k (an increase seen). This is how an incoming extreme loss observation increases hsVaR.

Also, the 4th largest loss ($16.8k) is scenario-220, a rather "old" scenario. In 30 days time, this scenario will become scenario-250 and will exit the observation window. All else being equal, the 8th largest loss (now scenario-71) will then move back up one rank to become the 7th rank, i.e. the VaR decreases to $15.3k.

Figure 6-3 Tail profile of the total PL distribution of the test portfolio

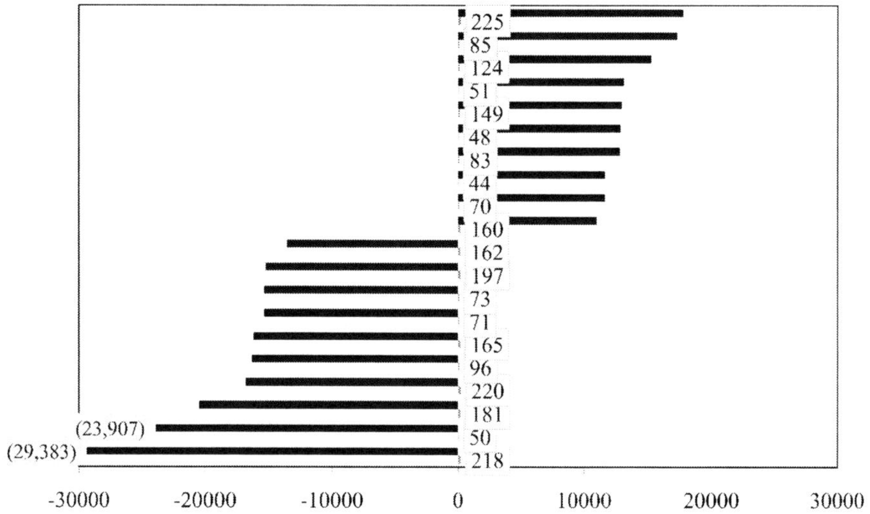

Component VaR

Individual VaR is not a useful way to show decomposition of risk for a portfolio because it ignores the power of diversification. In particular, it does not add up to the total diversified VaR. *Component VaR* partitions the portfolio VaR into parts that *add up* to the total diversified VaR. This additivity is a nice feature for the purpose of risk communication so that the report is more intuitive.

It uses the beta approach which *linearly* aggregates risks and implicitly assumes the joint distribution is normal. Recall that the beta is just the slope of the graph of return of asset *i* vs. portfolio return. If the relationship is non-linear, the slope is ill-defined. Thus, component VaR is good in the absence of non-linear products and when the portfolio is large. The component VaR of asset *i* is given by:

$$CVaR_i = VaR_i \rho_i \qquad\qquad (6.1)$$

where *VaR_i* is the individual VaR of asset *i* and ρ_i is the correlation of return of asset *i* with the portfolio return. Spreadsheet 6.3 is a worked-out example; the result is in Table 6-3. Notice the component VaRs, expressed as a percentage, sum up to 100% of the diversified portfolio VaR.

Table 6-3 Component VaR calculated using pVaR method

	Individual VaR	Component VaR	% of Total	Correlation
deal(1)	(12,709)	(9,034)	64%	0.71
deal(2)	(10,030)	7,388	-52%	(0.74)
deal(3)	(1,945)	(1,165)	8%	0.60
deal(4)	(2,542)	1,807	-13%	(0.71)
deal(5)	(11,874)	(8,641)	61%	0.73
deal(6)	(7,646)	(4,572)	32%	0.60
Total		(14,218)	100%	
Equity Portfolio	(10,167)	(7,227)	51%	0.71
Option Portfolio	(2,988)	(1,253)	9%	0.42
Bond Portfolio	(9,591)	(5,737)	40%	0.60
Total		(14,218)	100%	
Diversified VaR		(14,218)		

Component VaR is a convenient representation but it does not reflect diversification—the risks add up linearly whereas in reality they should really be sub-additive. Furthermore, component VaR is *not* additive in either a non-normal analytical setting or a Monte Carlo / historical simulation context. See

Hallerbach (2002) who investigated the decomposition of VaR in a general distribution-free setting.

Incremental VaR

Incremental VaR is the difference between diversified VaR with and without the position under investigation. This is the most correct decomposition method for use with hsVaR (full revaluation) since it accounts for the *full impact* of the position including any non-linearity.

Incremental VaR for asset *i* is given by:

$$IVaR_i = VaR_{P+i} - VaR_P \qquad (6.2)$$

where VAR_{P+i} is the portfolio VaR inclusive of asset i, VAR_P is the portfolio VaR after removing asset *i*. Clearly when $IVAR_i>0$ (for clarity we will express VaR as positive numbers) then this position contributes by increasing overall diversified VaR by the amount $IVAR_i$. If $IVAR_i<0$ it means the position is risk reducing—it hedges some of the portfolio risk by the amount $IVAR_i$.

Table 6-4 Incremental VaR calculated using hsVaR method

	Individual VaR	Incremental VaR
deal(1)	11,858	3,966
deal(2)	8,477	(8,622)
deal(3)	2,065	1,261
deal(4)	2,553	(1,518)
deal(5)	14,875	5,435
deal(6)	8,062	1,786
Sub Total		2,309
Equity Portfolio	9,487	3,335
Option Portfolio	4,412	1,778
Bond Portfolio	10,127	1,113
Sub Total		6,225
Diversified VaR		14,244

Spreadsheet 6.4 is a worked-out example; the result in Table 6-4 shows that deal 2 and 4 are risk decreasing—long index put option and short stock in an overall long equity portfolio. Note that the incremental VaR number is drastically different to component VaR. They are different things—one is the actual dollar impact, the other is a beta attribution. Also, the subtotals in Table 6-4 do not add up to anything meaningful and should never be used because such simple summations do not account for diversification.

Incremental VaR can be used in flexible ways to *study risk drivers* of the overall book. For example, one can run hsVaR for the entire portfolio as a base case, then run hsVaR again but *without* applying interest rate risk factor scenarios. The difference will give incremental VaR due purely to interest rate risk! Likewise, one can calculate incremental VaR due to FX risk alone, due to a portfolio belonging to one trader, due to one particular deal, due to volatility smile effect, or even due to time (theta) decay. The general idea is to run VaR twice—with the factor(s) you want to study and without—then take the difference. The combinations are limited only by the imagination.

The weakness of this approach is that it takes a long time to fully revalue the entire portfolio multiple times to work out the increments. And secondly the incremental VaR does not add up to overall VaR; this unintuitive fact will require some effort to explain to top management.

6.4 Scaling and Basel Rules

Basel Rules

Most banks calculate VaR using *daily* returns and at less than 99% confidence level. This is driven by practical considerations such as data availability, statistical accuracy and the need to ensure responsiveness to market changes.

However, regulatory reporting as stipulated by the *Basel Rules* (1995) requires VaR to be stated in terms of a 10 day horizon and 99% confidence level. The Basel Rules provide the formula to compute the *market risk charge* (*MRC*) at day t for a bank:

$$MRC_t = \max\left(\frac{k}{60}\sum_{i=1}^{60}VaR_{t-i}, VaR_{t-1}\right) + SRC_t \qquad (6.3)$$

which involves taking the larger of the most recent VaR or the average VaR of the last 60 days. The *specific risk charge* (*SRC*) captures the idiosyncratic risk coming from securities of specific issuers[3]. The supervisory multiplier k, which must be 3 or larger, is determined by the regulator depending on its assessment of the "goodness" of the bank's risk model (see *back testing* in Chapter 8).

Let's look at the merit of equation (6.3). The averaging over the last 60 days in the first term smoothens the VaR so that the *MRC* is stable. 60 days also reflects the liquidity horizon, which in Basel's opinion, is sufficient for a bank in trouble to raise funds or to unwind trading positions. The first term mostly dominates the *MRC* because of the multiplication by k. The second term (VAR_{t-1}) will overtake only when there is an extreme event (say in a crash) or when traders increase positions substantially. This design gives a less volatile capital charge and yet provides for higher penalty under exceptional situations.

Suppose the capital charge is volatile, since positions can seldom be adjusted quickly, a bank will need to maintain a conservative (spare) capital buffer to absorb the fluctuation and peaks in charges—it cannot be cost effective. Hence, a less variable, smoother capital charge is beneficial economically.

Time scaling

The 10-day horizon (also called *holding period* or *liquidity horizon*) stipulated by Basel corresponds to the estimated time required for corrective action by regulators should a bank run into liquidity problems. This could involve orchestrating a rescue plan or an orderly unwind of positions. To scale to 10 days, Basel has recommended the use of the "square-root of time" scaling:

$$VaR_{10day} = VaR_{daily}\sqrt{10} \tag{6.4}$$

The square-root of time scaling rests on the assumptions of i.i.d., normal distribution and constant position over the entire horizon. These are arguably weak assumptions. Consider a time series of returns X_t. The variance over two equal, non-overlapping periods (say $t=1, 2$) is given by:

$$\sigma(X_1,X_2)^2 = \sigma_1^2 + \sigma_2^2 + 2\sigma_1\sigma_2\rho_{12} \tag{6.5}$$

---

[3] Debt securities (corporate bonds) will contain idiosyncratic risk unique to the issuer of that security on top of the usual interest rate risk (which falls under MRC). These idiosyncratic factors include the risk coming from credit spread movement and a rating downgrade.

By i.i.d. the variance of X_1 and X_2 are identical ($\sigma_1=\sigma_2=\sigma$) and has zero correlation $\rho_{12}=0$, hence: $\sigma(X_1,X_2)= \sigma\sqrt{2}$. Extending this argument iteratively we have $\sigma(X_1,\ldots,X_T)= \sigma\sqrt{T}$. Because volatility is often quoted in annualized terms, to transform to a volatility of horizon T years, we use:

$$\sigma = \sigma_{annual}\sqrt{T} \tag{6.6}$$

To obtain daily σ for example, let $T= 1/250$. And since VaR is just σ times a constant, for a normal distribution, equation (6.4) is true.

Equation (6.6) underestimates risk in the presence of serial correlation (non i.i.d.). However, this can be corrected. Let's consider an AR(1) model of the form:

$$X_t = \rho X_{t-1} + \varepsilon_t \tag{6.7}$$

where the random element ε_t is white noise and ρ the autocorrelation. Once again, the 2-period variance is:

$$\sigma(X_1,X_2)^2 = \sigma^2 + \sigma^2 + 2\sigma^2\rho = \sigma^2(2+2\rho) \tag{6.8}$$

For T periods this can be generalized to:

$$\sigma(X_1,X_T)^2 = \sigma^2\left(T+2(T-1)\rho+2(T-2)\rho^2 +\ldots+2(1)\rho^{T-1}\right) \tag{6.9}$$

of which equation (6.6) is a special case when $\rho=0$. When $\rho>0$, equation (6.6) underestimates the true risk because equation (6.9) grows faster than (6.6) with increasing horizon T.

A technical point—the autocorrelation ρ needs to be computed *just once* at the bank-wide PL vector and not at each risk factor's scenario vector. This is because we want to capture the serial correlation caused by derivatives held by the bank as a whole. For example, range accruals are options that provide a fixed positive return (say 0.02% daily) for every day that a reference index trades within a predefined range. If a bank holds large amounts of range accruals and the index spends a large part of its life within the range, we can expect significant autocorrelation in PL. With ρ estimated, equation (6.9) can be used for more accurate scaling.

A more advanced method uses *power law scaling*, where volatility is assumed to scale with T^h, where h can be statistically determined. For more details, the reader may refer to Alexander (2008). Note that the naïve method of using a "rolling" 10-day return to calculate the 10-day VaR will produce a biased result, because it introduces an artificial serial correlation into the 10-day return series which would distort back testing. This is illustrated in Spreadsheet 6.5.

The second assumption that a bank's position remains constant for 10 days is simply untrue for investment banks which deal with huge trading volume. The disconnect with this assumption is that VaR will not be the 10-day forward looking measure Basel meant it to be. The truth is banks almost always know about incoming deals 10 days ahead of time especially when it comes to significant transactions. The trading desk knows about large deals in the pipeline and customers orders ahead of the transaction. This is particularly true for underwriting and securitization deals, which take weeks to put together. Also, if a trader needs to prehedge a large transaction or unwind a large portfolio, the plan is known ahead of time and usually executed over a period. Thus, the obvious alternative to the constant position assumption is to pre-book deals (for the purpose of VaR) if the trader is confident that the deal will happen. If the deal falls through later, it can be cancelled from the system.

In theory this idea could work but there are two critical weaknesses. Firstly, it is open to gaming—if the trader is about to breach his VaR limit due to losses, he may pre-book a hedge (without actually doing the transaction) on the pretext of intending to unwind in the next 10 days. If the market recovers, he could decide not to unwind. In this way, he could avoid the discipline to cut his losses. Secondly, if a large impending deal gets pre-booked, it is more susceptible to information leakage and insider trading, which would violate client confidentiality. For these reasons, perhaps, the naïve assumption of constant position is an unavoidable simplification.

Quantile scaling

Since Basel stipulates a 99% confidence VaR and most banks use an observation window of $1 - 2$ years, risk modelers often run into a data scarcity problem. For example, with a 250-day window, the 99% VaR is determined by just 2.5 data points. Such an estimate is hardly statistically meaningful.

To overcome this problem, banks often compute the VaR using a lower quantile such as 97.5% confidence and then scale up to 99% by assuming the tail belongs to a normal distribution. With this simplification, the VaR is scaled using the standard normal deviate $\alpha(q)$ of quantile q or confidence level $(1-q)$. In Excel function $\alpha(q)$=NORMSINV(q). Then:

$$VaR_{99\%} = \frac{\alpha(0.01)}{\alpha(0.025)}VaR_{97.5\%} = \frac{2.326}{1.960}VaR_{97.5\%} \qquad (6.10)$$

Basel's choice of 99% confidence level would translate to one occurrence of (non-overlapping 10-day) loss larger than VaR for every 4 years on average. This frequency of bank failures is still far too high for any regulators to tolerate. Hence, the multiplicative factor $k(\geq3)$ is meant to provide an additional capital buffer.

6.5 Spreadsheet

6.1 In historical simulation VaR, risks can easily be aggregated to arrive at portfolio VaR. Aim: illustrates the aggregation of VaR by adding PL vectors across scenarios for a portfolio containing 6 deals. It also illustrates the ranked tail profile of the PL distribution often used for analysis.

6.2 The benefit of diversification increases as the number of securities in the portfolio increases. Aim: illustrates the benefit of diversification, hence, the fall in portfolio VaR, as the number of securities n increase. Note: pVaR is calculated assuming a constant correlation ρ (for each pair-wise combination). The quantity of each security is equally weighted such that the undiversified VaR adds up to $1 million. Action: key in a different correlation ρ and observe how the pVaR declines with n. More interestingly, key in a negative ρ and observe that pVaR fails because the matrix is no longer positive semi-definite. For a small negative correlation ($\rho= -0.1$) the pVaR can still be calculated for small n. But as the n grows, the correlation matrix becomes too large and restrictive in terms of satisfying the positive semi-definite condition.

6.3 Component VaR is a method to decompose portfolio VaR by assuming its constituents are beta portions of the portfolio VaR. Aim: illustrates the computation of component VaR using pVaR and hsVaR methods. Note: under pVaR, the component VaRs add up to 100% of diversified portfolio VaR. Under hsVaR, the component VaRs do not add up to 100% of total generally. It works for pVaR because both pVaR and the beta approach assume normality.

6.4 Incremental VaR is a method to decompose portfolio VaR by calculating the actual contribution (including effects of diversification) of a deal to the portfolio VaR. This is done by removing that deal and recalculating portfolio VaR and taking the difference. Aim: illustrates the computation of incremental VaR using hsVaR method. Note: the incremental VaRs of constituents are not expected to add up to portfolio VaR because their contributions take into account diversification.

6.5 Is it valid to calculate a 10-day VaR directly using a 10-day log return applied over a "rolling" window? I.e. where the return series is $\ln(X_t / X_{t-10})$ where $t=10,11,...,T$. Aim: Use an ACF plot to illustrate that a serial correlation is artificially introduced into the 10-day return series even though the 1-day return series is i.i.d. Note: this problem can be resolved by using non-overlapping returns, where $t=10,20,...$ However, this requires 10 times as much historical data.

Chapter 7

The Physics of Risk and Pseudoscience

Great fortunes are made and lost on Wall Street with the power of mathematics. Quantitative or "quant" modeling is akin to an arms race amongst banks. The conventional wisdom is that a bank that has superior models can better exploit market inefficiencies and manage risk competitively.

Many of the modeling techniques and ideas were borrowed from mathematics and physics. In hard sciences, a mathematical law always describes a truth of nature which can be verified precisely by repeatable experiments. In contrast, financial models are nothing more than toy representations of reality—it is impossible to predict the madness of the crowd consistently, and any success in doing so is often unrepeatable. It really is pseudoscience, not precise science. The danger for a risk manager is in not being able to tell the difference.

Empirical studies have shown that the basic model assumptions of i.i.d., stationarity and Gaussian "thin" tailed distribution are violated under stressful market conditions. Market prices do not exhibit Brownian motion like gas particles. Phenomena that are in fact observed are fat-tailness and skewness of returns, and evidence of clustering and asymmetry of volatility. In truth, the 2008 crisis is one expensive experiment to debunk our deep-rooted ideas.

This chapter discusses the causes and effects of the market "anomalies" that disrupt the VaR measure. Due to its failings, VaR is increasingly recognized as a "peace-time" tool. It's like supersonic flight—the shock wave renders the speedometer useless in measuring speed when the sound barrier is broken; likewise our riskometer fails during market distress—the moments such as variance and kurtosis can no longer be measured accurately.

7.1 Entropy, Leverage effect and Skewness

In physics, *entropy* is a measure of disorder or chaos. The famous *second law of thermodynamics* states that entropy can only increase (never decrease) in an enclosed environment. For entropy to decrease, external energy must flow into the physical system (i.e. work needs to be done). Thus, in nature there is a spontaneous tendency towards disorder. For example, if we stack a "house of cards" (as shown in Figure 7-1), a small random perturbation will bring down the whole structure but no amount of random perturbation can reverse the process unless external work is done (restacking). Interestingly, entropy acts to suggest the *arrow of time*. Suppose we watch a recorded video of the collapse of the house of cards *backwards*—the disordered cards spontaneously stacking themselves—we know from experience this is physically impossible. In other words, manifestation of entropy can act as a clock to show the direction of time. Figure 7-2 shows two charts of an actual price series. Can you tell which one has the time scale reversed purely by looking at the price pattern? Could this be evidence of entropy?

Figure 7-1 Collapse of the house of cards and entropy

Note the asymmetry—it takes a long time to achieve order (work needed) but a very short time to destroy order (spontaneous tendency). There is evidence that entropy exists even in social interactions. For example, it takes great marketing effort for a bank to attract and build up a deposit base, but only one day for a bank-run to happen if there is a rumor of insolvency.

In information theory, entropy (or *Shannon entropy*) is a measure of uncertainty associated with a random variable used to store information[1]. The links

---

[1] The concept was introduced by Shannon (1948) the founder of information theory. More recently, Dionisio et al. (2007) explored the use of Shannon entropy as a financial risk measure, as an alternative to variance. Gulko (1999) argues that an efficient market corresponds to a state where the informational entropy of the system is maximized.

between physical, informational and social entropies are still being debated by scientists.

Figure 7-2 Which chart is time reversed? The intuition of entropy

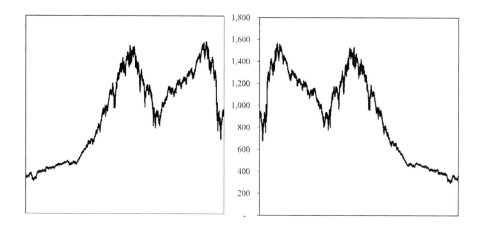

Financial markets' entropy is manifested as the *leverage effect*, the phenomena whereby rallies are gradual and accompanied by diminished volatility, while sell-downs are often sharp and characterized by high volatility. Destruction of wealth has more impact on to the economy than creation of wealth—it hurts the ability of firms to raise money and the individual's spending power. For investors, the rush to exit is always more frenzied than the temptation to invest (there is inertia in the latter)—fear is a stronger emotion than greed. For example, consider Figure 7-3 which shows the S&P 500 index and the VIX index[2]. There is an apparent negative correlation between a stock index and its volatility.

The leverage effect is also reflected in the equity option markets, in the form of an observed *negative* "volatility skew"—OTM puts tend to demand a higher premium compared to OTM calls of the same delta. The fear of loss is asymmetric; from investors' collective experience, crashes are more devastating than market bounces. Thus the premium cost for hedging the downside risk is more expensive than that for the upside risk. Interestingly, this volatility skew appeared after the 1987 crash and is with us ever since. The volatility skew is illustrated in Figure 7-4; the horizontal axis shows the strike price of options

---

[2] The VIX index is an average of the implied volatilities of S&P index options of different strikes. It is a general measure of precariousness of the stock market and is often used as a "fear" gauge.

expressed in percentage of spot (or "moneyness"). Points below 100% money-ness are contributed by OTM puts, while those above are contributed by OTM calls.

Figure 7-3 Negative correlation between an equity index and its volatility

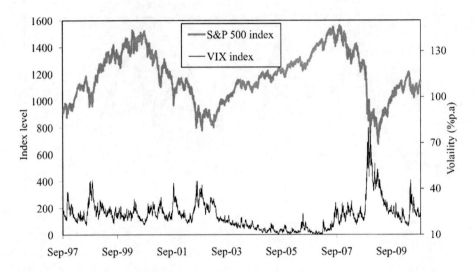

Figure 7-4 Illustration of "volatility skew" for an equity index

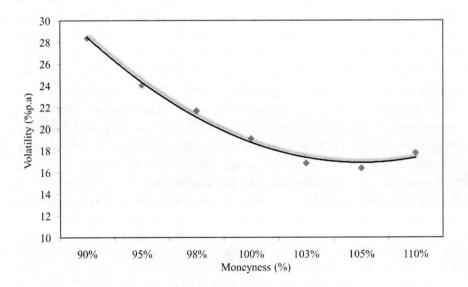

The asymmetry of risk causes skewness in distributions. In a bull trend, the frequency of positive observations is expected to be larger than negative ones. In this case the skew is to the *negative*. As illustrated by Figure 7-5 the frequency on the positive side of the hump is larger. Because the area has to sum up to a probability of 1.0 and skew is measured *on a centered basis*, it causes a "tail" which is skewed to the left. Conversely, in a bear trend, the skew is positive. Spreadsheet 7.1 lets the reader simulate these stylized examples. The rather unintuitive result is often observed in actual data. Figure 7-6 plots the S&P 500 index during a bull market (negative skew) and bear market (positive skew)!

Consider equation (2.4) for sample skewness; it can be rewritten in terms of centered returns $y_i = x_i - \hat{x}$:

$$skewness = \frac{1}{n-1}\sum_{i=1}^{n}(y_i^2)(y_i)\frac{1}{\hat{\sigma}^3} \qquad (7.1)$$

Figure 7-5 Stylized example of bull market and negative skew distribution

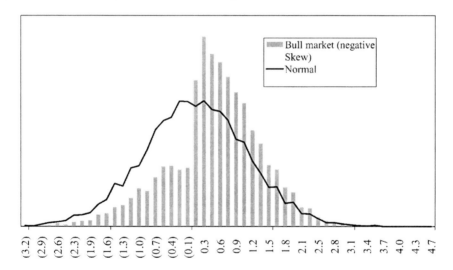

which shows the interesting idea that skewness can be seen (loosely) as *correlation* between the movement of the random variable (Y_i) and its volatility (Y_i^2)— by equation (2.16). Generally (but not always[3]) the correlation is negative during

---

[3] This is because the volatility is also affected by local features of the market- for example, as prices approach support and resistance levels, volatility may sometimes decline because traders place trading bets that these levels will hold.

a rally and positive during a sell-down. Note the relationship between Y_i and its volatility is quadratic hence is not well-described by linear correlation.

Unfortunately, skewness is an incomplete measure of risk asymmetry. In particular, it fails to account for price microstructure when prices approach important support and resistance levels. Consider a defended price "barrier" such as a currency peg like the USD/CNY. Speculators who sell against the peg will bring prices down to test the peg. This downward drift is gradual because the currency is supported by the actions of opposing traders who bet that the peg will hold and by the central bank managing the peg. On the other hand, each time the peg holds, short covering will likely see quick upward spikes. This will cause occasional positive skewness in the distribution even though the real risk (of interest to a risk manager) is to the downside—should the peg break, the downward move may be large. In fact, the risk shows up as a negative volatility skew in the option market[4]. Thus, statistical skewness is often an understated and misleading risk measure in situations where it matters most.

Figure 7-6 Skew of S&P 500 index during bull and bear phase

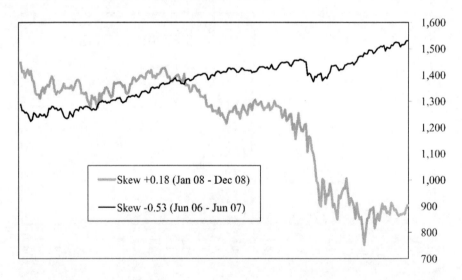

In conclusion, the leverage effect which depends on *price* path, critical levels and trend is too rich to be adequately described by simple statistics (of returns)

---

[4] This volatility skew (which looks like Figure 7-4) can be mathematically translated into a PDF which slants to the left side - this implied distribution will disagree with the observed distribution. Technically speaking, the risk neutral probability inferred from the current option market differs from the physical probability observed from historical spot prices.

such as skew and correlation. Measures such as VaR, made from moments and correlation describes an incomplete story of risk.

7.2 Volatility Clustering and the folly of i.i.d.

Volatility clustering is a phenomenon where volatility seems to cluster together temporally at certain periods. Hence, the saying goes that high volatility begets high volatility and low volatility begets low volatility. Figure 1-3 shows the return series of Dow Jones index—the clustering effect is obvious. This is caused by occasional serial correlation of returns—in stark violation of the i.i.d. assumption.

Under the assumption of i.i.d., return series should be stationary and volatility *constant* (or at least slowly changing). This naïve assumption implies that information (news) arrives at the market at a continuously slow rate and in small homogenous bits such that there are no "surprises" or shocks. But news does not come in continuous streams. Its arrival and effects are often lumpy—for example, news of a technological break-through, central bank policy action, H1N1 flu outbreak, 9-11 tragedy, a government debt default, etc. Each of these can cause a sudden surge in market volatility.

Many volatility models attempt to account for clustering by making volatility conditional on past volatility (i.e. autoregressive); for example, EWMA and GARCH models (see Section 2.7). VaR based on these models will be more responsive to a surge in volatility.

Some thinkers argued that if a phenomenon is non-i.i.d., the use of frequentist statistics becomes questionable in theory. The late E.T. Jaynes, a great proponent of the Bayesian school, wrote in his book "Probability Theory: The Logic of Science" that "The traditional frequentist methods . . . are usable and useful in many particularly simple, idealized problems; but they represent the most proscribed special case of probability theory, because they presuppose conditions (independent repetition of a 'random experiment' but no relevant prior information) that are hardly ever met in real problems. This approach is quite inadequate for the current needs of science . . .".

7.3 "Volatility of volatility" and Fat-tails

The phenomenon of volatility clustering implies another obvious fact, that volatility is not constant but *stochastic*. Volatility (like returns) changes with time in a random fashion. What is interesting is that stochastic volatility (or "volatility of volatility") can cause fat-tails.

Figure 7-7 shows two return series which can be simulated using Spreadsheet 7.2. The upper panel is generated by GBM with constant volatility, while the lower panel is by GBM with stochastic volatility given by a simple process:

$$\Delta\sigma_t = 0.02\sigma_{t-1}\varepsilon_t \qquad (7.2)$$

where the random element $\varepsilon_t \sim N(0,1)$. For a more realistic model, see Heston (1993). Notice the lower panel shows obvious clustering, characteristic of stochastic volatility. Figure 7-8 shows the probability distribution of both the series—constant volatility caused a normal distribution but stochastic volatility caused the distribution to be fat-tailed. For a discussion of the impact of variable volatility on option pricing, see Taleb (1997).

Figure 7-7 Return series with constant volatility (upper) and stochastic volatility (lower)

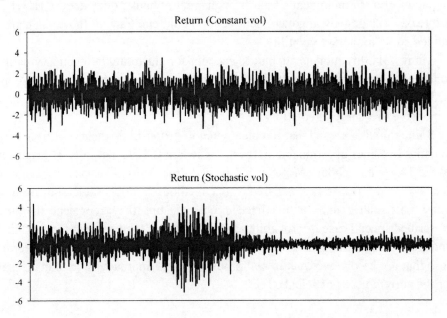

How does stochastic volatility create fat-tails? The intuitive way to under-stand this is to consider the mixture of normal distributions in Figure 4-5. The fat-tailed distribution (bar chart) is just a combination of two distributions of *varying* volatilities. The high volatility observations dominated the tail whereas the low volatility observations dominated the middle or "peak". So the net distribution is fatter at the tail and narrower in the middle as compared to a normal distribution. A distribution with stochastic volatility can be thought of as being a mixture of many normal distributions with different volatilities, and will thus result in a fat-tail.

Figure 7-8 Probability distributions with constant and stochastic volatility

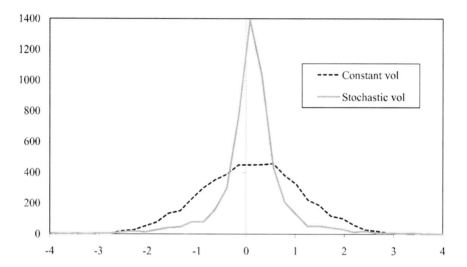

Figure 7-9 Scatter plot of quantiles of the Dow Jones index vs. the standard normal

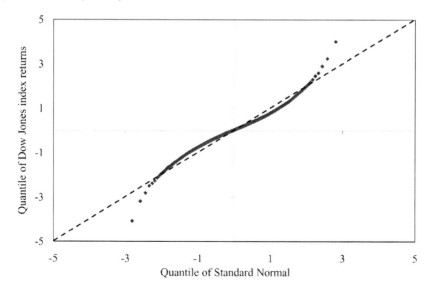

In Figure 7-8, it is hard to see any difference at the tails compared to a normal distribution. The histogram is an unsuitable tool to study the tail. A scatter plot is a better choice. For example, Figure 7-9 is a scatter plot of the quantiles (expressed in units of standard deviation) of the Dow Jones index daily returns from Jul 62 to Jun 09 vs. the standard normal. Had the empirical data been normally distributed, the plot would have fallen on the dotted line (with unit slope). But the empirical data is fat-tailed, so the tail quantiles are more extreme (more risky) than the normal, while the lower quantiles are less risky.

How far off are we if we use the tail of the normal distribution to model the risk of extreme events? Very. Empirical evidence of past market stress revealed that the normal distribution is an impossible proposition. Table 7-1 lists the ten largest one-day losses experienced by the Dow Jones index in 20 years (1988 – 2008). The third column shows the statistical frequency (in units of years) for each event assuming the normal distribution holds. These are calculated using the Excel function:

$$\frac{1}{250T} = probability(x) = NORMDIST(x,0,\sigma / sqrt(250), TRUE) \qquad (7.3)$$

where the observed event of log return x is calculated to occur once every T years (assuming 250 business days per year). We have also assumed an annualized volatility σ=25%, typical of equity indices.

Table 7-1 Top ten largest single day losses for Dow Jones index (1988-2008)

Event Date	Daily log return	Mean number of years between occurrences
19-Oct-87	-25.6%	1.86E+56
26-Oct-87	-8.4%	69,074
15-Oct-08	-8.2%	37,326
1-Dec-08	-8.0%	19,952
9-Oct-08	-7.6%	5,482
27-Oct-97	-7.5%	3,258
17-Sep-01	-7.4%	2,791
29-Sep-08	-7.23%	1,684
13-Oct-89	-7.16%	1,346
8-Jan-88	-7.10%	1,120

The results show the forecast of the normal distribution is ludicrous—"Black Monday" (19 Oct 87) is computed as a once in 1.86×10^{56} year event! In contrast, the age of the universe is only 14 billion years. We have already witnessed 10 such extreme events in a span of just 20 years—clearly extreme events occur more frequently than forecasted by the normal distribution.

From a modeling perspective, there are two schools of thought on fat-tails. One school believes that returns follow a distribution which is fat-tailed (such as the log-gamma distribution or stable Pareto distribution). The second school sees returns as normal at each instant of time but *look* fat-tailed due to time series fluctuations in volatility. In Section 13.2, we shall propose a third, whereby fat-tailness arises from a break or compression of market cycles.

7.4 Extremistan and the Fourth quadrant

Chapter 1 provided a prelude to the idea of extremistan. We shall continue by noting that financial markets are informational in nature and scalable. This gives rise to extremistan behavior of rare events such as crashes, manias, rogue trading and ponzi schemes. From the VaR perspective, attempts to forecast these events using Gaussian models will render us "fooled by randomness" because it will never let us predict Black Swans, but lull us into a false sense of security that comes from seemingly precise measures. Having a thick risk report on the CEO's desk does not make this type of risk go away. Black Swans are not predictable, even using fat-tail distributions (such as that of EVT) which are just theoretically appealing fitting tools. Such tools are foiled by what Taleb called "inverse problems"—there are plenty of distributions that can fit the same set of data, and each model will extrapolate differently. Modeling extremistan events is futile since there is no typical (expected) value for statistical estimation to converge to.

The idea of extremistan has serious consequences. The business of risk measurement rests on the tacit assumption that *frequency distribution equals probability distribution*. The former is a histogram of observations, the latter is a function giving theoretical probabilities. There is a subtle philosophical transition between these two concepts which is seldom questioned (most statistical textbooks often use the two terms interchangeably without addressing why). This equality is the great divide between the frequentist school and the Bayesian school (which rejects the idea). The frequentist believes that probability is objective and can be deduced from repeatable experiments much like coin tosses. This is simply untrue where extremistan is present—extreme events in financial markets and irregularities that happen in the corporate world are not repeatable experiments. Without the element of reproducibility, the frequency histogram becomes a bad gauge of probability and the quantile-based VaR loses its probabilistic interpretation. Extremistan also broke the lore of i.i.d. since if events are non-repeatable (and a-typical), they cannot be identical in distribution.

Do we really need to be fixated on *measuring* risk? Suppose we admit that the tail is *unknowable* and are mindful that Black Swans will occur more frequently than suggested by model, we are more likely to take evasive actions and find ways to hedge against such catastrophes. This is the message here. Taleb (2009) suggested the idea of the *fourth quadrant*—a zonal map to classify situations which are prone to Black Swan catastrophes so that protective actions can be taken.

Taleb observed that the fourth moment (kurtosis) of most financial variables is dominated by just the few largest observations or outliers. This is the reason why conventional statistical methods (which work well on more regular observations) are incapable of tracking the occurrence of fat-tail events. Furthermore, there is evidence that outliers, unlike regular events, are not serially dependent on past outliers i.e. there appears to be no predictability at all in the tail.

In Taleb's paper, distributions are classified into two types. Type-1 (mediocristan): thin-tailed Gaussian distribution which occurs more often in scientific labs (including the casino) and in physical phenomena. Type-2 (extremistan): unknown tail distributions which look fat (or thick) tailed. The danger with type-2 is that the tail is unstable and may not even have finite variance. This "wild" fat-tail should not be confused with just meaning having a kurtosis larger than the Gaussian's, like that of the "power-law" tail generated by EVT and other models. For this *mild* form of fat-tail, theoretical self-similarity at all scales means that the tails can always be defined asymptotically. This allows for extrapolation to more extreme quantiles beyond our range of observation, a potentially dangerous practice as we are extrapolating our ignorance.

Since measurements are always taken on finite samples, the moments can always be computed, that gives the illusion of finiteness of variance. This imperfect knowledge means that one can seldom tell the difference between the "wild" (type-2) and the mild form of fat-tails. In fact, evidence suggests financial markets are mostly type-2.

Payoffs are classified into simple and complex. Simple payoffs are either "binary", true or false games with constant payout, or linear, where the magnitude of PL is a linear function like for stocks. Complex payoffs are described by nonlinear PL functions that are influenced by higher moments. A good analogy is to think of the different payoffs as: a coin toss (binary), a dice throw (linear) and buying insurance (asymmetrical, non-linear, options).

The four quadrants are mapped in Table 7-2. The first quadrant is an ideal state (such as in casino games) where statistics reign supreme. In the second quadrant, statistics are predictive even though the payoff is complex. Most academic research in derivatives pricing in the literature assumes this idealized setting. In the third quadrant, errors in prediction can be tolerated since the tail does not influence the payoffs[5]. The dangerous financial Black Swans reside in the fourth quadrant. Unfortunately, market crises are found to be extremistan and positions held by banks are mostly complex.

Taleb argued that since one cannot change the distribution, one strategy is to change the payoff instead, i.e. exit the fourth quadrant to the third. This can be done using macro hedges to floor the payoff so that the negative tail will no longer impact PL. In practice this could require purchasing options, taking on specific insurance protection or changing the portfolio composition.

Table 7-2 The four quadrants

	Simple Payoffs	Complex Payoffs
DISTRIBUTION 1 (Thin tailed)	First Quadrant: Extremely safe	Second Quadrant: Safe
DISTRIBUTION 2 (Fat or unknown tails)	Third Quadrant: Safe	Fourth Quadrant: Exposed to Black Swans

A second strategy is to keep a capital buffer for safety. Banks are capital efficient machines that generally optimize the use of capital. However, optimization in the domain of extremistan is fraught with model errors; a simple model error can blow through a bank's capital as witnessed in the case of CDO mispricing during the credit crisis. Over-optimization can lead to maximum vulnerability because it leaves no room for error. Thus, one can argue that leaving some capital idle will be necessary for a bank's long term survival and protection against Black Swans.

---

[5] For example, option pricing usually assumes geometric Brownian motion (a second quadrant setting). But if the tail is actually fat, the real pricing formula will be different from the Black-Scholes equation. In contrast, simple linear payoffs will be the same even if the tail is fat.

7.5 Regime change, Lagging riskometer and Procyclicality

The lagging nature of VaR

In the field of technical analysis, any trend-following indicator is known to be lagging. Such indicators typically employ some form of moving-average (MA) to track developing trends. Because it takes time for sufficient new prices to flow into the MA's window to influence the average, this indicator always lags significant market moves. Figure 13-4 shows a simple 1000-day MA of the S&P 500 index. To reduce lag (i.e. make the indicator more responsive) traders normally shorten the window length, but this has the undesirable effect of making the indicator erratic and more susceptible to *whipsaws* (i.e. false signals). This is the catch-22 of using rolling-windows in general—timeliness can only be achieved at the cost of unwanted noise.

This is instructive for VaR, which also uses a rolling window of *returns*. The lagging behavior means that regime shifts will be detected late, often seriously so for risk control. Consider a situation whereby the government explicitly guarantees all banks. One can expect a sudden shift in the way bank shares behave—their volatilities will be lower than before, they move more in correlation as a group and may even exhibit some local behavior (microstructure) such as mean-reversion within certain price range. VaR will be late in detecting these changing risks, if at all.

To test how VaR performs when faced with a regime shift, we simulate a regime change and compare the responsiveness of pVaR, hsVaR and EWMA pVaR. In Figure 7-10 we simulated a doubling of volatility—the lower chart shows the return series, the upper chart shows various VaRs. The shaded area represents the 250-day window used to compute VaR, where the left edge marks the regime shift. The volatility to the right of this demarcation is twice that to the left. PVaR and hsVaR are able to detect this sudden shift but with a time lag—they increase *gradually* until the new volatility has fully rolled into the 250-day window. For EWMA VaR, its exponential weights shorten the effective window length. And by virtue of being *conditional* it is able to capture the regime shift fully in a fraction of the time. Unfortunately, timeliness comes with instability—the EWMA VaR is a lot noisier.

In Figure 7-11, the shaded area marks a regime shift in autocorrelation, suddenly changing from zero to +0.5; the volatility is kept constant. The new return series (lower panel) shows an obvious seasonal behavior which we have introduced artificially. This test revealed that none of the three VaR methods is able to detect the regime shift. This case study is worked out in **Spreadsheet 7.3**.

Figure 7-10 Simulated regime change—doubling of volatility

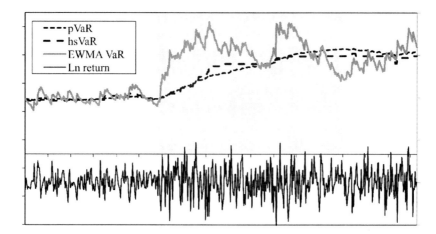

Figure 7-11 Simulated regime change—outbreak of seasonality and autocorrelation

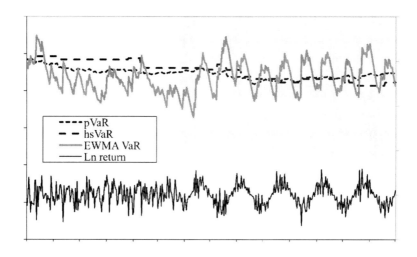

We conclude that VaR is able to capture changes in volatility regime (it is designed for this) but with an often fatal delay. Worst still, subtler regime changes such as that in correlation and market microstructure may not be detected at all.

Hardwired procyclicality

The Turner Review (2009) identified that procyclicality is hardwired into the VaR method. A dire combination of three factors makes this a potent threat to the financial system. Firstly, procyclicality is rooted in the lagging nature of VaR. Consider Figure 7-10—VaR took almost a third of the 250-day interval to increase noticeably after the regime shift. This means VaR may lag the onset of a crisis by months, and VaR-based regulatory capital will be late in pulling the brakes on rising risks. Secondly, the leverage effect comes into play by manifesting subdued volatility during a rally. As a result, the regulatory capital will be very business conducive (low) during the boom phase. Thirdly, mark-to-market accounting, a global standard for regulated fair accounting practice, allows banks to recognize their profits immediately in a rally. The gain is often used as additional capital for further investment and leverage. Otherwise, given so much liquidity (capital) and the general perception of low risks, banks will likely be faulted by shareholders for underinvestment. The net effect is banks are encouraged to chase an economic bubble.

When a financial bubble bursts, the incentives are completely reversed. History tells us VaR often spikes up the most during the initial fall of a bust cycle. This increases the VaR-based capital requirement and forces deleveraging among banks in order to stay within the regulatory minimum[6]. At the same time, volatility also grows by virtue of the leverage effect. The self-imposed discipline to mark-to-market the losses means that a bank's capital base will shrink rapidly as the market collapses, forcing further deleveraging. And since most of the money in the system is leveraged (paperless accounting entries of borrowed money), they can vanish as quickly as they were created—liquidity dries up. This could lead to a vicious spiral for the banking system[7].

As an overhaul, the Turner Review broadly recommended a "through the cycle" capital regime instead of the current "point in time" (VaR) regime. While specifics were not given, the FSA did mention "introducing overt counter-cyclicality into the capital regime"—reserving more capital during a boom which can be used to cushion losses during the bust phase. As we shall see in Part IV of this book, *bubble VaR* is in the spirit of this prescription.

---

[6] A well researched counter-argument is provided by Jorion (2002). The author found that the averaging of VaR over the last 60 days as required by Basel (equation (6.3)) means that market risk capital moves too slowly to trigger systemic deleveraging.

[7] Without liquidity, a bank risks not being able to pay its obligations on time which could lead to (technical) default. This has dire consequences and hence banks hoarded liquidity during the 2008 credit crisis.

7.6 Coherence and Expected shortfall

The purpose of VaR is to summarize the risk of the entire loss distribution using a single number. Even though features of the tail of the joint distribution are underrepresented, there is merit in using such a "point estimate"; it is convenient and intuitive for risk control and reporting.

Artzner et al. (1999) introduced the concept of *coherence*—a list of desirable properties for any point estimate risk measure. A risk measure (denoted here as *VaR*) is said to be coherent if it satisfies conditions (7.4) to (7.7).

Monotonicity: if $X_1 \leq X_2$ then $VaR(X_1) \geq VaR(X_2)$ $\qquad$ (7.4)

If a portfolio has values lower than another (for all scenarios), its risk must be larger. X corresponds to the P&L random variable of a risky position.

Homogeneity: $\qquad\qquad VaR(aX) = aVaR(X)$ $\qquad\qquad$ (7.5)

Increasing the size of the portfolio by a factor a will linearly scale its risk measure by the same factor.

Translation invariance: $VaR(X + k) = VaR(X) - k$ $\qquad\qquad$ (7.6)

Adding riskless cash k to the portfolio will lower the risk by k.

Subadditivity: $VaR(X_1 + X_2) \leq VaR(X_1) + VaR(X_2)$ $\qquad$ (7.7)

The risk of the portfolio is always less than (or equal to) the sum of its component risks. This is the benefit of diversification.

A few key points regarding coherence are worth knowing. Firstly, the quantile-based VaR is not coherent—it violates the property of subadditivity, except in the special case of the normal distribution. This could lead to an illogical situation where splitting a portfolio decreases the risk.

Secondly, and more generally, coherence holds for the class of *elliptical distributions*, for which the contour of its joint distribution traces an ellipsoid. The (joint) normal distribution is a special case of an elliptical distribution. An elliptical distribution has very strict criteria—it is necessarily unimodal (single peaked) and symmetric. Hence, most realistic distributions are just not elliptical.

Why does'nt incoherence wreak havoc on the lives of risk managers[8]? It is because incoherence violates the integrity of the VaR measure in a stealthy and non-overt way. Consider the truism: an elliptical distribution is surely coherent. But the reverse is not true i.e. a non-elliptical distribution need not be incoherent. We can only say that *coherence is not guaranteed* i.e. we cannot say for sure that subadditivity is violated in realistic portfolios. Furthermore, even if subadditivity is violated, for a large portfolio, its effect may not be obvious (or material) enough for a risk manager to take notice, and may be localized within a specific subportfolio. The problem will be felt when the risk manager tries to drill down into the risk for small subportfolios containing complex products—he may get a nonsensical decomposition.

Fortunately, there is an easy backstop for this problem called *expected short-fall* proposed by Artzner et al. (1999). This brings us to the third point—expected shortfall, sometimes called *conditional VaR* (cVaR) or *expected tail loss* (ETL)—satisfies all the conditions for coherence. It is defined as the expectation of the loss once VaR is exceeded:

$$ETL = \mathrm{E}(-X \mid X \leq -VaR) \tag{7.8}$$

For all practical purposes, it is just the simple average of all the points in the tail left of the VaR quantile, and thus can be easily incorporated using the existing VaR infrastructure. For example, the ETL at 97.5% confidence using a 250-day observation period is given by the *average* of the 6 (rounded from 6.25) largest losses in the left tail. For most major markets, assuming linear positions, the 97.5% ETL works out to be in the order of magnitude of three sigmas. Hence, under regular circumstances expected shortfall is roughly 50% higher than pVaR (which is 2 sigma) if positions are linear.

The ETL is sensitive to changes in the shape of the tail (what we are really after). VaR, on the other hand, is oblivious to the tail beyond the quantile level. In Section 13.6, we will show using simulation that ETL is superior to quantile VaR as a risk measure in terms of coherence, responsiveness and stability.

---

[8] The issue of coherence (and subadditivity in particular) currently gets little attention from practitioners and regulators. It is debated more often in academic risk conferences.

7.7 Spreadsheet

7.1 Empirically, bull markets tend to show negative skew in return distributions, and bear markets tend to show positive skew. Aim: illustrate a stylized bull (bear) market distribution and its corresponding negative (positive) skew using random simulation.

7.2 Fat-tail distributions can be caused by stochastic (or variable) volatility. Aim: illustrates using Monte Carlo simulation that stochastic volatility gives rise to a fat-tailed distribution.

7.3 As a risk measurement tool, VaR is often accused of being late in detecting crises and regime changes in general. Aim: explore the timeliness of VaR by comparing the performances of pVaR, hsVaR and EWMA VaR when encountering a simulated regime change. Two regime shifts are tested: a doubling of volatility and an introduction of serial correlation of +0.5.

Chapter 8

Model Testing

Regulators require banks to test their VaR systems regularly to ensure they are in working order. We review three common tests. Precision test, which is actually a *measurement* of the precision of the VaR number given a chosen method and a data set. Frequency back test, which is a requirement to ensure model "goodness" and is used by regulators to determine a bank's multiplier for minimum capital. Bunching test (or independence test) which checks that VaR exceedences are i.i.d., otherwise the VaR quantile understates what it is meant to measure. There are many more sophisticated statistical tests available for VaR; the interested reader can refer to Campbell (2005) for a good review.

8.1 Precision Test

Precision is an important element in any scientific measurement. For example, when one reports the weight of an item in a lab experiment as 2.5 kg $\pm$ 0.2 kg, one really means the object's weight lies within [2.3, 2.7] kg. So it may come as a surprise that such error bands are seldom included in VaR reports. To appreciate why, let us first see how such an error band can be computed.

Since this book favors hsVaR as a basic method, we shall illustrate a method called *statistical bootstrapping* which uses empirical observations. This method does not make any prior assumption about the shape of the distribution. It involves the following steps:

1. Compute the VaR of the original sample data (T data points).
2. Perform resampling from the *same* sample set *with replacement* and then recompute the VaR—i.e. draw T points from the sample one at a time, putting each back into the sample before the next draw, so that the sample remains undepleted.
3. Repeat step (2) K times such that a distribution of VaRs is obtained.
4. The error band (with a c% confidence interval) of the original VaR number can be determined from this distribution, and is given by the lower $0.5(1-c)$ quantile and the upper $1-0.5(1-c)$ quantile.

Spreadsheet 8.1 implements this method for the S&P 500 index for the period
Jul08 – Jun09 with T=250, K=1000, c=0.95. The results (which can be re-
simulated) indicate a 97.5% VaR of 6.2% move in the index with a confidence
interval between 5% to 9%, a huge error band of 4%! This statistic means there
is a 95% chance or confidence that the "correct" value of VaR is in that range[1].

To express it in dollar terms, consider a portfolio of S&P index stocks of
$100 million. The VaR is reported as $6.2 million, but could range anywhere
from $5 million to $9 million. Small wonder VaR is seldom reported with error
bands—it would have been astounding (and possibly incapacitating) to the top
management. More importantly, it also highlights the hazard of the false sense of
security provided by seemingly precise numbers.

Figure 8-1 Graphical illustration of statistical bootstrap

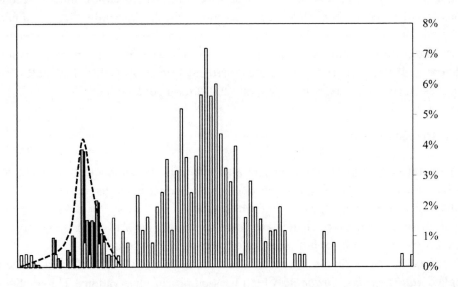

VaR numbers are often reported to a few decimal places. In the above case, if
VaR fell to $5.65 million the next day, a less quantitative senior executive would
have concluded, with some relief, that risk have fallen by $0.55 million. Yet,
with such a large error band, his/her conclusion has very little statistical meaning. Worse still, if the senior executive believes the real "risk" (however she/he
may interpret it) is at $6.2 million—he/she would have been precisely wrong (or

---

[1] The confidence interval idea rests on the (often unquestioned) assumption that samples have
finite variance and are distributed nicely in a bell shape (localized). In the presence of extremistan,
the distribution could be asymptotically explosive (has infinite variance).

fooled by randomness). The true *expected loss* could be multiple times bigger than the reported VaR!

To see graphically what bootstrapping does, see Figure 8-1 (which can be generated using Spreadsheet 8.1). The central distribution is the actual return distribution which is resampled many times. For each sample (250 points resampled 1000 times), the quantile is computed. The quantile's distribution is shown as the dark histogram to the left (we have rescaled it to look nicer, so ignore the vertical axis values). This histogram is centered on the VaR. The 95% confidence interval for VaR is just the bounds that ring fence 95% of the area of the dark histogram. We can see the error range is wide and is left skewed.

8.2 Frequency Back Test

Frequency *back test* (also called *unconditional coverage test*) measures the "biasness" of the VaR model to see how precisely its results follow the quantile definition. Regulators use this to decide the "goodness" of a bank's internal model and to adjust the multiplier for capital charges accordingly. When a bank's VaR model passes back testing, its internal model is deemed acceptable by regulators. Otherwise, a more penal minimum capital is levied using the "traffic light" approach outlined by Basel Rules:

$$k = \begin{cases} 3.0 & \text{if } N \leq 4 \quad \text{green} \\ 3 + 0.2(N-4) & \text{if } 5 \leq N \leq 9 \quad \text{yellow} \\ 4.0 & \text{if } N \geq 10 \quad \text{red} \end{cases} \tag{8.1}$$

where k is the multiplier in equation (6.3), N is the number of days realized PL exceeds daily 99%-VaR in the last 250 days. Daily PL as published by *product controllers* is used.

If VaR is truly an *unbiased* estimate of the quantile, by definition we expect 2.5 violations per year statistically. Basel uses this knowledge to scale its parameter k: as long as the number of violations is 4 or less, the multiplier remains at its lowest level of 3. If the VaR is violated more frequently than expected theoretically, a bank is penalized proportionally by the capital charge. In the red zone, the VaR model is deemed inaccurate (biased or systematically understates risk) and that calls for immediate corrective action to improve the risk management system. In contrast, too few violations would imply that the bank's model is overly conservative—it systematically overstates risk.

Gross violation of back testing could be symptomatic of a few potential problems:

1. Deals are not marked-to-market properly and published PL is wrong.
2. The universe of risk factors is poorly-designed and is not representative of the risks affecting the portfolio.
3. The VaR model is biased (bad assumptions or bad implementation).
4. The market data exhibits clustering (non-i.i.d.) behavior characteristic of a stressful situation.

Problem (4) is beyond the bank's control and will cause the VaR model to understate the true quantile risk.

Figure 8-2 illustrates a typical back testing diagram as reported to regulators. This is implemented in Spreadsheet 8.2 for Dow Jones index for the period Jan06 – Mar09. Every day that a return exceeded the 99% VaR (on either tails), the *hit* counter will register 1 count. For the final 250-day rolling period, the hits add up to $N=18$ (red zone). Since this is an error-free example, the only possible cause is problem (4)—the market was exhibiting a strong degree of clustering during the 2008 crisis period.

Figure 8-2 Regulatory back testing diagram for Dow Jones index

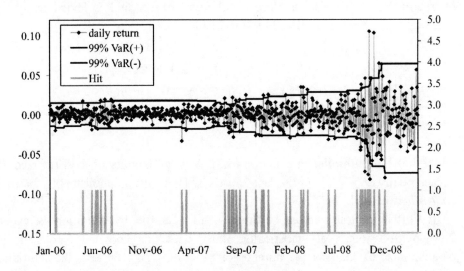

In fact, a widespread breakdown of back tests can be an important signal that the market is entering a stressful period in which VAR models are less accurate (assuming model and data errors have already been ruled out). Some markets, such as pegged currencies, are prone to occasional volatility clustering which undermines back tests. In this case, rather than attempting to justify the model, resources are better spent on measuring the risks using other tools such as stress tests specifically targeted at positions that are causing the back test breaks, or on hedging such exposures.

8.3 Bunching Test

This test, also called *independence test*, is targeted at measuring clustering. In Figure 8-2 we plotted the occurrence of a VaR violation by marking its time with a "hit" function. The *hit* is actually given by the indicator function:

$$I_t(p) = \begin{cases} 1 & \text{if } x_t \leq -VaR_{t-1}(p) \\ 0 & \text{if } x_t > -VaR_{t-1}(p) \end{cases} \tag{8.2}$$

where $\{x_1,...,x_N\}$ is the sequence of daily PL for the portfolio, p is the quantile (i.e. for 97.5% VaR, p=2.5%).

For a VaR model to be accurate in its prediction, violations must be independent across time—the hits must be evenly spread out in time; they must not be "bunched up" or clustered together. To see why, suppose hypothetically that whenever a VaR violation occurs (for p=2.5%), it always occurs in pairs, so that when one violation occurs it is immediately followed by another of the same loss. Let's say VaR is at $10 million. When one violation has occurred with $10.5 million loss, the probability of the second violation is 100% and no longer 2.5%. Hence, the reported VaR, now at $10.5 million, no longer represents a 2.5% probability of (left side) exceedence—it is understating the true risk. To be correct, the VaR result should be farther out in the tail (say $30 million) so as to reduce its exceedence probability back to 2.5%. This example shows that in the presence of bunching, VaR is inaccurate because its probability interpretation is distorted.

This encouraged research in academia for better VaR models—"better" in the narrow sense of low bias and low bunching. Some conditional models such as GARCH, EWMA and Hull-White VaR can achieve this by being more responsive to market innovation (new prices). These fast-moving systems are more adept at moving the VaR number farther out into the tail when multiple hits occur, such that the VaR number remains an unbiased measure of the real quantile.

In testing if the hits are evenly dispersed in time, we need to determine if they are serially independent. There are many sophisticated tests of independence, for example the Christoffersen test (1998) and subsequent development of this test in this area. Here we will content ourselves with a simpler test, the *Ljung-Box statistic* (1978) which tests that the autocorrelations of different lags are jointly zero. We use the $h=15$ lagged autocorrelation of the hit function I(.). The statistics $Q(h)$ follows a chi-squared distribution with h degrees of freedom. A value of $Q(15)$ less than 25 indicates that zero correlation cannot be rejected at the 95% confidence level. This critical value can be determined from Excel function: CHIINV(0.05,15)=25.

$$Q(15) = n\sum_{k=1}^{15} w_k \rho_k^2 \qquad (8.3)$$

where n is the number of observations, ρ_k is the autocorrelation with lag k days and $w_k = (n+2)/(n-k)$.

Figure 8-3 The plot of the hit function I(0.01) for pVaR, EWMA VaR and hsVaR.

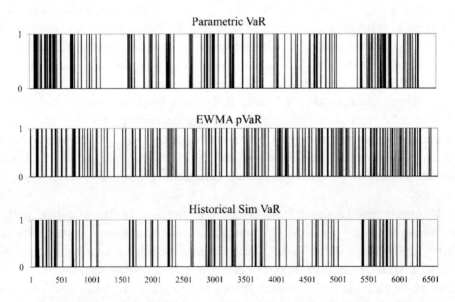

Spreadsheet 8.3 implements the Ljung-Box statistic for the 99%-VaR back test violation (i.e. the hits I(0.01)) for Dow Jones index for period Jan82 –

Mar09. Comparison is made for various VaR models all calculated based on *ex post* 250 days of data (i.e. I_t violation is determined by looking at VaR_{t-1}). The Ljung-Box statistics are $Q(15)$ = 478, 18, 165 for pVaR, EWMA VaR and hsVaR respectively which indicates that only EWMA VaR shows statistically insignificant bunching at 95% confidence level.

Figure 8-3 plots the hit function I(0.01) for the three VaR models. It is apparent that the EWMA VaR shows the most spread-out hits. The other two unconditional models show clustered exceedences of VaR. In case Figure 8-3 misleads you into thinking that EWMA VaR *removes* clustering, let me clarify that it doesn't. Clustering is a market behavior which obviously cannot be influenced by its measurement. The advantage of EWMA VaR is just that its quantile interpretation is less distorted by the clustering effect.

8.4 Spreadsheet

8.1 A method to determine the confidence interval or error band of a VaR result is statistical bootstrap. Aim: illustrates use of the statistical bootstrapping method to calculate the error band (or 95% confidence interval) for VaR. Note: a VB code resamples 1000 times 250 random draws (with replacement) from an empirical distribution of 250 data points.

8.2 Back testing is a regulatory requirement to monitor the "goodness" of a VaR model. It checks that the number of days the PL exceeded the VaR level during the observation period is in agreement with the definition of the quantile. Aim: illustrates the back testing method stipulated by Basel Rules (the traffic light approach). Note: there is an increased number of back test "breaks" during the 2008 crisis period.

8.3 Bunching tests check how evenly the VaR back test "breaks" are distributed over time. If the "breaks" are bunched up in time, it suggests the presence of strong serial correlation and VaR becomes a biased estimate of the real quantile. Aim: illustrate how a simple bunching test can be performed using the Ljung-Box statistic on "breaks" of the 99%-VaR. Three VaR models are tested—pVaR, hsVaR, EWMA pVaR. The *hit* function is also plotted to illustrate the effect of bunching. Action: modify the spreadsheet to test at 97.5%-VaR. What are the limitations of using the Ljung-Box statistic for a test of bunching?

Chapter 9

Practical Limitations of VaR

Chapter 7 discussed the theoretical flaws of VaR. Here we consider the practical limitations when implementing and using a VaR system. These are practical blind-spots that are beyond the ability of VaR to cover.

9.1 Depegs and Changes to "Rules of the game"

Like any measurement device, VaR is a function of its information input. To the extent that a market event does not produce timely data for input to the VaR system, it follows that the risk for that event can never be captured. This is the case for some types of events which are not registered in prices even though it may be anticipated by a knowledgeable risk manager.

The classic examples are currency controls and depegs. During the Asian currency crisis (1997 – 98), the Malaysian ringgit was attacked by currency speculators due to contagion from a currency crisis that started in Thailand. The Thai central bank devalued the baht on 2 Jul 97, after which the ringgit depreciated from 2.52 to a high of 4.77 against the dollar, a whopping 47% fall. To fend off currency speculators, the Malaysian central bank imposed capital control in Sep 98—pegging the ringgit to the dollar at 3.8. After 7 years, the central bank officially lifted the peg on 21 Jul 05. The ringgit is still semi-controlled to this day.

Figure 9-1 shows this chronology of events and the effects on VaR. At point A, VaR was late to register the onset of the devaluation even though traders and banks already knew the ringgit was under attack—the central bank was openly defending the ringgit and the baht had already devalued. Currency control was imposed at point B and for some time the price was untraded until point C when the peg was removed. The lesson is that VaR could not predict the imminent events at A, B and C because these events are not reflected in prior prices even though market participants knew about the currency attacks and expected some extreme price breakouts.

Figure 9-1 Currency control of the ringgit and the impact on VaR (97.5%-hsVaR)

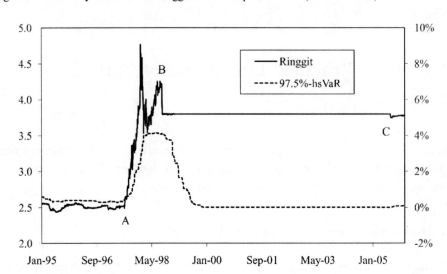

Had a risk manager relied solely on VaR, he would have detected the risk very late and rather abruptly, and may have lost his job. This highlights the importance of the subjective experience of risk professionals. If a depeg risk is anticipated subjectively, quantifying it can easily be done using stress testing. The market participants normally have some consensus (sometimes even an opinion poll) of the size of the revaluation if it happens. Hence, if a bank knows its position in a pegged currency (such as the HK dollar and the Chinese yuan) and the estimated magnitude of revaluation, it can conservatively estimate the potential loss, and take a suitable capital buffer or hedge out the risk.

Currency control is an example of sudden changes to the "rules of the game" i.e. to the way the market is traded. It causes an artificial segregation between onshore and offshore forward markets which then behave differently because arbitragers cannot bring equilibrium to bear. Other examples are: a government nationalizing a bank, causing the bank shares volatility to diminish, and a corporate takeover causing the target company's shares to trade differently after the acquisition. In all these cases, a regime shift took place, after which the old data history is no longer reflective of future risk. The VaR forecast will be biased temporarily until the old data rolls out of the 250-day window.

9.2 Data Integrity Problems

VaR is only as good as its data. Since VaR is a point estimate, a single number result for the entire portfolio and the joint distribution, it is difficult to tell if it is tainted by erroneous data. Back testing is too crude for the diagnosis. The solution is prevention. As such, most banks invest substantially in data maintenance work which consist of proper sourcing of data, capturing of end-of-day data (EOD data snapping), rates cleaning (removing bad points and filling up holes in the data set) and data interpolation.

We list below certain data problems that can undermine the integrity of the VaR system:

1. Mis-specified risk factor universe. The resulting VaR will not represent accurately the true risk of the portfolio.

2. Operational error in data handling—data is filled wrongly during holidays causing a misalignment of scenario sequence across different risk factors. The affected PL vector is out-of-step with the other vectors. This will give a meaningless aggregated VaR because the correlation structure is broken.

3. Asynchronous data. Some markets close at different times of the day even though all data are snapped at the same EOD moment. For example, consider an Asian corporate dollar bond hedged by USD swaps. The former ceases trading after Asian hours while the latter trades 24 hours. If data is snapped at the New York session close, the collected last price will be a few hours apart; the VaR of the hedged position will be misstated. One solution is to use interpolation to forecast the Asian bond price at the New York closing time.

4. Using in-house trader input is inferior to third party vendor data, and may run into conflict of interests. Data vendors are independent and their data is often poll-based, whereas a trader has incentive to massage the data because the same prices are often used to determine P&L, and eventually his bonus. This is akin to what analysts call accounting "window dressing" where companies smooth out earnings in order to show above-target profits consistently every year. At times, using in-house data is unavoidable for emerging markets not well-covered by data vendors.

5. Stale data and bad proxies. Data problems are especially prevalent in credit trading where, because of the issue-specific and bespoke nature of the derivatives, prices are not actively quoted, resulting in missing data and discontinuity in the time series. Such data will contain a high degree of random error. As one may recall from the study of high school physics, if we measure A with error of 5 units, and B with error of 2 units, the result for (A+B) will show at least an error of 5 units. This can be a problem when we aggregate the VaR of a credit book (with large

error) to the rest of the portfolio. The aggregated VaR will have an error dictated by the worst bad data—to be exact, the factor that has the largest dollar error in quantile estimation. The lesson here is that when performing risk factor mapping, it is often better to choose a less perfect proxy with good data (the basis risk can at least be estimated) than the correct risk factor with bad data.

The above problems are by no means exhaustive. Since VaR is a regulatory reported number and is used for minimum capital charges for banks, it is ultimately one of the safeguards for the financial system. There is a moral obligation to be accurate.

9.3 Model Risk

We next consider model risks which are outside the scope of the VaR engine but that nevertheless affect the VaR result.

Pricing model risk

The VaR method is just a system to shock risk factors and to calculate the quantile from the resulting PL distribution. The translation from shifted prices to actual PL involves full revaluation (for simulated VaR) or derivation of Greek sensitivities (for parametric VaR). In both cases, we need to use a pricing model specific to the product. In a bank's risk architecture (see Section 3.1) this component is stored in a pricing library and can be called from the VaR engine. An erroneous pricing model will result in a wrong (or at least inaccurate) VaR number. The error could be due to the wrong choice of pricing model, bad calibration[1] or a plain coding mistake.

More profoundly, the idea of correctness of pricing is sometimes not clear cut except for "vanilla" products which use standard pricing models that are well accepted by the industry. This ambiguity gives rise to model risk. We use a definition of model risk adapted from Rebonato (2003): "Model risk is the risk of occurrence of a significant difference between the mark-to-model value of a complex and/or illiquid instrument and the price at which the same instrument is revealed to have traded in the market." This difference will not exist if the *efficient market hypothesis* (EMH) holds true. This school of thought argues for

---

[1] Many advanced models used by banks today (such as Heston model and local volatility model which attempt to account for the "volatility smile" effect) do not price options directly using observed volatilities. Rather, the implied volatility surface needs to be calibrated first. This is computationally complex.

the "law of one price" since any violation will be arbitraged away by pseudo-arbitragers. But when pseudo-arbitragers are hindered by cost-concerns, illiquidity or regulatory constraints, market prices can stray from model prices significantly.

A popular parable to illustrate this: An illiquid option market has been observed at 20% volatility irregularly. After due analysis, traders decided that the theoretical price should be centered around 20% and used this as the mark-to-model price in the bank's risk system. One day, there is a sudden market quote of 10% (perhaps from a customer) and the option trader quickly buys the option cheap (at 10%) and delta-hedges the position (with a hedge ratio calibrated at 20%). Which volatility (10% or 20%) should be used for risk pricing? The trader would naturally argue for 20% since this would let him realize an immediate profit for the "arbitrage". On the other hand, a risk manager who strictly follows the mark-to-market accounting "cook book" would mark the option at 10% and provision the profit. The two approaches have very different risk management implications. If the risk system is marked at 20%, there will be no difference in models used by traders and risk controllers, the VaR will be very small, reflective of a delta-neutral position. On the other hand, if the risk system is marked at 10%, the position will appear to be not fully delta neutral—VaR will be material. The right approach depends on the subjective information and intelligence gathered by the prudent risk manager i.e. the nature of the counterparty, the consensus view on choice of models and price levels among professional players, etc. The paper by Rebonato (2003) provides a topical discussion.

Strategies and futuristic information

The VaR framework is based purely on *past* data and rests on the premise that past risk measurement is an unbiased predictor of future risk (i.e. the next day's). The VaR method does not accommodate *futuristic* information even if available. Here I am referring to trading strategies—which is a trader's *intention*, formalized and committed but not yet traded upon. VaR by definition does not include such things.

Suppose a trader holds $100 million in stocks and runs a 5% daily VaR. He has his stop-loss at 2% below current levels. Is his risk more than $5 million or just $2 million? His real risk is just $2 million assuming no loss from slippage when exiting positions (a reasonable assumption for very liquid markets). As a second example, consider the popular quant trading strategy called the *constant proportion portfolio insurance* (CPPI) scheme where the position is leveraged up when the portfolio gains, and deleveraged when the portfolio loses. There are well-defined models to execute such a trading strategy, often automatically buying and selling at pre-determined levels. In a deep market, such a CPPI program can never lose money beyond a certain fixed amount. In other words, it has a floored payoff similar to a call option. Unfortunately, because VaR does not account for strategies, it will overlook the downside protection and overstate the risk.

This is less of a concern for regulatory capital since the overstatement of risk leads to a more conservative capital number. However, it does blunt the VaR risk measure as a monitoring tool. In particular, for program trading desks and hedge funds that use predetermined trigger levels for trading, the VaR number is completely misleading.

The solution is to use other tools. For CPPI-type strategies, one can use Monte Carlo methods to simulate the path dependence of the *strategy* and look at the PL distribution at a future horizon (say 10 days). For trades with predetermined stop losses, the PL distributions of such deals should be floored at the stop loss levels. Both methods are compatible with the VaR approach and can be integrated into the VaR system.

9.4 Politics and Gaming

Since a VaR system has many moving parts, it is open to manipulation and negligence. For example, a trader can "game" his VaR by altering the distribution of the desk's PL to reflect a fixed VaR but with a much larger tail risk by taking on long-short "market neutral" positions or by selling default swaps. The trader effectively gains from small frequent premiums or positive carry by taking on the long term risk of an infrequent tail event (large loss).

This human or behavioral aspect is possibly the weakest link in the VaR system. It arises from the imbalance of power and skewed incentives in the way banks are organized. There is a "principal-agent" problem at play—decision-making in banks is an arm-wrestle between risk and return, between risk managers and risk-takers. While the front office (trading) is a profit generating center, risk management is often seen as a support function in most banks. Regulation calls for an independent reporting line for risk management to reduce the conflict of interest, but the culture is often the case that profit generating functions are usually the "sponsors" of support functions.

A trader earns his profit-sharing bonus (often very high by earthly standards) by making profits and taking risks. The risk manager who controls risk on the other hand is almost never rewarded for stopping a bad deal or criticizing a suspicious position or profit. Risk management is about loss avoidance and it is difficult to measure what has been avoided and hence has not occurred. The lopsided compensation encourages a culture which is not prudent. Traders have the incentive to paint a picture of low risk - stable profitability to top management. If a lower risk number can be achieved by gaming the technicalities of the risk engine, then this will allow more room for trading, since risk-taking activity is ultimately controlled by VaR limits.

On the other hand, the reward system in risk policing creates potential incentive for politics and lobbying. There is also a propensity to suppress bad news, the "don't rock the boat" culture. When things do go wrong, it is convenient to blame the models, which few could understand anyway. We have seen this during the 2008 credit crisis where the popular press sensationalized the blame on quants for creating credit derivatives (similar to blaming all physicists for the atomic bomb).

Regulators are beginning to realize the importance of the risk culture in a bank. If critical risk information is not escalated to decision makers, even a state-of-the-art risk system is ineffective. In this respect, moral courage is an important trait of a risk controller. Justifiably most people will not put their jobs on the line unless they are financially and ethically very secure. And leaving banks to correct the power imbalance is impractical. We have seen how self-regulation and bad corporate governance had led to the downfall of prestigious institutions in 2008[2]. Perhaps the solution is to legislate and provide a whistle-blowing avenue for insiders. Another possible solution is to outsource the VaR reporting to an independent policing entity thereby creating a layer of protection against potential gaming and negligence.

---

[2] For an insightful read of the corporate culture of Wall Street, please refer to "A colossal failure of commonsense - the insider story of the collapse of Lehman Brothers" by L.G. McDonald and P. Robinson (2009).

Chapter 10

Other Major Risk Classes

The recognition of major risk classes by the *Basel Committee* for inclusion into the regulatory capital regime has been the driving force for the development of their risk models. The original Basel I Accord (1988) focused on *credit risk*, which is by far the largest risk class faced by banks. An Amendment (1996) included *market risk* into the capital regime and introduced the "internal models" approach (by de facto VaR). The Basel II reform (2004) established *operational risk* as a major risk, following the fall of Enron and WorldCom, two of the largest corporate bankruptcies caused by unauthorized trading and accounting scandal. The 2008 credit crisis brought forth another major risk—that of *liquidity*. Basel's consultative paper on a liquidity risk framework (Dec 2009) introduced tools to contain firm liquidity risk. This Chapter is a brief overview of risk classes (other than market risk) and the conventional models used to quantify them.

From a regulatory capital perspective, one challenge is in aggregating these diverse classes of risk—credit, market, operational and liquidity. This so-called "problem of aggregation" to merge the various risks under a unified theory has attracted much interest from academics. The last section addresses the challenges of aggregating these very different items.

10.1 Credit Risk (and Creditmetrics©)

Credit risk refers to the risk of default and risk of ratings downgrade of companies. Such events are company (or "name" or "issuer") specific and often happen when the credit worthiness (credibility to raise funds) of a company is fundamentally impaired or is perceived by the market to have deteriorated.

Since banks and investors often hold exposures to companies, they are exposed to credit risk. Such exposures come in various forms. If the exposure is in the form of a (non-tradable) loan to a company, then this is technically a banking book credit risk. If the exposure is in bonds or securities issued by that company, or credit derivatives written on that company, then this credit risk is a component of trading book[1] market risk. If the exposure exists because the bank traded with that company and funds are owed, then it is considered a counterparty risk. Such distinctions are inconvenient but necessary because the nature of data, modeling method, accounting rules and regulatory capital treatment—are all very different.

In this section, we will look at the modeling of credit risk of loans and traded instruments using Creditmetrics© developed by JP Morgan in 1997. There are a few other popular models available; see Crouhy et al. (2000) for a comparative analysis.

Creditmetrics asks: "Over a one-year horizon, how much value will a loan portfolio lose within a given confidence level (say 5%) due to credit risk?" The answer, expressed as credit VaR, will incorporate both risk of default and rating downgrades. Our example uses simple Monte Carlo simulation and will illustrate all the key ingredients of Creditmetrics. It helps to divide the calculation process into three steps:

Step 1: defining various states of the world

A bond issuer's credit worthiness is often rated by credit rating agencies such as Standard & Poor's and Moody's. For loans, banks typically use internal credit scores. To measure the risk of deterioration in credit quality, we need the probabilities of migrating from the initial state to another rating level. This information is contained in the *transition matrix* published regularly by rating agencies. Table 10-1 is an example. The numbers reflect the average *annual* transition probability from initial state to final state one-year later. These statistics are compiled based on actual observations of firm defaults bucketed by specific industry sectors and ratings over a long history (i.e. there will be one matrix per industry sector).

While the rating transition matrix has been generally accepted by the industry for risk modeling, it is often criticized for being backward-looking. Observations of actual bankruptcies occur very slowly and will not capture the shift in market expectations of a credit deterioration of a company (expectation is forward-looking). Hence, some banks attempt to model the transition probabilities as a function of credit spreads and macroeconomic variables which are more contemporaneous.

---

[1] See Section 11.1 for the difference between banking book and trading book.

Table 10-1 One-year transition matrix (%) (numbers below are hypothetical)

Initial Rating	Rating at year-end (%)							
	AAA	AA	A	BBB	BB	B	CCC	Default
AAA	90.87	8.25	0.70	0.06	0.12	0.00	0.00	0.00
AA	0.69	90.45	7.99	0.65	0.06	0.14	0.02	0.00
A	0.09	2.25	91.02	5.58	0.74	0.26	0.01	0.06
BBB	0.02	0.33	6.03	86.76	5.36	1.19	0.12	0.18
BB	0.03	0.15	0.66	7.79	80.51	8.76	1.02	1.09
B	0.00	0.11	0.24	0.43	6.55	83.42	4.17	5.08
CCC	0.22	0.00	0.22	1.31	2.36	10.85	65.52	19.52

Step 2: revaluation of loan portfolio

The loan portfolio will need to be revalued using the 1-year forward credit spread curve. For simplicity we consider the case of a simple bond with fixed annual coupon, c. The value of the bond in one year including the next paid coupon (first term) is:

$$\text{Forward value: } P = c + \sum_{i=1}^{n} \frac{c}{(1+f_i+s_i)^i} + \frac{100}{(1+f_n+s_n)^n} \qquad (10.1)$$

where there are n coupons left after one year, s_i is the forward spread[2], f_i is the forward risk-free discount rate which can be derived from today's discount curve[3] r_i from the simple compounding relation:

$$\exp(r_{i+1}t_{i+1}) = \exp(r_i t_i)\exp\left(f_i(t_{i+1} - t_i)\right) \qquad (10.2)$$

where $i=1, \ldots, n$, time t_i is expressed in fractional years and $(t_{i+1} - t_i)$ is the coupon period. Since we can observe from the market a unique spread curve s_i for every rating in the matrix, we can compute the value for each bond in the portfolio for

---

[2] The spread curve for a particular issuer is a market observable. For simplicity, we assume a static curve i.e. S_i observed at the one-year horizon gives the same values as S_i observed today.
[3] In practice, the observed curve is the swap curve which is then bootstrapped to obtain the zero coupon curve or discount curve.

all the seven ratings using (10.1). The defaulted state's value is simply given by the recovery rate[4] multiplied by the forward bond value.

Spreadsheet 10.1 is a toy implementation of Creditmetrics for a portfolio of three bonds. In order not to digress from the main presentation, we will not show the valuation of the bonds as per equation (10.1), but simply state the results in Table 10-2. This table will be used subsequently to lookup the bond values at each simulated credit rating end state.

Table 10-2 Bond values of different end states at the one-year horizon ($/million)

	Bond 1	Bond 2	Bond 3
Initial Rating	BBB	A	CCC
Rating at 1-year			
AAA	5.375	3.132	1.171
AA	5.368	3.13	1.165
A	5.346	3.126	1.161
BBB	5.302	3.113	1.157
BB	5.081	3.063	1.142
B	4.924	2.828	1.137
CCC	3.846	2.174	1.056
Default	1.8557	1.2504	0.3168

Step 3: building correlation

Credit migrations of different companies are expected to show positive correlation because companies tend to be influenced by common macroeconomic drivers and the business cycle. But how can we measure a *default* correlation which cannot be observed?

The solution is to consider Merton's model (1974) which sees the equity position of the borrowing firm similar to holding a call option on the assets of that firm. The idea is that because of "limited liability", equity holders can never lose more than their original stake. Company default is then modeled as the fall in asset prices below the firm's debt (i.e. the option "strike"). Thus, default correlation can be modeled by the correlation of asset returns which in turn can be measured as the correlation of readily-observed equity returns.

---

[4] The recovery rates depend on bond rating and seniority. Normally they are internally estimated by the bank. Typical values range from 20% to 40% of par.

Once the correlation matrix is derived using equity returns, it needs to undergo Cholesky decomposition before it can be used to simulate correlated random asset returns. The asset returns are assumed to follow a normal distribution. A common misconception is that by assuming normal distribution, we are somehow not capturing the well-known fat-tail effects in credit spread changes. This is not the case, however, because we are assuming normality for the (stochastic) *drivers* of credit changes, not the asset changes themselves. In fact, as will be seen later, the final portfolio distribution (Figure 10-2) is heavily fat-tailed.

To translate a random draw from the multivariate normal distribution to an asset value in the end state, we need a mapping table. This is created by partitioning the scale of end ratings according to the normal distribution scale by matching the transition probability. See Figure 10-1.

Figure 10-1 Partition of asset change distribution for BBB issuer (Bond 1)

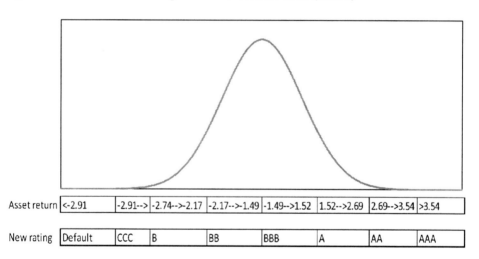

Asset return	<-2.91	-2.91-->	-2.74-->-2.17	-2.17-->-1.49	-1.49-->1.52	1.52-->2.69	2.69-->3.54	>3.54
New rating	Default	CCC	B	BB	BBB	A	AA	AAA

To obtain the portfolio distribution, Monte Carlo simulation is employed to generate three correlated random variables (one for each bond) for a large number of scenarios. Based on the drawn asset returns, we can read from the partition the corresponding end states of the bond's rating. And based on the end states we can read off Table 10-2 the final dollar value of the bond at the horizon. The three bond values are added per scenario to give the final portfolio distribution.

Credit VaR is then defined as the loss quantile of this distribution at a given confidence level. Figure 10-2 shows that the 95% worst case loss from the mean is $0.6 million. See Spreadsheet 10.1 for a worked-out example.

Figure 10-2 Portfolio distribution and Credit VaR

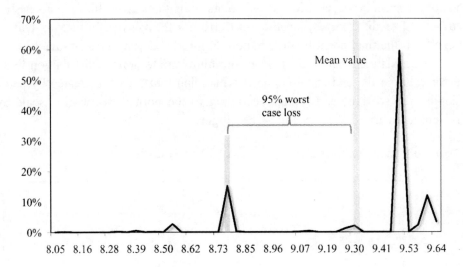

10.2 Liquidity Risk

What exactly is liquidity risk?

Liquidity risk has long been identified as a key risk in financial assets. To quantify it, it helps to first define what liquidity risk is. The common term liquidity risk is loosely defined and could mean a few things:

1. The risk of not being able to meet funding obligations as a firm leading to a bank's failure or bankruptcy. This is *funding* liquidity risk or *firm* liquidity risk.
2. The risk in paying the *bid-ask cost* when forced to liquidate a position during normal market conditions. Forced liquidation can happen for a variety of reasons—closure of business unit, bankruptcy of the bank, a VaR limit being exceeded, stop-loss being triggered, etc. In all cases, it is a reluctant and almost immediate unwind of positions. Since there is uncertainty in bid-ask costs, there is risk.

3. The *slippage loss* when liquidating a *large* position. When the forced-sale position is substantial and the market is illiquid, interbank players can be easily "tipped off" by large irregular transactions (what traders call "smelled blood"). The bid-ask quote will widen against the bank which is trying to exit the position.

4. In a disrupted market environment, such as in a crisis, risk averse participants will either not quote any bid-ask prices or quote them with unrealistically wide spreads. This increased cost reflects the risk of *mark-to-market (MTM) uncertainty*.

Consider the first in the list. In banks, the management of day-to-day liquidity is run by the *asset & liability management* (ALM) traders and risk controllers. The sub-prime crisis in 2008 has witnessed how the sudden appearance of funding liquidity risk almost caused the complete collapse of the world financial system. The fear of counterparty default had made banks reluctant to lend money to each other, which resulted in the hoarding of liquidity. The global payment system choked as liquidity "dried up". After the credit crisis, the BIS tightened regulations by requiring a *liquidity coverage ratio*, which stipulated the minimum liquid assets banks must hold to cover a stressful period of 30 consecutive days. This is discussed in Section 11.4.

The last three risks in the list are collectively known as *market liquidity* risk. MTM uncertainty is a risk that gained notoriety during the credit crisis and is caused by the "insidious growth of complexity"—unchecked product innovation driven by the speculative needs of investors. As such products are OTC derivatives—bespoke and illiquid—their risk is difficult to regulate and is stealthy in nature. No single regulator monitors the total outstanding notional globally or the identity of the counterparties holding such derivatives.

For example, the models used to price CDOs broke down during the 2008 crisis and led to a loss of confidence in using such models (price quotes disappeared), even though trillions of dollars of such derivatives had already been issued. With complex products, MTM uncertainty is intricately linked to *model risk*. By the definition in Section 9.3, model risk is the difference in theoretical and observed traded prices. During the CDO debacle, both were indeterminate and indeed this eventually led to the setup of the *Troubled Asset Repurchase Program* (TARP) in the US. The TARP was tasked with disposing of these "toxic" products over time in an orderly fashion in order to reduce further fallout to the financial markets.

Liquidity adjusted VaR or L-VaR

In recent years, there has been development in incorporating market liquidity risk into the VaR framework. For a review of such models please refer to Sebastian et. al (2009). Generally, the models attempt to include the bid-ask costs into the VaR distribution (or return scenarios).

In the more advanced models, the bid-ask cost is weighted by transaction volumes using data from exchanges. Such models not only consider the bid-ask cost but also the "depth" of the limit order book. As an example, suppose the bank has $q=1000$ lots of shares of a company. The liquidity cost may be given by:

$$L(q)_t = 0.5\left(\frac{a(q)-b(q)}{x_{mid}}\right)_t \tag{10.3}$$

where $a(q)$ is the "average" ask price weighted by transaction volumes as a trader "sweeps" the limit orders on the offer side in the limit order book, to fill 1000 lots. Likewise, $b(q)$ is similarly defined on the bid side. Since most banks mark their position at mid price x_{mid}, the multiplier of 0.5 reflects that only half of the "round trip" transaction cost is incurred. This percentage liquidity cost is converted into continuous terms by: $l(q) = \ln(1-L(q))$. Then, the asset's return net of liquidity cost is given by:

$$rnet(q)_t = r_t + \begin{cases} -l(q)_t & \textit{if long} \\ +l(q)_t & \textit{if short} \end{cases} \tag{10.4}$$

where r_t is the asset return on day t. To calculate the liquidity-adjusted VaR (L-VaR), we use $rnet(q)_t$ in place of r_t for scenario deal re-pricing and taking of the quantile. Equation (10.4) essentially widens both sides of the return distribution by an amount given by the liquidity cost as observed on individual past dates.

L-VaR rests on two unrealistic assumptions. Firstly, it assumes past liquidity cost (of the last 250-day observation period) is a good predictor of future liquidity cost (in the next 10-day horizon). This is difficult to justify if we reflect that the CDS bid-ask cost prior to 2007 would have understated liquidity costs during the credit crisis in 2008, and the bid-ask cost in 2008 would have overestimated liquidity costs since the crisis.

Secondly, L-VaR assumes the entire bank's positions were unwound every-day in the past observation period. Clearly a bank will only liquidate entire holdings when it is in credit difficulties. The probability of such a mass liquidation event is small and is not accounted for in L-VAR, leading to possible overstatement of risks.

A possible add-on formula

In this section we propose a simple "add-on" that can be used for reserve purposes. First, we attempt to include slippage in the bid-ask spreads by defining the adjusted spread as:

$$Aspread_n = \frac{q_n d_n}{N_n} - \frac{d_n}{2} \tag{10.5}$$

where q_n is the bank's net notional holdings of asset n. For an asset n, d_n is its bid-ask spread, N_n is the quoted maximum size that can be traded in a single transaction *without moving the bid-ask quote*. Equation (10.5) mimics the "sweeping" of a limit order book. For example, if N_n is 200 lots, and a bank needs to liquidate immediately $q=1000$ lots. The transaction will consummate five levels of bid-ask spreads in the order book, assuming the limit orders are homogenously queued. The second term reflects that a bank only crosses half the bid-ask spread at the first level.

The latest N_n and d_n can be subjectively observed from OTC markets, or automatically collected for exchange-traded products. For illiquid and bespoke products, a bank can use the spreads it quotes to a typical client. A bank would have a good idea how much transactional cost it wants to charge a client based on traders' assessment of the complexity, liquidity and hedging costs of the product.

When "crossing the bid-ask" we can assume linearity in pricing even for option-related products because the difference in price levels between bid and ask is relatively small. A sensitivity approach is thus valid:

$$BidAskLoss = \sum_{n=1}^{j} p_n Abs(sensitivity_n \times Aspread_n)_{primary} \tag{10.6}$$

where j is the number of assets, and p_n a probability factor (explained in the next section). We include only the *primary* risk factor's bid-ask spread for each asset n. This recognizes the way products are traded between professional counterparties—the bid-ask of only *one* primary risk factor is crossed. For example, the risk factors for an FX option are spot, interest rates and volatility, but actual trading is quoted in volatility terms, hence the volatility bid-ask is the *only* cost. The relevant sensitivity is vega in this case.

Equation (10.6) is calculated and summed across all j assets without any offsets. Since liquidity cost cannot be diversified away, netting between long and short is not allowed, except for instruments that are strictly identical in risks. Another exception should be made for "non credit risky" cash flow products because cash flows of two such deals are considered fungible[5]. One way is to bucket such cash flows into time pillars (with offsets) and then treat each pillar as a separate asset for the purpose of equation (10.6).

Taking probability into account

The p_n in equation (10.6) accounts for the probability of a mass liquidation event. A rough estimate is the probability of default for the bank or its interbank counterparty (for asset-n), as implied by their CDS spreads. After all, it is reasonable to assume that when a bank fails, it has to liquidate its holdings, or when its counterparty fails, the bank has to hedge outstanding positions.

As regulators use a 10-day horizon for safety capital, it makes sense to use a 10-day default probability derived from a 10-day CDS spread. (If this is not readily observed, the benchmark 5-year CDS spread can be used). The marginal default rate is related to CDS spread by:

$$p_n = 1 - \exp[-s\Delta t / (1 - R)] \tag{10.7}$$

where s is the larger of the bank's own CDS spread and the counterparty's CDS spread. $\Delta t = 10/250$ and $R = 0.45$, an assumed average default recovery rate for the banking sector.

To get a sense of magnitude of the add-on using this simple model, consider a credit derivative position of just one issuer with a notional of $500 million and maturity of 5 years. The add-on calculation is shown in Table 10-3.

---

[5] For example, in swaps, when credit riskiness is deemed absent (due to a netting agreement between professional counterparties), one cash flow is no different from another if they fall on the same date.

Table 10-3 Calculation of market liquidity risk add-on for $500 million position

Exposure to a single credit derivative issuer:	
Holdings of 5yr CDS	$ 500,000,000
Bid-offer spread (BP)	5.00
Maximum liquid size	$ 20,000,000
Adjusted Bid-ask spread	122.50
Credit sensitivity per BP	$ 250,000
Bid-offer loss	$ 15,312,500
Calculation of default probability:	
Own CDS spread (BP)	200
Counterparty CDS spread (BP)	300
Recovery rate	0.45
Horizon (Year)	0.04
10-day default probability	0.2179%
Expected liquidity loss	$ 33,373

The add-on may seem small for a $500 million position but since netting or diversification is not permitted (in general) these costs will add up very quickly on a firm-wide basis as the portfolio size grows.

10.3 Operational risk

Operational risk modeling is still in its infancy. There is no consensus on the definition of operational risk yet. Some banks broadly define this as risks other than credit and market risks—clearly not a very useful definition. Others define operational risk by identifying what it includes—as risk arising from human error, fraud, process failure, technological breakdown and external factors (such as lawsuits, fire hazards, natural disaster, customer dissatisfaction, loss of reputation, etc.). With such a broad definition, risk identification and classification (also called *taxonomy*) is an enormous challenge. Compounding the problem is the general lack of statistical data for all these individual items. Banks normally make do with a combination of in-house data and external data provided by vendor firms.

Fortunately, the Basel Committee provided some guidelines. For the purpose of compiling statistics—frequency and severity of losses—identified items should be bucketed into a grid similar to Figure 10-3. The grid represents various combinations of business line (BL) and event type (ET). Ideally the grid must be comprehensive and each cell should not contain overlapping risk types.

Figure 10-3 Operational risk factor grid

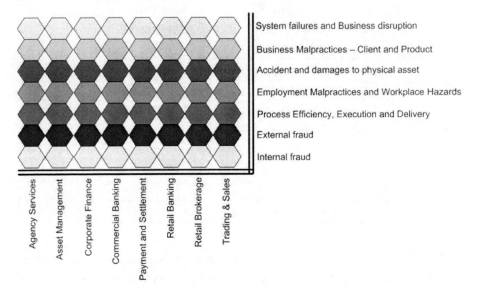

Of course not all items need to be modeled. It really depends on materiality. Consider Figure 10-4 which shows a zonal map of operational risk. Clearly resources should not be spent on items which are of low likelihood and low severity (for example, staff being late for work). On the other extreme, an event which occurs very frequently and of high severity represents an anomaly that should be investigated immediately, not modeled (for example, a bank experiencing 10 robberies in a single year). Hence, the focus for quantitative modeling is the zones marked "expected loss" and "unexpected loss/exceptional loss". Expected loss (EL) is the loss due to process failures, unexpected loss (UL) is typically due to internal control weakness, and exceptional loss (XL) is often a Black Swan event. This division is shown in the loss distribution (Figure 10-5).

A popular way to model operational risk (if data is available) is by using an actuarial approach. The result can be expressed in terms of loss quantile consistent with VaR used for market risk and credit risk. This loss number is called operational risk VaR or *OpVaR*. Each cell of the grid in Figure 10-3 is assumed to be a standalone risk factor independent of others. Thus, the OpVaRs for each risk factor are simply summed without considering correlation.

Figure 10-4 The zonal map of operational risks

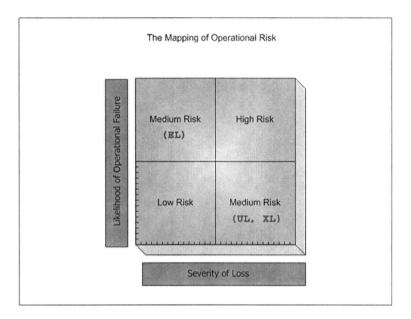

For a particular risk factor, historical data on loss are collected for observed events. These are used to model the *frequency distribution f(n)* and *severity distribution g(x|n=1)* where x is the loss for the event, n is the number of events per annum. Hence, $g(x|n=1)$ is the loss density function conditional on a single event (i.e. loss per event). These are shown in the upper two charts in Figure 10-5. Since OpVaR is normally measured at a one year horizon, the density *f(n)* is the probability of n events per annum.

We then use a process called *convolution* to combine *f(n)* and $g(x|n=1)$ to derive a *loss distribution*. Simplistically, this can be done by *tabulation* i.e. systematically recording all possible permutations of severity for every n. Table 10-4 shows an example of frequency and severity distributions. Table 10-5 illustrates the tabulation process used to derive the loss distribution. For example, for $n=2$, there are 9 ways to obtain two events given three possible severity values. For each permutation, the total loss is just the sum of losses for those two events. The probabilities can simply be read off Table 10-4. For example, for the sixth row, the joint probability of $n=2$, loss of 1000 and loss of 10000 is 0.15*0.5*0.3 = 0.0225. Spreadsheet 10.2 provides a worked out example.

Table 10-4 Frequency and severity distributions

Frequency Distribution		Severity Distribution	
Frequency (p.a.)	Probability	Severity	Probability
0	50%	$1,000	50%
1	30%	$10,000	30%
2	15%	$100,000	20%
3	5%		
Expectation	0.75	Expectation	$23,500

Table 10-5 Tabulation of loss distribution

Number of loss	Loss #1	Loss #2	Loss #3	Total Loss	Probability
0				-	0.5
1	1000			1,000	0.15
1	10000			10,000	0.09
1	100000			100,000	0.06
2	1000	1000		2,000	0.0375
2	1000	10000		11,000	0.0225
2	1000	100000		101,000	0.015
2	10000	1000		11,000	0.0225
2	10000	10000		20,000	0.0135
2	10000	100000		110,000	0.009
2	100000	1000		101,000	0.015
2	100000	10000		110,000	0.009
2	100000	100000		200,000	0.006
3	1000	1000	1000	3,000	0.00625
3	1000	1000	10000	12,000	0.00375
3	1000	1000	100000	102,000	0.0025
3	1000	10000	1000	12,000	0.00375
3	1000	10000	10000	21,000	0.00225
3	1000	10000	100000	111,000	0.0015
3	1000	100000	1000	102,000	0.0025
3	1000	100000	10000	111,000	0.0015
3	1000	100000	100000	201,000	0.001
3	10000	1000	1000	12,000	0.00375
3	10000	1000	10000	21,000	0.00225
3	10000	1000	100000	111,000	0.0015
3	10000	10000	1000	21,000	0.00225
3	10000	10000	10000	30,000	0.00135
3	10000	10000	100000	120,000	0.0009
3	10000	100000	1000	111,000	0.0015

3	10000	100000	10000	120,000	0.0009
3	10000	100000	100000	210,000	0.0006
3	100000	1000	1000	102,000	0.0025
3	100000	1000	10000	111,000	0.0015
3	100000	1000	100000	201,000	0.001
3	100000	10000	1000	111,000	0.0015
3	100000	10000	10000	120,000	0.0009
3	100000	10000	100000	210,000	0.0006
3	100000	100000	1000	201,000	0.001
3	100000	100000	10000	210,000	0.0006
3	100000	100000	100000	300,000	0.0004

The expected loss (EL) is given by the product of the expectation of the frequency distribution and the expectation of the severity distribution; 0.75*23500= 17625. It can also be calculated from Table 10-5 by taking the product of total loss and probability, and then summing the products across all permutations. The plot of the total loss vs. probability is the loss distribution shown in Figure 10-5 (note that the horizontal axis is not scaled uniformly). It is clearly fat-tailed. The 99.9%-OpVaR is then defined by the loss quantile at the tail. We consider the region beyond OpVaR as representing exceptional loss (XL). The region between EL and XL gives the unexpected loss (UL). From the diagram, OpVaR=EL+UL.

Figure 10-5 Operational risk loss distribution

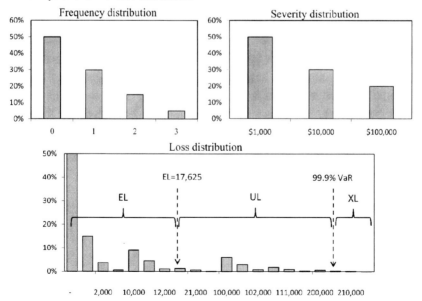

Under Basel II's *loss distribution approach* (an "internal model" approach), the operational risk capital for banks is a function of the sum of OpVaR for all combinations of business line vs. event type (BL-ET). The OpVaR is defined on a 99.9% quantile over a one-year horizon. For a discussion about the challenges of OpVaR see Coleman (2010).

10.4 The Problem of Aggregation

The danger of "adding apples to oranges"

As directed by Basel, capital charges for various risk classes are calculated separately—some based on internal models (as for market risk) and others on a set of rules given by regulators (as for credit risk). To compute the total charge, the regulator's current treatment is to just sum them up. This is nothing more than a recipe to obtain the aggregated final charge—there is little conceptual justification. This method suffers from at least three drawbacks which we will examine closely: (1) It ignores the possibility of risk diversification or offsets, (2) under certain situations the aggregated risk can actually be less conservative, and (3) the final number is difficult to interpret.

Firstly, one can argue that diversification is the hallmark of a good risk measure, without which a risk model tells us an incomplete story. For example, while diversification is not captured in operational risk VaR, we intuitively know its necessity. Why do banks normally fly their top executives to overseas functions on separate flights? The bosses know intuitively to diversify this operational risk (accident hazard). Likewise, a bank that relies on multiple sources of funding has diversified its firm liquidity risk as compared to a bank that relies solely on wholesale borrowing. Yet presently there is no standard approach for modeling firm liquidity risk, let alone its diversification effect.

It is important to realize that the simple summation method implicitly assumes a correlation of one, which is more conservative than the assumption of zero correlation. In other words, "no correlation" does not equate zero correlation. Clearly, when $\rho=0$,

$$VaR_A + VaR_B > \sqrt{VaR_A^2 + VaR_B^2 + 2\rho VaR_A VaR_B} \qquad (10.8)$$

Empirical analysis, say by comparing market risk and credit risk time series, would suggest that zero correlation is often a more realistic (and hence preferred) assumption than perfect correlation.

Secondly, the popular wisdom that the simple summation rule is conservative (thanks to equation (10.8)) does not hold true in some situations, especially if we are not clear what exactly we are adding. Breuer et al (2008) showed that simply adding market risk and credit risk may result in a *less conservative* aggregate in some cases.

A good example[6] is foreign currency loans. Consider a foreign bank lending US dollars to a local borrower. The loan contains market risk (FX risk) and credit risk (default risk of the borrower). The two risks are measured separately. In a scenario where the domestic economy slows and the local currency depreciates, from the bank's perspective, the loan appreciates in value and the credit risk of the borrower increases—the two effects should somewhat offset at first sight. But this diversification argument neglects the fact that the ability of local borrowers to repay depends in a non-linear way on currency fluctuations. Unless the borrower has other revenues in US dollars, it may be pressed to default on the loan if the currency loss is unbearable. This is what happened to many local borrowers during the Asian financial crisis in 1997. Such trades where credit risk and market risk amplify each other are known as *wrong-way trades*.

More generally, under Basel, the capital charge for credit and market risk are required to be modeled separately and then simply summed up. However, most products contain both risks, which cannot be decoupled easily because of the complex interaction between credit and market risk. It is unclear whether the diversification benefits are positive or negative. As in the example of a foreign currency loan, its risk may be higher that the simple summation of credit and market risks that exist separately.

Finally, if we add the risk up without a unifying conceptual framework, the aggregated VaR will have little meaning. What does it really mean to add a ten-day 99% market VaR to a one-year 99.9% OpVaR? Also a 99.9% confidence level is incomprehensible and not empirically verifiable. It is impossible to make intelligent decisions if one cannot interpret what the risk numbers really mean.

The problem of aggregating these diverse risk classes is a difficult one; they are very different in almost all aspects. Table 10-6 summarizes their characteristic differences.

---

[6] The example is taken from BIS Working Paper No. 16 "Findings on the interaction of market and credit risk" (May 2009) which discusses the latest progress in unifying market and credit risks.

Table 10-6 Summary of characteristics of major risk classes

Risk class	Methodology	Risk factor mapping	Data general availability	Result reliability
Market risk (including specific risk)	Quantile based 99%/10 day	Well defined	Good (vendor/ priced based data)	Good (within definition of quantile)
Credit risk	Quantile based ,99.9%/1 year	Chosen grades/ grids	Subjective (internal/ scoring based)	Poor (wide error)
Operational risk	Quantile based ,99.9%/1 year	Loosely-defined taxonomy	Poor (ill-defined)	Poor (wide error)
Firm Liquidity risk	Liquidity coverage ratio	N.A	Excellent (internal/ positional based)	Deterministic but risk misspecification of scenarios

In the list, only market risk has enough quality data to be analyzed precisely using a statistical distribution. Even here, problems in the tail can undermine accuracy. Credit and operational risks are known to be fat-tailed and very likely extremistan in nature. On the other hand, liquidity risk will be handled using coverage ratios (see Section 11.4), an appropriate choice of solution and not really a model. It is a good example which shows that we need not model risk precisely to protect against it. Can this be aggregated?

Adding across different forecast horizons

The unavoidable part about forecasting probabilities of future events is that one needs to specify a horizon. For example, Basel's market VaR is a forecast for 10 days ahead. If different risks are estimated at *different horizons*, simply adding them up can lead to undesirable side effects.

As an illustration, suppose there is a casino that offers a game that has a 60% chance of winning for the customer. The casino has a bad fire safety record—it was burnt down twice in the last four years. So the hazard rate measured at the 1-year forecast horizon is 0.5 fires per year. Would you play the game (assuming you can bet on-line so there is no personal safety concern)? Are the odds of winning simply 30% (=0.6*0.5) or 60% (=0.6(1-0.5/365))? The situation is not unlike that of a credit risky bond where there is a stochastic price risk and a default risk element. There are two lessons here: (1) In order to have a meaningful interpretation, the risks need to be scaled to the same "unit" before adding, and (2) the risk changes with forecast horizon (i.e. frequency of visits to the casino). If you visit just once, the odds are 60%, but if you gamble the whole year round, the odds are 30%.

Scaling the risk from one horizon to another is not straightforward. Firstly, volatility scales with the square-root of time, whereas, default probability scales linearly with time. This implies that the choice of measurement horizon will have an impact on the relative importance of these two risks. Secondly, the popular scaling method is laden with naïve assumptions which are often taken for granted. For example, the square-root of time scaling that is commonly used to bring a 1-day VaR to 10-day assumes that returns are i.i.d. (see Section 6.4) and that positions remain constant (frozen) in the interim ten days. These assumptions do not reflect the real trading environment.

The general problem of aggregation can be addressed using the following logic: first scale all risk numbers to the same "units" (i.e. same quantile and same horizon) before adding them up. Are there any diversification effects and complex relationships that need to be accounted for in the summation? If so, is it material? Scaling often requires unrealistic assumptions. Is the error due to these assumptions material at a portfolio level? If the error is unacceptable, to avoid making such assumptions one really has to model the various risk classes within a unified framework. For a realistic example of a model used by a bank, see the paper by Brockmann and Kalkbrener (2010).

10.5 Spreadsheet

10.1 Creditmetrics© is a popular credit model used by banks to capture credit default and rating migration risks on a portfolio basis. Aim: illustrates a simple implementation of Creditmetrics for a portfolio of three bonds. Note: all figures are hypothetical, the valuation of the forward values of each bond at each rating is not shown. The illustration focuses on the Monte Carlo simulation of rating migration and the resulting loss distribution.

10.2 Operational risks VaR (OpVaR) is a commonly-accepted method to measure operational risks at banks if a bank chooses an actuarial approach. While theoretically appealing, this method is fraught with data scarcity and classification challenges. Aim: derives the operational risk loss distribution using tabulation method given the data on frequency distribution and severity distribution. Action: run the VB macro to generate all permutations of number of events $n=0,1,2,3$. The loss distribution of the permutations is computed; OpVaR is just its loss quantile.

PART III

THE GREAT REGULATORY REFORM

Chapter 11

Regulatory Capital Reform

The *Basel Committee of Banking Supervision* (dubbed "Basel") is instrumental in the design and development of the current framework for banking regulation and capital requirements. Though not legally binding, these rules have become the de facto standard adopted globally.

This chapter begins with a short background of the Basel framework and guidance[1]. We then explore the recent policy development in response to the credit crisis of 2008. Most of these policy papers came in a scramble in 2009 and are slated for implementation in 2012. The policy response is very comprehensive, covering many aspects of banking regulations, even though it is fair to say that the industry is still looking for all the right tools to do the job. We focus our discussion on the capital adequacy aspect of risk regulation and the calculation of minimum capital, in line with the purpose of this book.

11.1 Basel I and Basel II

The Basel committee comprises of the central bank governors of the group of 10 most industrialized nations (or G-10). The role of Basel is to promote the safety of the global financial system and to create a level playing field among international banks. Basel is a high level policy body. Local regulators such as central banks and banking supervisors use the Basel framework as a guide to write rulebooks for national banks under their supervision.

A core element of supervision is the idea of capital adequacy—a bank has to hold sufficient capital (in proportion to the risk taken) for the business it is engaged in. For example, for every \$100 engagement in risky activities, the bank is required by regulation to maintain \$8 (say 8%) of capital. This *minimum* (or regulatory) capital acts as a safety buffer for a bank during times of crisis to prevent bankruptcy, and to give it time to source emergency funding. A larger

---

[1] The interested reader is referred to the Basel's website: www.bis.org which publicly discloses all frameworks, revisions, consultative papers and documents.

minimum capital is more conservative but will also take a toll on a bank's profitability (return-on-capital) since the spare capital is not put to productive use. In the EU, this element of Basel is written into the *Capital Adequacy Directive* (CAD) which stipulates various rules and methods to derive the minimum capital.

The Basel Accord (1988) or Basel I was a pioneer capital framework. It focused only on credit risk (the largest risk class faced by banks) and was a first attempt at designing a risk-based capital charge i.e. penalizing banks more for holding riskier assets. However, it is a simple "rules-based" approach[2]—risky positions (or claims) held by a bank are simply categorized according to Table 11-1 which also gives their risk weights. Multiplying a position by its risk weight will give its *risk weighted asset* (RWA). The minimum capital is then just 8% of RWA summed across all positions.

Table 11-1 Risk weights for claims under Basel I regime

Weights	Asset Type
0%	Cash
	Claims on OECD governments
	Claims on governments in local currency
20%	Cash to be received (in collection)
	Claims on OECD banks and regulated securities firms
	Claims on non-OECD banks below 1 year
	Claims on multilateral development banks
	Claims on foreign OECD public-sector entities
50%	Residential mortgage loans
100%	Claims on the private sector (loans, equity, etc.)
	Claims on non-OECD banks above 1 year
	Real estate
	Plant and equipment

In 1996, the committee amended Basel I to include market risks. The total capital charge is now given by:

---

[2] From here on, the term *rules-based* will generically mean that the risk weights are read mechanically from tables provided in regulatory rulebooks and used in capital charge formulas stated in these rulebooks as opposed to model-based (internal model) approaches such as VaR which attempt to model the underlying risk phenomena.

$$MinimumCapital = 8\%[CRC + (1/8\%)MRC] \qquad (11.1)$$

where credit risk charge (*CRC*) is the RWA for loans. The market risk charge (*MRC*) is computed using either the *Standard Approach* (another rules-based method) or *Internal Models* (VaR-based).

The introduction of internal models is a milestone development in Basel and is a tacit recognition by regulators that banks have developed sophisticated models to measure risks and can be counted on to advance on this frontier. To qualify for internal models, a bank has to show that it has a robust risk management infrastructure, a culture of risk awareness and reliable models. Since the use of internal models can lead to significant capital savings (thanks to diversification and offsets), needless to say, banks are well-motivated in this direction of research.

The rules-based regime of Basel I had some serious loopholes. It gave preferential treatment to OECD claims and there was no differentiation between corporate loans of different ratings (see Table 11-1). This led to widespread "regulatory arbitrage" where banks attempt to obtain a better return-on-capital by divesting high quality (hence low-yielding) assets in favor of low quality (high yielding) assets if they attracted the same capital charge. It motivated US banks for example to securitize high quality loans on their books and on-sell them to investors, and also to lend heavily to Asian corporations in the run up to the Asian crisis (1997). The dollar loans were used for unproductive speculation in local assets which were giving high yields at that time because of the Asian currency pegs to the US dollar. Quite unintentionally Basel I encouraged undesirable behavior by banks and led to a deterioration of banks' credit quality.

The Basel II was published in 2004 to overcome some of these weaknesses. Basel II is based on three "pillars" of supervision: i) minimum capital requirements, ii) supervisory review process, which gives greater powers to the regulator, and iii) market discipline, which outlines the disclosure requirements for banks. Operational risk charge was introduced following the high-profile scandals that bankrupted Enron in 2001 and Worldcom in 2002.

As shown in Table 11-2, a menu of methods is available under Basel II to compute various capital charges. For credit risk (loans, claims) a bank can choose the rules-based standardized method (legacy of Basel I) or the *internal ratings based* (IRB) approach. Generally speaking, under IRB, the credit risk charge for each category of asset is given by:

$$CRC = LGD\times[K_V - PD]\times M \times EAD \qquad (11.2)$$

where *PD* is the probability of default (of the loan) at 99.9% confidence level at a 1-year horizon, *LGD* is the loss given default, *EAD* is the exposure at default and *M* is the loan's maturity adjustment factor. K_V is the *Vasicek formula*. *PD* and *LGD* are in percentage whereas *EAD* is in currency units. In the foundational IRB, only *PD* is estimated by banks, and in the advanced IRB, all inputs are estimated using banks' own models. The IRB formula is a simplified portfolio credit risk model—a simple function of PD, LGD and EAD—derived based on the assumptions of a single risk factor and normal distribution[3].

Table 11-2 Methods approved for calculation of capital charges under Basel II

Credit risk	Market risk	Operation risk
Standardized	Standardized	Basic indicator
Foundational IRB	Internal Models (VaR)	Standardized
Advanced IRB		Advanced measurement

For market risk, the standardized approach is rules-based and expensive on capital charges. Given the advances in VaR modeling nowadays, most banks have upgraded to use internal models where the *MRC* is described by equation (6.3).

The *MRC* is divided into two components: the *general* market risk charge (*GMRC*) and *specific* risk charge (*SRC*), where the latter captures the *idiosyncratic* risk of *tradable* instruments, such as the issuer default risk of corporate bonds. Note that there is no overlap between the *CRC* of a loan and a *SRC* of a bond of the same corporate name because *CRC* is a *banking book* treatment whereas *MRC* (i.e. *GMRC* plus *SRC*) is solely for the *trading book*[4]. Basel has decided to exclude the banking book from (general) interest rate charge since it contains mainly loans held to maturity. Market fluctuations are not important since the loans will not be traded. The treatment for equities and options is beyond the scope of this book.

---

[3] The model is attributed to Vasicek (1991). Thomas et al. (2005) provides a clear interpretation and good critique of this formula.

[4] A trading book contains positions held with *trading intent* and for short-term resale. This may come from proprietary trading, arbitrage or market-making activities. Mark-to-market accounting applies. The banking book consists of other instruments, mainly loans that are held to maturity. Accrual accounting applies (except for derivatives hedges). A banking book (unlike a trading book) is usually net long.

For operational risks, the basic indicator and standardized approaches are rules-based. The advanced measurement approach is in fact a nascent internal model quite similar to VaR. To calculate the operational risk charge (*ORC*) the model takes the quantile based on 99.9% confidence level and over a 1-year horizon (see Chapter 10). The total capital charge for a bank is then given by:

$$MinimumCapital = 8\%[CRC + (1/8\%)MRC + (1/8\%)ORC] \qquad (11.3)$$

11.2 The Turner Review

The *Turner Review* (2009) published by the FSA is a comprehensive (126-page) diagnosis of the 2008 credit crisis which contained a list of prescriptive policy actions points. It will likely become the blue print for the coming regulatory reform. Here we will digest two sections of the review pertinent to this book: on fundamental theoretical issues, and on avoiding procyclicality in Basel II.

Fundamental theoretical issues

The review questioned the intellectual assumption of efficient market theory on which previous regulatory approaches have largely been built. This indirectly shaped the supervisory and risk management mindset and practices of today. Five points were mentioned:

1. We can use market prices as good indicators of rationally-evaluated economic value, for example, as unquestionable valid inputs to a risk model. Evidence from the crisis: The markets can be irrational, illiquid and inefficient under stress.
2. Development of credit securitization will improve financial stability by reallocating risks and by allowing for hedging. Evidence from crisis: credit securitization concentrated risk in a systemically harmful way— banks were all on the same side of the trades.
3. Market discipline can be used as an effective tool in constraining harmful risk-taking. The market self-regulates. Evidence from crisis: As a result of procyclicality and positive feedback, it seems prices and market pressures have played vicious roles in exacerbating the crisis.
4. Financial innovation is a good thing—it adds value to the real economy. Any non-beneficial product would be snuffed out by competition. Evidence from crisis: The credit product innovation that contributed to the crisis had very little economic value, except for the illusionary effect of

wealth creation due to mark-to-market in a rising market. Also investors were overcharged in terms of high margins—made possible by pricing opacity and asymmetric information between banks and customers—what the review called the harmful effect of "rent extraction".

5. The risk characteristics of financial markets can be inferred from mathematical analysis, delivering robust quantitative risk measures. Evidence from crisis: The VaR method broke down. Four inherent limitations were highlighted by the review (listed below).

First, a short observation period (i.e. 12 months) introduced dangerous procyclicality. Second, the effective assumption of a normal distribution meant that VaR models systematically underestimated the chance of fat-tail events and "Black Swan" losses. Third, risk models implicitly assume that individual participants' reactions to price movements are sufficiently small and are mutually independent such that they do not affect market equilibrium. In other words, risk models do not account for "network externalities" or contagion effects (see Chapter 12). This could explain why VaR was at its long-term low in spring 2007 just before the credit crisis when in fact systemic risk was brewing—it wasn't designed to detect network risk.

Finally, the assumption that information contained in past distributions can be used to infer future distributions rests on insecure grounds, but has gained widespread acceptance in financial modeling. Variants of this idea are used in many areas including derivatives pricing (the "Markov property") and risk modeling (i.i.d.). But economic regime shifts can and do happen that will invalidate the usefulness of past data. Credit risk is a good example—past observations are of no use at all to predict future defaults since a company can only default once, i.e. past observations that a company did not default does not tell us when or if the company will default in future. This point is thought-provoking.

It is true only because present-day risk models are not accustomed to interpreting past data in unconventional ways. Default of Company A could well contain useful information on the near term future defaultability of Company B from the same sector. Compression of credit spreads in spring of 2007 could signal (in a contrarian sense) that a blow-up in spreads was imminent. Some irregular escalation in credit *spreads* of Company A could well be the harbinger of a *default* of Company A. In other words, today's risk models are rigidly formulated to predict based on the logic that: A→A, or today's distribution is i.i.d. or "more of the *same* occurrence in future". But from the examples I have given, other applications seem promising: A→B, A→non(A) (i.e. contrarian logic), spread(A)→default(A). We really have to get past the i.i.d. paradigm!

Interestingly, the Turner review also mentioned we should distinguish between risk and uncertainty, and touched on the idea of *Knightian* uncertainty:

"The term 'risk' as loosely used in everyday speech and in economic discussions really covers two things which, functionally at least, ... are categorically different. The essential fact is that 'risk' means in some cases a quantity susceptible of measurement, while at other times it is distinctly not of this character; and there are far reaching and crucial differences in the bearings of the phenomenon depending on which of the two is really present and operating." (Frank Knight, "Risk, Uncertainty and Profit", 1921)

Knight insisted that we really should name the unquantifiable risk as "uncertainty". Compare the following problem statements: A dice throw is a repeatable experiment. What is the probability of getting three zeros in a row? This is quantifiable risk. But, what is the probability the US president will win the next re-election? The problem cannot be cast as a repeatable experiment. It is at best a function of expert judgment (opinion poll perhaps) and is subjected to occasional update as new information is gathered (subsequent opinion polls). This is uncertainty.

In a Bayesian sense, uncertainty measures our state of ignorance or incomplete knowledge. The less informed we are, the more uncertainty we face.

At times, we face similar situations in finance where no mathematical exactness is possible, even though we may choose to use percentage probabilities as a language device. And herein lies the danger—we may unknowingly "outsource" our good judgment and commonsense to mathematical models if we confuse uncertainty for risk. To make things worse, the line between risk and uncertainty can be changing. During the 2008 crisis, the normal market mechanism was disrupted and price discovery became unreliable, especially for "toxic" derivatives—risk turned into (Knightian) uncertainty.

Avoiding procyclicality in Basel II

The herd actions of rating agencies to upgrade (or downgrade) firms during a business cycle upswing (or downswing) can lead to harmful procyclicality in credit risk scores. Likewise, the short observation period used in VaR also leads to a safety capital which is procyclical. These factors ultimately encourage reckless investment behavior by borrowers and market players. The review prescribed three ways to dampen such "hard-wired" procyclicality:
1. The use of *variable scalars* targeting specifically the IRB (banking

book) framework. Banks will be tasked to model the credit cycle on a long-term basis or "through-the-cycle" instead of on a short-term basis or "point-in-time". The assessment is done for each credit grade and ultimately expressed as a variable scalar. This factor is applied to the *PD* (in equation (11.2)) as a correction so that the effect of procyclicality is dampened.

2. Introducing an *overt countercyclical* capital buffer such that the required capital would increase in good years when loan losses are below long run averages, creating capital buffers which can be drawn down during a financial crisis. The review favors a formula-driven approach which can be calibrated at the discretion of the supervisor. At the time of writing, the BIS has just released a working paper on countercyclical capital buffer. See BIS working paper no 317 (July 2010).

3. Changing the current accounting system which is known to cause procyclicality. Today's accounting philosophy is focused on communicating facts to shareholders at the publication date (i.e. PL marked at current prices) and should not anticipate probable future events. But this makes the reported balance sheet hostage to irrational and cyclical price swings (which were not seen before in that accounting year). The review proposed the set-up of a non-distributable *Economic Cycle Reserve* in published accounts, which would set aside profits in good years to anticipate losses in the future.

While the general principles are set forth, the FSA is still working with the UK banking industry to establish the detailed framework and necessary tools. The proposals must be implemented in a consistent way and across all banks globally to avoid the possibility of "regulatory arbitrage".

11.3 Revisions to Basel II Market Risk Framework

July 2009 saw the release of the final version of the revision to the Basel II market risk framework and the guidelines for computing the incremental risk charge. We shall discuss three important new requirements stated in these papers:

Incremental risk charge

We recall from equation (6.3) that *MRC* consists of *GMRC* (VaR-based) and *SRC* (rules-based, does not differentiate issuers). Major banks are already using internal models for *GMRC* and are in a transition phase to extend the VaR model to capture (issuer) specific risk as well. However, the explosive growth in credit derivatives and credit securitization in the mid-2000's has prompted Basel to introduce an incremental charge. The *incremental risk charge* (IRC) was incorporated into the trading book capital regime in recognition that default risk of illiquid credit products is not well-reflected in VaR. Note that there is no overlap between the specific risk charge modeled as part of VaR (at 99%, 10-day) and the IRC. The former captures risks from spread movement, thus often called *credit spread VaR*, whereas the latter captures default risks, rating migration risks and default correlation risks at a much longer horizon of one year.

Basel did not favor any particular model for IRC but provided high-level guidelines summarized below:

1. Scope: A bank that has approval to internally model specific risks as part of its VaR will also be subjected to an IRC. IRC covers all positions that are internally modeled for specific risks with the exception of securitization products.

2. IRC must be based on losses at 99.9% confidence level, 1-year horizon, and should have a soundness standard comparable to IRB. This is to avoid possible "regulatory arbitrage" between the trading and banking books.

3. Assumes a constant level of *risk* (as measured by VaR or other metric) over a one-year horizon. This reflects the fact that banks can seldom respond efficiently in the short-term when in distress, such as by selling off all positions or by raising emergency capital. Also, consistent with a "going concern" view of a bank, a one-year horizon is appropriate because a bank must continue to take risks to support its income-producing activities despite losses.

4. Must have a *liquidity horizon* of at least 3 months. Banks must explicitly model the liquidity horizon of different credit products. In principle, this horizon represents the fastest time taken to sell off/hedge a position in a stressed market without tipping over prices.

5. Cross correlation effects must be modeled such as the correlations between default, migration and other risk factors.

6. Concentration risk of issuers and sectors must be properly reflected.

7. Risk-netting and diversification rules. These rules are very strict and would disallow netting for most long-short positions in a typical trading book. Instead, the longs and shorts will need to be summed on a gross basis. Diversification between gross long and gross short positions will need to be modeled separately.

8. The IRC must reflect optionality.

The IRC is a turning point that may open up an exciting but arduous path of development. The current VaR assumes a constant level of *position* in the forecast period (10 days). So banks do not care what happens to positions in the interim and can use a simple square-root-of-time scaling. But now, rules (3) and (4) together require banks to model the *dynamic* rebalancing of positions (simplistically speaking, rolling over positions) to maintain a constant level of *risk* throughout a one-year period. In theory, the liquidity horizon determines the rebalancing interval (and frequency) for each credit product. In effect, the new legislation forces banks to think about what happens to positions in the interim period between today and the measurement horizon. But in keeping a constant level of risk (VaR), Basel is hinting that it wants to model effects other than market risks that will also influence the risk charge. This could be sunken costs that arise from exiting illiquid products, a term structure of liquidity/ default risks, PL accruals from premiums of credit derivatives, etc. It is a leap in sophistication and possibly the first serious attempt to blend asset liquidity risk into the credit VaR framework.

See Finger (2009) for an industry comment on these guidelines. There are presently many portfolio credit models available. One possible prototype for the IRC is Creditmetrics© (see Chapter 10) even though quite a bit of plumbing is required in order to satisfy all the IRC guidelines.

The initial consensus is to use a multi–step Monte Carlo simulation on each product to model the dynamic rebalancing. Suppose positions A, B, C, D have liquidity horizons 1, 3, 6, 12 months, then the number of steps for the simulations of default risk are 12, 4, 2, 1 steps respectively—conceptually speaking. For an example of a multi-period model, the reader may refer to the paper by Brockmann and Kalkbrener (2010).

Banking book treatment of securitized credit products

Note that the IRC is meant for *unsecuritized* credit products. The Basel is unconvinced that current state-of-the-art models adequately capture the risks of *securitized* credit products such as tranched securities and correlation products (n'th-to-default swaps) given that many of them turned into "toxic" assets during the CDO debacle in 2008.

Hence, for securitized products, the more punitive capital charges of the banking book (IRB approach) will apply with a limited exception for correlation trading activity, where banks may be approved by supervisors to calculate a *comprehensive risk capital charge*. This exception is recognition by Basel that such businesses will not be viable under the IRB regime where there are effectively no offsets between longs and shorts. Closing down such business activities is also not possible due to the trillions of dollars of outstanding notional that is already issued.

The comprehensive risk charge will be modeled internally by banks and must include *all* risks pertinent to correlation trading. This will be a challenging task as it includes a host of complex risks[5]. The comprehensive charge will be floored by a percentage of the comparative charge as calculated using the banking book approach.

Stressed VaR

The Basel II revision also requires banks to calculate a "stressed VaR", which is just the conventional 99%/10-day VaR calculated using a 1-year (fixed) observation period of high stress. The 12-month period ending Dec 2008 qualifies for this purpose. Unlike normal VaR, the stressed VaR is a "static" risk measure that does not depend on the arrival of market movements although it varies with positional changes, and as such, is really a *stress test* result. The idea is to use this stressed VaR (*SVaR*) as a first buffer against procyclicality.

In summary, if a bank's specific risk (*SRC*) is not approved for internal models, the market risk charge for the trading book, equation (6.3) now becomes:

$$MRC_t = \max\left(\frac{k}{60}\sum_{i=1}^{60}VaR_{t-i},VaR_{t-1}\right)+\max\left(\frac{m}{60}\sum_{i=1}^{60}SVaR_{t-i},SVaR_{t-1}\right)+SRC_t$$

(11.4)

where the multipliers k and m are set by regulators subject to $k\geq3$, $m\geq3$ and k is determined by back-testing of normal (non-stressed) VaR. On the other hand, if a bank's internal model is able to include specific risk, then the market risk charge is given by:

$$MRC_t = \max\left(\frac{k}{60}\sum_{i=1}^{60}VaR_{t-i}^*,VaR_{t-1}^*\right)+\max\left(\frac{m}{60}\sum_{i=1}^{60}SVaR_{t-i}^*,SVaR_{t-1}^*\right)+IRC_t$$

(11.5)

---

[5] Explicitly mentioned inclusions are default, migration, multiple-default, spread risk, cross-gamma effects, volatility of implied correlation, correlation between spread and implied correlation, basis risk, recovery rates, benefit of diversification and hedge slippage.

where the subscript * denotes that specific risk is included. The BIS estimated[6] that the new rules will increase the *market risk* charge by an average of 224%. This figure excludes capital charges for securitization exposures and the comprehensive risk capital charges; thus the actual increase will likely be higher.

11.4 New Liquidity Framework

Liquidity stress testing has long been a traditional risk management practice at banks. Even so, the credit crisis revealed how unprepared banks were to a sudden dry-up in funding liquidity—clearly, liquidity stress testing has been an underdeveloped discipline. In 2008, the BIS published a set of (rather high level) principles to guide banks in funding liquidity risk management. To fortify this critical area, the BIS introduced two new *minimum* requirements in Dec 2009—these two *liquidity ratios* are now included in Basel III:

Liquidity coverage ratio = (stock of high quality liquid assets) / (net cash outflows over a 30-day period), with a minimum of 100%.

and,

Net stable funding (NSF) ratio = (available amount of stable funding) / (required amount of stable funding), with a minimum of 100%.

where the terms are briefly described in Table 11-3. More details can be found in the BIS document *"Basel III: International framework for liquidity risk measurement, standards and monitoring"* (Dec 2010).

The liquidity coverage ratio is designed to ensure that a bank has enough liquidity to cover a 30-day "mini bank run" scenario as defined by Basel[7]. The scenario emphasizes the danger of over-reliance on wholesale funding (as opposed to deposit funding) which can disappear quickly in a crisis. The goal is to set up a liquidity buffer to defend the balance sheet if it suddenly comes under stress.

---

[6] See *Analysis of the trading book quantitative impact study*, BIS, October 2009.
[7] Broadly speaking, this stress scenario is whereby the bank is simultaneously hit by: a 3-notch credit rating downgrade, partial loss of deposits, loss of wholesale funding, increase in secured funding haircuts, and margin calls. This features the shocks experienced during the recent credit crisis.

On the other hand, the NSF ratio aims to promote more medium-to-long-term funding of assets and activities of banks—it discourages over-reliance on short-term wholesale funding. It dictates an overall funding structure where long-term commitments must (largely) be financed using long-term liabilities. This explicitly constrains the "maturity transformation" activities of a bank.

The weights in Table 11-3 under *required* stable funding, approximate the amount of that asset that could *not* be monetized through sale or pledged for collateralized borrowing, during a liquidity stress lasting one year. Hence, this portion of the asset will need to be supported by the available *stable* funding.

Table 11-3 Brief description of terms that define the liquidity ratios

Term	Brief description
Stock of high quality liquid assets	Central bank eligible collateral such as cash, government bonds and covered bonds which are unencumbered (not pledged for other purposes).
Net cash outflows over a 30-day time period	Represents a run-off of liquidity under a Basel defined stress scenario ("mini bank run") where the bank will need to survive for 30-days. The run-off portions are given per category. Example: Loss of 7.5% of stable retail and small business deposits, 100% of interbank funding with maturity <30 days, and so on.
Available amount of stable funding	Funding (liability) with weighting scheme given. Example: 100% of Tier 1, Tier 2 capital, preferred stock, 90% of "stable" deposits from retail customers and small businesses, 50% of large deposits by non-banks <1yr, and so on.
Required amount of stable funding	Weighted sum of the asset side of the balance sheet. Example: 5% of sovereign/supra-national debt >1yr, 50% of gold, 85% loans to retail customers <1yr, and so on. All items must be unencumbered.

11.5 The New Basel III

Basel III was finally released in Dec 2010 in the BIS paper *"Basel III: A global regulatory framework for more resilient banks and banking systems"*. It details new regulatory requirements (primarily additional capital) over and above what is already stipulated by Basel II and its revisions in 2009. Here is a short summary:-

First, Basel III calls for the redefinition of capital—more stringent criteria for what qualifies as the capital base for a bank[8], and standardization across jurisdictions. The *minimum* capital (as a percentage of RWA) has been raised to 4.5% for common equity, and to 6% for Tier 1 capital, but total capital remains at 8% of RWA. The increase will be phased in by 1 Jan 2015.

Second, it proposes several initiatives to enhance risk coverage—to cover the gaps seen during the 2008 crisis. Credit securitization risks and procyclicality are addressed by the revisions to Basel II (see Section 11.3). Counterparty risks arising from derivatives and SPVs are dealt with by a new set of rules— counterparty credit risk to be computed using stressed inputs, additional capital for *credit valuation adjustment* or CVA (i.e. the potential MTM loss due to counterparty credit deterioration), incentives to move OTC trades to centralized clearing to minimize systemic risk, treatment of wrong-way trades, etc.

Third, the new Basel will require minimum capital to cover funding liquidity risk. These are the two liquidity ratios mentioned in Section 11.4.

Fourth, it introduces a *leverage ratio* [9] (ratio of capital-to-total exposure, initially set at 3%) to constrain the build-up of leverage in the banking system, which effectively dampens the positive feedback loop so that harmful systemic

---

[8] A short note on capital: A bank raises capital (equity and debt) to fund the asset side of the balance sheet. Regulators require that at least 8% of RWA must be funded by Tier 1&2 capital, with the goal of influencing the capital (liability) structure of a bank. This minimum funding from common equity ensures that the balance sheet has more loss absorbing capacity, in the sense that equity holders will absorb the first loss, whereas any losses to debt holders (including depositors) will trigger a default. Tier 1 capital is meant to protect a bank's solvency, Tier 2 capital to protect depositors—together they form total (regulatory) capital. The lowest quality Tier 3 capital instruments will be phased out. Common equity and retained earnings, often called core Tier 1, are the highest quality subset of Tier 1 capital. Common equity is money paid up originally to purchase common shares of the bank, and not the value of those shares now traded at the exchange. Basel II allowed for hybrid securities to qualify for Tier 1 capital. These are bonds issued with equity-like characteristics—perpetual (no maturity), discretionary coupons (dividend like). However, innovative hybrids have callable and coupon step-up features, e.g. after 10 years, that encourage the bank to call back the bonds for cheaper refinancing. During the 2007 credit crisis, bond yields were above the coupon, which made it uneconomical for refinancing, but many banks still called back in order to manage investor's expectation, thus depleting the banks' capital. Inconsistent definition by different regulators of what qualifies for Tier 1 compounded the matter. In Basel III, innovative hybrids will be phased out of Tier 1 capital.

[9] Leverage ratios are already used by US banks, which have not fully adopted the Basel II framework. Basel III looks to standardize its definition. The numerator is Tier 1 capital. The denominator follows the definition of exposures in financial accounts. Netting between deposits and loans, and credit risk hedging of on-balance sheet exposures are not recognized in computing exposures.

deleveraging is less likely during a downturn. The leverage ratio is a good supplement to the risk-based (VaR) approach because it does not depend on any models (no modeling risk) and measures very different aspects of a bank's strength. It is also more difficult for banks to arbitrage around two capital methods at the same time.

Fifth, Basel III includes a *capital conservation buffer* over and above the minimum capital to cushion against stressful events (fat-tail risk). Banks will need to set aside another 2.5% of RWA in terms of common equity by 1 Jan 2019. A bank can draw on this buffer, but as the buffer shrinks, the bank will be restricted by law from paying dividends and bonuses.

Finally, there is an additional *countercyclical capital buffer* meant to protect the banking system from the procyclicality of credit growth. The buffer will fluctuate within the range of 0% - 2.5% depending on the credit-to-GDP ratio of the country of the credit exposure. This targets the credit growth cycle of the country where the creditor or counterparty is located, regardless of the location of the entity granting the credit. The level of the buffer and timing of release are decided by the host regulator of the creditor, using the credit-to-GDP as a common reference. More details can be found in the BIS working paper No. 317 (2010) and Basel III document *"Guidance for national authorities operating the countercyclical capital buffer"* (2010). There is a genuine concern from the industry that such a method may be prone to regulatory arbitrage and double counting with other capital buffers if not implemented carefully.

11.6 The Ideal Capital Regime

In closing this Chapter, it helps to get an ideological view of the previous capital regimes from the perspective of responses to the economic cycle, in order to appreciate where the future could lead. Figure 11-1 is a stylized representation of Basel I, Basel II and the *ideal* capital regime which, for lack of a better name, we shall call "Basel III". This is plotted against a hypothetical business cycle (the dotted line).

Basel I is an ultra-conservative regime that imposes a capital surcharge, a thick buffer against losses. In fact, it is not responsive to gyrations in the economic cycle and can be seen as a crude stress test that only differentiates positions by simple categories.

Basel II, geared for internal models, is a market-sensitive capital regime. It responds to market volatility in a *contemporaneous* way, a behavior now referred to as "point-in-time". VaR is prone to procyclicality—it is hard-wired to encourage leveraging and deleveraging just at the wrong times because, in a boom cycle, VaR understates risk and in a bust-cycle, VaR overstates risks.

"Basel III"? While we do not yet have an ideal capital regime, we do know how it should behave in theory, as Figure 11-1 illustrates. The risk charge is sensitive to the economic cycle in a *preemptive* or *countercyclical* way. The capital increases during a boom to restrain an overheated market and to build a safety buffer that can be dipped into during a future crisis. In the bust phase, for a fixed dollar position, VaR will be higher because volatility has gone up. This means that to pare back VaR (deleverage) a bank will have to sell even more positions. This pressure can be alleviated if regulatory capital is less demanding (understated) during the bust. The additional buffer that was built up earlier can now be used to buffer potential fat-tail losses.

Figure 11-1 Business cycle vs. capital held

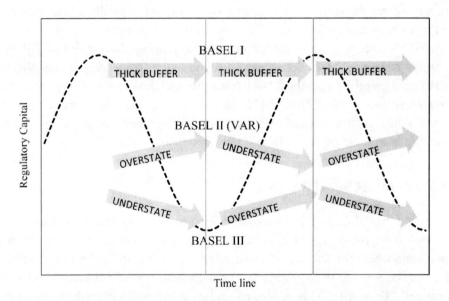

Time line

In short, the ideal capital regime will have three properties (at least): 1) it is risk-based[10], 2) it is countercyclical (thus preemptive), and 3) it is large enough to buffer against most (even if not all) extreme events.

After the 2008 credit crisis, there is a natural push among regulators to move towards a more penal regime. The Turner Review even called for a trading book

---

[10] An ideal risk model will reflect the reality of risk diversification (and risk amplification in the case of wrong-way trades) and will not suffer from double counting of different risk classes.

capital of about three times conventional levels, understandably to protect against fat-tail events. But we have to be vigilant not to sacrifice market sensitivity, lest we regress back to Basel I. Basel I is like a socialist program—everybody gets the same charge (one-size-fit-all) during good or bad economic times, whereas Basel II, notwithstanding procyclicality (which can and should be fixed) allows a bank with better risk management sophistication to conduct business more efficiently using capital charges which are commensurate with the risk. It gives the right incentives for progress.

Generally speaking, basing capital rules on traditional stress tests, or by choosing a very long observation period (multi-year) for risk measurement, has the effect of dulling the response to the market cycle. Stress testing is an unsuitable metric [11] for *capital requirements* since the risk controller is constantly fighting yesterday's battles. The next crisis will surely come, but the scenario will likely be completely different from any one selected from past history, or constructed by controllers. Stress tests are easy to perform but difficult to act on. What do you do with this very big number, especially when you know it could have easily been some other big number if your colleague had designed the stress test? What if the real probability of occurrence of the chosen scenario is one trillionth of a percent? Is the scenario worth considering? Without considering probability, stress testing may be an incomplete exercise—it will mean that financial firms are permanently braced for crisis, an approach that would be neither practical nor economical.

At the time of writing, the general sense in the industry is that the new Basel proposal is too fragmented in design and lacks a unified strategy. This may lead to significant double counting of capital buffers in some cases. In the trading book capital for example, a credit derivative will have a capital charge coming from VaR, SRC, IRC and SVaR. It is possible the total charge could be higher than that of a similar position held in the banking book (which uses the IRB model), which would encourage "regulatory arbitrage" by parking positions in the banking book. In certain situations, it may even be possible that the total charge is higher than the full notional loss of a product, which does not make intuitive sense.

---

[11] A good exception is the use of stress testing to determine the liquidity coverage ratio. Here the variables are accounting items (amounts held) and under stress they can only fall. Thus, the set of sensible scenarios to consider is rather limited, and it is possible to think of a standard stress scenario for all banks. In contrast, for market risk, the variables are market prices/ rates—each can move up or down by a large range without a clear bound. The problem is compounded by differing trading positions of banks, which can be leveraged, non-linear, long or short.

The dilemma is mainly in the area of credit securitization where trades are illiquid and may be arbitrarily classified as trading book or banking book based upon *trading intent*. These artificial boundaries in the regulation lead to similar assets having different capital requirements and modeling approaches. See a discussion paper on this topic by the FSA (2010), "The prudential regime for trading activities". Recognizing the timely need for an overhaul, the BIS is targeting for a "fundamental review" of the trading book by end of 2011.

Chapter 12

Systemic Risk Initiatives

The idea of reflexivity[1] and its connection to market crashes and systemic risks has been studied and even published since 1987. Ironically, two decades and three crises have passed and we still lack the tools to measure and safeguard our financial system from such a danger. Until very recently, most research was focused on phenomenology—explaining but not solving the problem. This chapter describes some key milestones in our understanding of the causes of systemic risk.

12.1 Soros' Reflexivity, Endogenous Risks

"The salient feature of the current financial crisis is that it was not caused by some external shock like OPEC raising the price of oil or a particular country or financial institution defaulting. The crisis was generated by the financial system itself. This fact that the defect was inherent in the system contradicts the prevailing theory, which holds that financial markets tend toward equilibrium and that deviations from the equilibrium either occur in a random manner or are caused by some sudden external event to which markets have difficulty adjusting. . . . I propose an alternative paradigm that differs from the current one in two respects. First, financial markets do not reflect prevailing conditions accurately; they provide a picture that is always biased or distorted in one way or another. Second, the distorted views held by market participants and expressed in market prices can, under certain circumstances, affect the so-called fundamentals that market prices are supposed to reflect. This two-way circular connection between market prices and the underlying reality I call reflexivity."

(George Soros's testimony during Senate Oversight Committee hearing, on the role played by hedge funds in the 2008 crisis)

---

[1] We use this term generically to mean what many researchers also call feedback loop, vicious cycle, endogenous risk and network externalities.

Soros first described the idea of market reflexivity in his book "The alchemy of finance" in 1987. His ideas ran against conventional economic theory that markets tend towards equilibrium as suggested by efficient market theory. Soros argued that the market is always biased in either direction (equilibrium is rare), and markets can influence the event they are supposed to anticipate in a circular, self-reinforcing way. This he termed reflexivity. However, this early reflexivity idea was couched in philosophy and behavioral science, not risk management.

Trading is decision-making under uncertainty. Conventional risk modeling sees trading as a "single-person game against nature" where price uncertainty is driven by exogenous factors, and not impacted by the decision maker. This is frequentist thinking—an impartial observer scientifically taking measurements, inferring conclusions and ultimately making decisions. This paradigm originates from the tradition of *general equilibrium theory* developed by Samuelson (1947), where macroeconomics is the aggregate behavior of a model where market participants or "agents" are rational optimizing individuals. Under this paradigm, statistical techniques can be used and indeed have been applied with great success, especially during normal market conditions.

However, during crises, conventional risk models break down. Market dynamics behave more like a "game against other gamers"—the drivers can be endogenous. Irrational herding behavior can occur without any external shocks. Prices can spiral out of control during a crash purely due to sentiment within the market. This could be caused by feedback loop effects between the actions of participants and outcomes, and spillover effect among participants within the system. Hence, after the 2008 crisis, there is a paradigm shift towards viewing the market as a complex adaptive system.

In the late 1990's, researchers began to formulate these effects in terms of game theory, Bayesian thinking and network science. The *network externalities* (spillover) arise because each trader's decision does not take into account the collective interest but ultimately affects it. For example, in a crash each participant hopes to beat the others to the exit. This risk of contagion increases with positional uniformity and leverage. It argues for the role of the regulator to intervene in free markets and to monitor for systemic risks on behalf of the collective interest.

Morris and Shin (1999) pointed out a blind spot in conventional risk management practice—VaR does not take into account the feedback loop between actions and outcomes. When many dominant players in the market follow a uniform strategy, the consequences of the feedback loop can be disastrous. For example, the 1987 crash was caused by *portfolio insurance*, a popular program trading strategy whereby institutions increase leverage in a rising market and deleverage in a falling market[2]. The selling frenzy fed on itself on "Black Monday". In 1997 – 1998, the Asian crisis was caused by concerted currency attacks by speculators, while local governments defended their currency pegs. Here, key players were amassing highly uniform positions.

Figure 12-1 Bi-modal distribution of a "switching strategy"

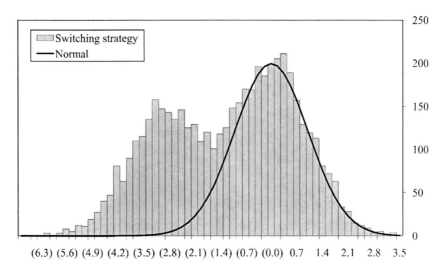

The authors proved that when a collective strategy is dominant, the usual "bell-shaped" return distribution can become distorted. Using the yen carry unwind in Oct. 1998 as an example of a *switching strategy*[3], the return distribution was shown to be bi-modal (has two peaks!). Hence, VaR will completely underestimate the true risk. If you plot the *empirical* distribution during that turbulent period, you will *not* see any evidence of bi-modality. This is because the bi-modal behavior happens only during the brief period of panic selling, too short to be captured by statistics. We can however simulate this behavior (see Spreadsheet 12.1). Figure 12-1 illustrates the bi-modal distribution of a switch-

---

[2] The program effectively tries to mimic the payoff of a call option so that the downside of the portfolio is protected. It does this by calculating all the correct sizes and levels to buy or sell. Execution is automated.

[3] Hedge funds attacked the yen in 1998 while the central bank, BoJ, was hopelessly defending the yen. The tide turned after the Russian debt default (Aug 98) and the LTCM debacle (Sep 98) caused nervous speculators to abandon the attack. In this case, certain events or price levels caused the market (which held a uniform position) to switch strategy en-masse. The rush-to-exit (unwind) caused the yen to rise by 15% in the week of 5-9 Oct.

ing strategy where speculators have a stop-loss exit strategy slightly below the current level.

Adrian and Shin (2008) analyzed the role of feedback loops in exacerbating the 2008 crisis. The key idea is that *leverage targeting* by banks gives rise to procyclicality in the system which accelerates the boom-bust cycle. Consider a stylized bank's balance sheet presented in Figure 12-2. Assets and liabilities are always balanced; the balancing variable is the (share holder's) equity. Hence:

$$equity = asset - debt \tag{12.1}$$

and we define:

$$leverage = \frac{asset}{equity} \tag{12.2}$$

Figure 12-2 A stylized bank's balance sheet illustration

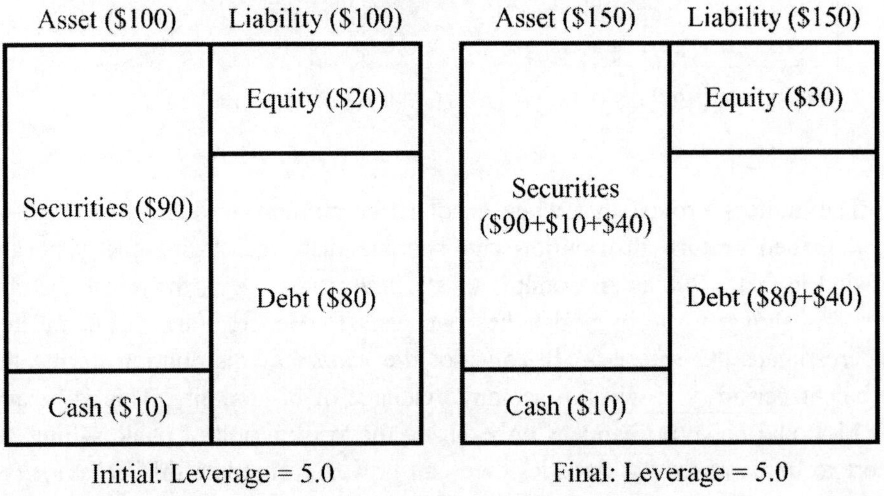

Asset ($100)	Liability ($100)
	Equity ($20)
Securities ($90)	Debt ($80)
Cash ($10)	

Asset ($150)	Liability ($150)
	Equity ($30)
Securities ($90+$10+$40)	Debt ($80+$40)
Cash ($10)	

Initial: Leverage = 5.0   Final: Leverage = 5.0

In the left panel, leverage is 5(=100/20) times. Suppose the price of (risky) securities goes up by $10, assets will increase to $110 by mark-to-market accounting and leverage will fall to 3.67(=110/30). In other words, asset growth and leverage growth should be *inversely* correlated if there is no change in positions. Surprisingly, empirical evidence by the authors showed that asset growth and leverage growth are *highly positively correlated* across US financial institutions as a cohort. This suggests that banks actively manage their positions to maintain some target leverage.

Hence, leverage is procyclical and that in turn can cause perverse asset price behavior. Consider the right panel; in order to maintain its initial leverage of 5 (suppose this is the target), the bank will borrow $40 more in debt to buy more securities that will bring assets to $150. Contrary to textbook norm[4], the demand curve for the asset becomes upward-sloping. The greater demand for the asset will put upward pressure on prices, price rally will lead to a stronger balance sheet, which necessitates even more purchases of assets to maintain the leverage target. Demand generates more demand in a self-reinforcing loop and this can cause an asset price boom as shown in Figure 12-3 (left panel).

Figure 12-3 Asset price boom and bust caused by procyclicality of leverage

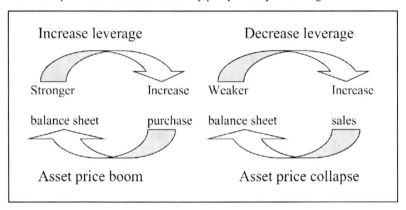

In an economic downturn, the mechanism works in reverse (right panel). Falling asset prices cause losses to the balance sheet, and leverage as defined in (12.2) increases. This will prompt banks to deleverage to maintain the target by selling off assets to pay off debt. The selling into a falling market can cause a downward price spiral and a sudden increase in supply (more people wanting to sell)—the supply curve becomes downward-sloping. This is called the *loss spiral*.

Another negative feedback is the *margin spiral*. Regulators require a minimum amount of capital to be set aside as a safety buffer (like a trading margin) usually determined by VaR. This can be represented simplistically as the cash

---

[4] In classic economic theory, the typical demand curve (plot of Price vs. Quantity) is negatively sloping, and the typical supply curve is positively sloping. The crossover of the two curves (on the Price vs. Quantity plot) gives the equilibrium price where demand is satisfied by supply.

portion on the asset side in Figure 12-2. The problem is VaR is low during a boom and high during a downturn (see Chapter 7). Therefore, the same amount of cash margin can support a lot more risky securities during a boom than during a downturn—encouraging leverage during a boom and loss-cutting during a bust.

The *"Geneva report"* (2009)[5] identified key systemic risk drivers and negative feedback loops which contributed to the 2008 crisis; policy recommendations to address systemic risks were also discussed. Taleb (2009a) wrote that markets are subjected to positive feedback loops, which cause fat-tails—it prevents the workings of the Central Limit Theorem (which requires i.i.d.) that establishes thin-tails under aggregation of risks.

12.2 Crashmetrics©

Crashmetrics was developed by Wilmott and Hua in 1998. Its purpose is to locate and estimate the worst-case scenario loss for a bank as a firm. The idea is that, since crashes cannot be delta-hedged in a continuous manner, especially with the presence of non-linear derivatives, it makes sense to ask what is the worst loss for a bank given its positions. If a bank knows that this loss can threaten its survival then it can *static hedge*[6] this vulnerability. The static hedging with derivatives can be optimized to make the worst-case loss as small as possible. This is called *Platinum Hedging* (not covered here) and is proprietary to Crashmetrics.

Crashmetrics for one stock

Unlike VaR, Crashmetrics does not make any assumptions on return distributions. There are also no prior assumptions on the probability, size and timing of crashes. The only assumption made is that crashes will fall in certain ranges (say from +100% to -50% price change).

Let's consider a portfolio of derivatives on a single underlying asset. If the asset price changes by δS, the portfolio value will change by:

---

[5] Brunnermeier, M., Crocket, A., Persaud, A., Shin, H. S. (2009) "The Fundamental Principles of Financial Regulation", Geneva Reports on the World Economy 11.

[6] Dynamic hedging (or delta hedging) of a derivative involves continuously buying and selling the underlying asset of that derivative in such as way that the combination has a delta (and perhaps also other risk sensitivities) of zero at any point in time. A static hedge, in contrast, is not adjusted over time and is targeted to protect very specific vulnerabilities.

$$\delta\Pi = F(\delta S) \tag{12.3}$$

where $F(.)$ represents the sum of all pricing functions of the derivatives. So if it is an option, $F(.)$ is the Black-Scholes equation, if it is a bond, $F(.)$ is the bond pricing formula, and so on.

We need to find the worst-loss for the portfolio i.e. the minima for $F(\delta S)$. In practice, to perform this minimization we need to constrain the domain of δS to within a finite range $[\delta S^-, \delta S^+]$. The risk controller just needs to assume a large but realistic range. The minimization problem then becomes:

$$\min_{\delta S^- < \delta S < \delta S^+} F(\delta S) \tag{12.4}$$

For complicated portfolios, it is possible to have local and global minimas (to be explained later). We are interested in finding δS which gives the global minima.

If the portfolio contains a vanilla option, $F(.)$ will be a continuous function and we can approximate $\delta\Pi$ using a Taylor expansion:

Delta-gamma approach: $\delta\Pi = \Delta\delta S + 0.5\Gamma\delta S^2 + ... \tag{12.5}$

where Δ and Γ are the delta and gamma as defined in Section 4.1. The worst-case loss can be found by making the first derivative $\delta\Pi/\delta S = 0$ which leads to the result:

$$\delta\Pi_{worst} = -\frac{\Delta^2}{2\Gamma} \tag{12.6}$$

Although this example is unrealistic (most banks would trade in non-vanilla options), it illustrates the procedure. Geometrically speaking, the minimization procedure involves searching the whole solution profile of $\delta\Pi$ to find the lowest trough[7] with slope $\delta\Pi/\delta S = 0$. For two assets, the profile is a surface; for N assets, the profile is an N-dimensional hypercube.

---

[7] It can happen that, for a complicated portfolio, there may be multiple troughs in the solution space. The lowest trough is called the global minimum, all other toughs are local minima. A good optimization program is able to find the global minimum while avoiding all the local minima.

Extension to multi-asset / multi-benchmark model

To extend the model to multi-asset, we need to relate the extreme moves of each asset to the extreme moves of one (or more) benchmark index. For example, we can map all US stocks to the S&P 500 index. The benchmark mapping is necessary to reduce the dimension to a manageable size. If the benchmark moves by X% then the i'th asset moves by k_iX% where k_i is the *crash coefficient* for asset-i. The crash coefficient is estimated using the beta approach (see equation (2.37)) except that we only use the 40 largest (extreme tail) daily moves in the history for asset-i.

Figure 12-4 shows a scatter plot for HK Electric's stock price returns versus its benchmark, the Hang Seng index, using the last 25 years of data. The circle and the oval show two distinct return regimes—normal and extreme. The slope of the (dotted) regression line for the full data set is the beta, whereas the slope of the extreme data set (line with higher slope) gives the crash coefficient, k=0.84. Because of its shape, the diagram is called the *Saturn ring effect*. The crash coefficient is higher compared to the beta because assets are expected to be highly correlated during a crash. Furthermore, the crash coefficient is found to be more stable than the beta, which makes this method more robust.

Figure 12-4 "Saturn ring" effect showing different return regimes

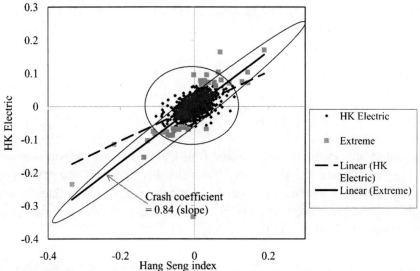

With the presence of exotic options, the delta-gamma approach will not work and a bank will need to do re-pricing of each deal in finding the worst-loss. For a

multi-asset/ single index model, the minimization problem then becomes:

$$\min_{\delta X^- < \delta X < \delta X^+} \sum_i g_i(k_i \delta X) \qquad (12.7)$$

where δX is the change in the index, constrained to a finite range $[\delta X^-, \delta X^+]$. The sum is across i assets, all benchmarked to the same index. $g_i(.)$ is the pricing function for asset i.

The idea can be extended to multi-risk factor where each factor is mapped to a benchmark. For example, we can have benchmarks for equities, rates, volatility, foreign exchange and commodities. A deal may be mapped to one or more benchmarks. For example, an equity option can be mapped to an equity index benchmark and a volatility benchmark (such as the VIX index). Suppose there are i risk factors and j benchmarks ($j < i$), then the minimization problem becomes:

$$\min_{\delta X_j^- < \delta X_j < \delta X_j^+} \sum_n g_n(k_{ij} \delta X_j) \qquad (12.8)$$

where the crash coefficient k_{ij} is the sensitivity of risk factor-i to an extreme move in benchmark-j. We need to solve for the set $\{\delta X_1, \delta X_2, .., \delta X_j\}$ where each element (a benchmark) is constrained by a user-defined range, such that the overall portfolio value is the lowest. Note, the summation is across n number of *deals*, where the pricing function of a deal $g_n(.)$ can be a function of multiple risk factors generally.

Simple illustration

It is possible to program an optimization algorithm to locate the global minimum in an N-dimensional hypercube efficiently and to compute the relevant hedge ratios (the so-called *Platinum hedges*). This is a sophisticated exercise and is proprietary to Crashmetrics. Here we will illustrate using a simple "brute force" implementation which can be used as a bank's stress/scenario testing to supplement VaR. The advantage is that whilst conventional scenario testing points to the risk of some hypothetical made-up situations which could be unrealistic, Crashmetrics points objectively to a bank's individual vulnerabilities. This should be appealing to regulators who can then compare worst-case losses among banks.

We first map the universe of all risk factors to five benchmark indices as shown in Table 12-1. The crash coefficient (k_i) for risk factor-i is estimated with respect to its benchmark index. When the benchmark index is stressed by δX, that risk factor is stressed by $k_i \, \delta X$. In effect, the crash coefficients link risk factors to benchmarks. Hence, by stressing all 5 benchmarks, we effectively stress *all* risk factors.

Secondly, we grid the hypercube. Suppose we have a small bank whose core business is in rates, FX and options trading, thus, we only need 3 benchmarks. Suppose today's state of the world is given by: (USD 10yr swap, US dollar index, VIX index) = (3%, 78, 27%). We assume a range where the extreme moves can happen for each benchmark for example: (USD 10yr swap, US dollar index, VIX index) = (0 – 10%, 50 – 100, 2 – 70%), and grid each range into 20 equal segments. Then the hypercube will contain 20x20x20= 8,000 states (or scenarios).

Table 12-1 Mapping of risk factors to Crashmetrics benchmarks

Risk factor class (across all countries)	Crashmetrics benchmark
Equities	S&P 500 index
Interest rates	USD 10yr swap
Foreign exchange rate	US dollar index (measures dollar strength relative to a basket of currencies)
Volatilities (all asset types)	VIX index (measures implied volatility)
Commodities	S&P Goldman Sachs commodity index

Thirdly, we perform *reverse stress tests*. The bank determines the maximum loss ψ that will cause it to fail. This critical level of loss is a function of the bank's own balance sheet strength and its ability to raise emergency funds. The bank's positions are re-priced for all scenarios in the hypercube. The scenarios that create a loss larger than ψ are highlighted as "red" zones in the hypercube.

Lastly, expert judgment is required of the risk controller. What is the *probability* of occurrence of the "red" zones? This is a function of how far they are from the current state and known structural relationships of the markets. It requires expert knowledge of probability and correlation. For example, if a "red" zone happens when rates are at 10%, the odds are really immaterial for say a one-year risk horizon. Is it likely for rates to move from 3% to 10% in a recessionary, low policy-rate environment? Also if the "red zone" suggests a scenario of extreme sell-down in equities and extremely high rates; this is also highly unlikely (perhaps even unrealistic) because equities and rates are known to be structurally correlated due to fund flows, flight-to-quality and central bank policy responses.

This "brute force" method illustrates a rough way to locate a bank's vulnerabilities. The method is crude because errors can arise from the estimation of crash coefficients and the choice of benchmarking. It should always be followed by stress tests targeted at a bank's specific vulnerabilities (or risk concentration).

But the problems with traditional stress test are that the scenario is subjectively determined and the resulting loss number prohibitively large. Without any assessment of the probability of occurrence, such a risk measure is difficult to act on. As a step to overcome this problem, Rebonato (2007, 2010)[8] developed a non-frequentist approach for stress testing extreme events which incorporates the risk manager's prior beliefs or expert judgment.

12.3 New York Fed CoVaR

Contagion VaR or CoVaR was introduced by Adrian and Brunnermeier (2009) to measure the spillover risk across financial institutions. Specifically, it is defined as the VaR of institution-i conditional on another institution-j being in distress i.e. j's return being at its VaR level.

CoVaR measures *volatility* spillover in a non-causal sense. The idea is that institutions often hold similar positions or are exposed to common systemic risk factors. These "crowded trades" give rise to dynamic co-opetition games which can cause liquidity spirals. For example, in an asset fire-sale or banks' hoarding of liquidity, individual actions by banks may appear prudent for the bank but the impact on the system is often not macroprudential. CoVaR measures this spillover or network effect.

We recall the definition of VaR as the q-quantile:

$$\Pr(X^i \leq VaR_q^i) = q \qquad (12.9)$$

where X^i is a variable of institution-i and VaR is a negative number. The time series X^i may be the daily PL vector of the bank's positions, or *changes* in the

---

[8] A book by Rebonato R. (2007), *Plight of the fortune tellers: why we need to manage financial risk differently.* Some of these ideas are formalized in the paper by Frankland et al. (2008).

bank's total financial assets in its balance sheet, depending on what type of spillover risk we want to measure.

The CoVaR of institution-j conditional on institution-i being in distress is then defined as:

$$\Pr\left(X^{j} \leq CoVaR_{q}^{j|i} \mid X^{i} \leq VaR_{q}^{i}\right) = q \qquad (12.10)$$

We are most interested in the case where j is the entire financial system (j=system). In this case, the institution-i's *contribution of spillover* to the financial system (j) is defined by:

$$\Delta CoVaR_{q}^{j|i} = CoVaR_{q}^{j|i} - VaR_{q}^{i} \qquad (12.11)$$

Studying data on US financial institutions, the authors found evidence of spillover—that CoVaR tends to be larger than VaR in general, making equation (12.11) positive. Furthermore, a linear regression of ΔCoVaR and VaR shows an absence of a linear relationship, which suggests that conventional VaR does not contain information on systemic risks at all, hence, the need for CoVaR.

Figure 12-5 Schematic of CoVaR network (numbers are hypothetical)

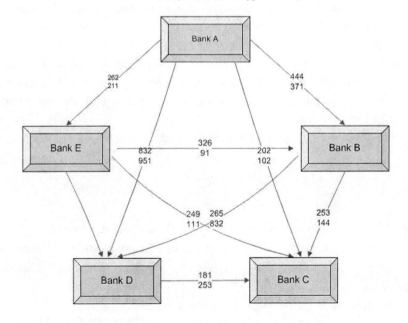

Figure 12-5 shows a schematic of CoVaR between various institutions. CoVaR of institution-i depends on the risk-taking activities of other institutions in the network. CoVaR is also directional—CoVaR of institution-i conditional on j does not equal CoVaR of institution-j conditional on i in general. This is illustrated as two different numbers on each connecting line in Figure 12-5.

The systemic risk regulator would in principle be able to collect all the required information X^i from each institution and calculate an institution's contribution to systemic risk using equation (12.11). Regulatory risk capital should then be a function of not just VaR but also ΔCoVaR—large contributors to systemic risk should be surcharged with higher capital.

Estimation of CoVaR

A convenient way to estimate CoVaR is by quantile regression (see Section 2.13). Here we assume j is the financial system and is related to bank-i's return variable by a linear model[9]:

$$X^j = \alpha + \beta X^i + \varepsilon^j \tag{12.12}$$

where X's are a function of time t (which we have suppressed for brevity), and the error term ε^j is i.i.d. We denote the inverse CDF by $F^{-1}(q)$ for a given q-quantile. Then the inverse CDF for (12.12) is written:

$$F_j^{-1}(q \mid X^i) = \alpha_q + \beta_q X^i \tag{12.13}$$

where the new parameters α_q and β_q contain also the inverse CDF of ε^j. From the definition of VaR as a quantile function or inverse CDF, equation (12.13) actually represents the VaR with confidence level $(1-q)$ of system-j *conditional on the returns of institution-i.*

We estimate the conditional quantile function (12.13) by solving for the parameters α_q and β_q that minimize:

---

[9] For ease of explanation, we illustrate a simplified version of the authors' paper. In the original paper, X^i is conditional also on a vector of external state variables M_{t-1}, and the stochastic third term (hence volatility) is also conditional on X^i.

$$\min_{\alpha_q,\beta_q}\sum_{t}\begin{cases} q\,|\,X^{j}-(\alpha_{q}+\beta_{q}X^{i})\,| & if\ X^{j}-(\alpha_{q}+\beta_{q}X^{i})\geq 0 \\ (1-q)\,|\,X^{j}-(\alpha_{q}+\beta_{q}X^{i})\,| & if\ X^{j}-(\alpha_{q}+\beta_{q}X^{i})<0 \end{cases} \quad (12.14)$$

Since CoVaR is defined as the VaR of *j* conditional on bank-*i*'s return being at its VaR level (i.e. set $X^{i}=VaR^{i}_{q}$), the CoVaR is thus given by:

$$CoVaR_{q}^{j|i} \equiv \hat{F}_{j}^{-1}(q\,|\,VaR_{q}^{i})=\hat{\alpha}_{q}+\hat{\beta}_{q}VaR_{q}^{i} \quad (12.15)$$

The parameters with the ^ are estimates from (12.14). Spreadsheet 12.2 illustrates the calculation of CoVaR using the Excel Solver.

In the original paper, the idea of CoVaR was extended to make X^{i}, X^{j} and (12.12) conditional on other lagged variables M_{t-1}. These could be systemic macro variables—such as the VIX index, repo spreads, T-bill yields—or a firm's institutional characteristics—such as maturity mismatch, leverage, relative size, etc. In particular, the authors found that, on a one-year lagged basis, a more negative ΔCoVaR is associated with higher values of the institutional characteristics just mentioned. The implication is that if regulators can predict, based on today's firm characteristics, what the ΔCoVaR will be for next year, it can levy a preemptive capital surcharge. This means ΔCoVaR capital could potentially offset the procyclicality weakness of conventional VaR. For further details, the reader can refer to the paper by Adrian and Brunnermeier (2009).

12.4 The Austrian Model and BOE RAMSI

In 2006, researchers at the Austrian Nationalbank (OeNB) introduced a model to measure the *transmission* of contagion risk in the banking system. Called *Systemic Risk Monitor* (SRM), it is based on the work of Elsinger et al. (2006a, 2006b) which combines standard risk management techniques with a network model[10] to capture the interbank feedback and potential domino effect of bank defaults. Only by looking at risk from the system perspective can regulators spot two key problem areas that could lead to financial system instability—correlated exposures and financial inter-linkages.

This section gives a simplified illustration of a highly complex series of models. The interested reader is referred to the original papers[11]. Figure 12-6 is a

---

[10] The network model is due to an earlier work by Eisenberg and Noe (2001).
[11] For a non-technical overview please see "Systemic Risk Monitor: A model for systemic risk

schematic of the SRM that was applied to the Austrian banking system. Each bank in the system is represented by a portfolio.

Figure 12-6 Basic structure of the SRM

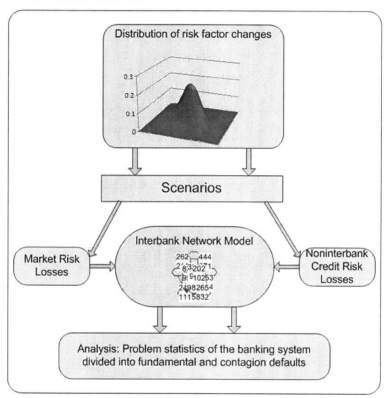

The model structure splits a bank's risk into three parts—a collection of tradable assets i.e. stocks, bonds, forex ("market risk losses" box), loans to nonbanks ("non-interbank credit risk losses" box) and interbank positions ("interbank network model" box). The third part captures the mutual obligations or counterparty risks which are highly contagious.

The model uses a group of risk factors including market and macroeconomic factors. The (marginal) distribution of each factor is estimated separately every quarter for a one-quarter horizon. The correlation structure is modeled separately using a copula. The SRM model then draws random scenarios from this multivariate distribution (the top box in Figure 12-6). The scenarios are then translated to portfolio PL. For market risk losses, this is a straightforward revaluation of

analysis and stress testing of banking systems", OeNB Financial Stability Report 11.

deals based on new scenarios. But for loans to nonbanks, we need to use a credit
risk model to calculate portfolio losses. For this purpose, SRM uses CreditRisk+
developed[12] by Credit Suisse in 1997.

The innovation of the Austrian model is its network model of the interbank
which checks whether a bank is able to fulfill its financial obligations as a result
of simulated movements in assets prices and loans, given its balance sheet
situation and mutual obligations with other banks. It does this by using a
clearing procedure which we shall illustrate using a toy example from the
original paper Elsinger et al. (2006a).

Suppose there are N banks in the system; bank-i is characterized by net value
e_i and liability l_{ij} against bank-j in the system. The entire banking system is thus
described by an $N \times N$ matrix L and a vector of values $e=\{e_1, e_2, .., e_N\}$.
e represents asset positions such as bonds, stocks, nonbank loans, minus liability
positions such as deposits and bonds issued by the bank itself.

Consider a three-bank system with $e=(1, 1, 1)$ and with liability structure
given by:

$$L = \begin{pmatrix} 0 & 0 & 2 \\ 3 & 0 & 1 \\ 3 & 1 & 0 \end{pmatrix} \tag{12.16}$$

where the numbers are in $ billions. For instance, bank 2 has a liability of $3
billion with bank 1 and a liability of $1 billion with bank 3. The diagonals are all
$0 since a bank will not have a liability with itself. The total liabilities of each
bank *due to* the system is given by the vector $d=(2, 4, 4)$, the row sum of L. Note
that the total income *due from* the system is given by the column sum of L.

The clearing mechanism is a redistribution scheme—if the net value of a
bank becomes negative, the bank becomes insolvent. This net value is the
income from non-interbank activities e_i plus income received from other banks
(part of L) minus its liabilities to other banks (part of L). Once a bank becomes
insolvent, the claims of the creditor banks are satisfied proportionally, i.e.
distributed according to the percentage of total liability owed. To implement this
proportion sharing, we need to divide L by d to get a normalized matrix in
percentage:

[12] This model (unlike Creditmetrics) models only default risk, migrational risk is excluded. The
default risk is not related to the capital structure of the firm but is modeled simply as a Poisson
distribution.

$$\pi_{ij} = \begin{cases} \dfrac{l_{ij}}{d_i} & \text{if } d_i > 0 \\ 0 & \text{otherwise} \end{cases} \tag{12.17}$$

In our example, this becomes:

$$\Pi = \begin{pmatrix} 0 & 0 & 1 \\ 0.75 & 0 & 0.25 \\ 0.75 & 0.25 & 0 \end{pmatrix} \tag{12.18}$$

The network model is represented by a *clearing payment vector, p.* The model has to respect the limited liability of banks (i.e. it cannot pay more than what it has in capital) and proportion sharing. p_i represents the total payment made by bank-i under a clearing mechanism.

$$p_i = \begin{cases} d_i & \text{if } \sum_{j=1}^{N} \pi_{ji} p_j + e_i \geq d_i \\ \sum_{j=1}^{N} \pi_{ji} p_j + e_i & \text{if } d_i > \sum_{j=1}^{N} \pi_{ji} p_j + e_i \geq 0 \\ 0 & \text{if } \sum_{j=1}^{N} \pi_{ji} p_j + e_i < 0 \end{cases} \tag{12.19}$$

The first condition says the bank has enough income to pay off its total liability, and so it pays d_i due to the system. In the second condition, it pays proportionally as determined by weights π_{ji}, and in the third, its payment is floored at zero due to limited liability. In the last two cases, because $p_i < d_i$, bank-i has defaulted with recovery rate p_i/d_i.

To solve for the vector p, Eisenberg and Noe (2001) proposed a procedure called "*fictitious default algorithm*" and proved that the procedure converges to a unique solution after at most N iterations. The procedure starts by assuming all banks fully honor their obligations i.e. $p=d$. After this payment, if all banks have positive value the procedure stops. Second iteration: if a bank now has a negative value, it is declared insolvent and its payment is given by the clearing formula (12.19). In the example, this is the case for Bank 2. We keep the other banks payments fixed as per the previous iteration. It can happen that another bank which was positively valued in the first iteration becomes negatively valued (defaulted) in the second iteration because it only received partial payments from Bank 2. This is indeed what happened to Bank 3. Then Bank 3 has to be declared insolvent and we move on to the third iteration and so forth.

A bank that becomes insolvent in the first iteration is considered fundamentally defaulted i.e. due to macroeconomic shocks. A bank that defaults in subsequent iterations is "dragged into insolvency" and represents a case of *contagion default*. Using the algorithm we can show that the clearing solution is $p=(2, 1.87, 3.47)$, Bank 2 is fundamentally defaulted and Bank 3 experienced a contagion default. Spreadsheet 12.3 provides a worked-out solution.

In practice, L comes from balance sheet information of banks and e is a function of risky positions held by banks—both of which are at the disposal of an ardent regulator. Market/economic scenarios sampled from the joint distribution are applied to e to simulate the risks caused by external shocks over a 3-month horizon. Spreadsheet 12.3 also provides an example where e is randomly simulated to calculate the probabilities of fundamental and contagion defaults of the three banks.

The SRM system is a powerful tool that can simulate systemic risk conditions and identify vulnerabilities in a banking system. Some analyses that could be carried out include:

1. Stress testing—the user can simulate specific scenarios, for example, a 5% fall in GDP.
2. Estimation of probabilities of fundamental and contagion defaults of each bank in the system.
3. By judiciously selecting relevant risk factors for simulation, one can study the loss distribution due purely to credit migrations, market risk, contagion risk, or combinations of various sources of risk.
4. The loss distributions from (3) can be used for VaR-type analysis for the whole banking system or for segments of the banking system.
5. The central bank can perform policy experiments, for example, to test the impact of a one-time rate hike of 200bp.

In 2009, the Bank of England (BOE) embarked on a project to model the network funding liquidity risk of the UK banking system. The model is a more sophisticated extension of the Austrian model and is known as RAMSI (*Risk Assessment Model for Systemic Institutions*). RAMSI is a sequence of models designed in a modular architecture (see Figure 12-7).

Figure 12-7 RAMSI framework

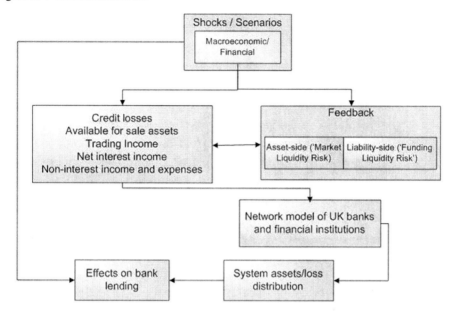

Figure 12-8 RAMSI model dynamics

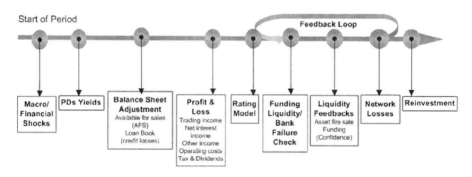

The innovation of RAMSI is in its modeling of feedback effects: the feedback associated with asset fire-sales following a bank default and the liability-side funding liquidity feedback. Unlike the single-period Austrian model, RAMSI is a multi-step model with a three-year forecast horizon (see Figure 12-8). A preliminary model description is available from the BOE[13].

---

[13] See BOE working paper No. 372, "Funding liquidity risk in a quantitative model of systemic stability" (June 2009).

12.5 The Global Systemic Risk Regulator

The 2008 crisis has highlighted the complete absence of regulation of systemic risk. The Turner Review aptly described this situation as "global finance without global government: faultlines in regulatory approach". National regulators do not have cross-jurisdiction powers and coordination among regulators is not effective and timely. Even within the same country, supervision is often fragmented with multiple regulators looking at different but overlapping aspects of the financial system such as securities houses, futures trading, banking, insurance and financial accounting. Quite the opposite, global banks operate across international borders, often exploiting differences in regulations so as to be as capital-efficient as possible, for example, by "migrating" operations to regulatory-or-tax-friendly jurisdictions.

There is asymmetry of information here: a bank knows exactly what its offshore branches are doing, but not what other banks are doing. An individual regulator knows only what the banks within its borders are doing and not about offshore banks. The informational disconnect creates a faultline where systemic risks can grow undetected by any one party.

Compounding the problem is that a new class of institutions (what is now known as "shadow banking") has emerged that functions like a bank but is not regulated as a bank. These are entities such as SIVs (special investment vehicles), pure investment banks and mutual funds, which perform the essential banking function of "maturity transformation"—effectively borrowing on short-term (liability), and lending or investing on long-term (asset). It is a crucial function that provides social and economic value but it creates risks—there is price risk on the asset side and liquidity risk on the funding side. This large shadow banking system contributes to systemic risk (contagion) because their positions are often "on the same side" as regulated banks. In a crisis, they may face investor redemptions in the same way that a bank may face "bank runs", even though they are off the radar screens of regulators, and are often "too big to fail".

These faultlines argue for the creation of systemic risk regulators, of which three were set up in 2009: the *Financial Stability Board* (FSB) which represents the G-20 nations, the *European Systemic Risk Board* (ESRB) from the EU and the *Financial Services Oversight Council* (FSOC) from the US. It seems logical that a *single* global regulator would solve some of the coordination problems previously mentioned and reduce political lobbying. But, in the near term, this will unlikely materialize for the same reasons that one cannot find a global government today.

Let's for the moment envision how such a regulatory body would work. It should have executive powers to investigate a bank[14] (in a more intrusive way), technical expertise, political independence and a modus-operandi not unlike that of a tsunami warning center. Some of the technical roles it will perform may include:

1. Determine the optimal parameters for VaR systems and standardize these for banks.
2. Provide a common set of risk factors and market data history for all banks so that their VaRs are comparable.
3. Collate daily all the PL vectors from banks in the most granular format, say by deal vs. risk factor breakdown (a bank still computes its PL vector using its own system). Counterparty information per deal is also collected. Let us call this multidimensional dataset a *hypercube*. The hypercube contains all information on positions and risks of each bank.
4. Use "smart" computer programs to analyze the data hypercube. This could ferret out information such as: pockets of risk concentrations, hidden correlation risk clusters[15] in a bank or within the banking system, counterparty risk concentrations between systemically important firms, etc.
5. Collate from banks the aggregated PL vector for the computation of a bank's VaR.
6. Collate balance sheet information and counterparty names for interbank funding activities.
7. Calculate CoVaR of each bank to analyze the spillover risk in the banking system. This measures potential *market risk* contagion and could highlight banks which are most "contagious".
8. Use network models to simulate potential *default risk* contagion in the banking system. The PL vectors from each bank can be used to generate a (empirical) joint distribution for the simulation, thereby accounting for non-linear positions held.
9. Issue warnings if overall systemic risk is above a certain threshold, or if there is undue concentration of systemic risks in certain markets or institutions.

Most of these ideas are within reach of today's risk technology and knowledge. At the time of this writing, U.S. legislation is pushing for over-the-counter derivatives to be processed, or cleared, with an independent third party. This

---

[14] We use the word "bank" generically to also include all other systemically important institutions (shadow banks).
[15] For example see the article "Detection and Analysis of Correlation Clusters and Market Risk Concentration" by Oest and Rollbuhler, *Wilmott Magazine July 2010.*

would set the stage for greater transparency and availability of data for a system-ic regulator.

For example, in the testimony to the U.S. House of Representative, Lo (2009) recommended the data collection and centralized monitoring of seven aspects of systemic risks: leverage, liquidity, correlation, concentration, sensitivities (to market movement), implicit guarantees, and connectedness. For a recent devel-opment in systemic risk measurement, read Billio et al. (2010).

12.6 Spreadsheet

12.1 Researchers have found that trading strategies which involve "switching" can cause systemic contagion when the majority of participants are collec-tively applying the same strategy. The usual "bell-shaped" return distribution can become distorted (bi-modal) even though this is *not* reflected in empiri-cal distribution. When this happens, VaR is an inaccurate measure of risk. Aim: simulate a stop-loss strategy where the stop-loss is 0.2 standard devia-tions (s.d.) below the current price, and plot the resulting return distribution. Note: the main process is simulated using a standard normal distribution. When the stop-loss is triggered, players will sell into a falling market and cause a 3 s.d. fall in the *next* time step. This switching strategy generates a bi-modal distribution.

12.2 CoVaR (contagion VaR) is a recent development that measures the spillover risks among financial institutions. It is the VaR of an institution conditional on another institution being in distress (i.e. having a loss at/beyond its VaR level). CoVaR is estimated using quantile regression. Aim: illustrates CoVaR using two hypothetical return time series from two institutions (i and j). Action: CoVaR of j conditional on i is solved by using the Excel Solver. Try to solve for CoVaR of i conditional on j instead. Are they the same?

12.3 The *Austrian model* is one of the earliest models for network risks of the banking system. Using a clearing procedure, it checks whether a bank is able to fulfill its payment obligations to the system as a result of simulated movements in assets prices and loans, given its balance sheet situation and mutual obligations with other banks. Aim: illustrate a simple network model for a banking system with three banks, and illustrate the *fictitious default algorithm* used to solve the model. Note: the first sheet shows a static exam-ple and the second shows a dynamic example where the vector e is simulated using geometric Brownian motion (using VB macros). You may change the blue cells to modify the banks' balance sheet initial conditions.

PART IV

INTRODUCTION TO BUBBLE VALUE-AT-RISK (BuVAR)

Chapter 13

Market BuVaR

"I can calculate the motion of heavenly bodies, but not the madness of people?"
(Sir Isaac Newton, mathematician and physicist, 1642 – 1727)

13.1 Why an Alternative to VaR

The 2008 credit crisis has challenged the foundation and the tradition of VaR as the standard risk measure and the de facto metric for minimum capital. As we have seen in Part II, the weaknesses in VaR had been well-known and debated in the academia for some time, for example, see Danielsson et al. (2001). It is only in 2008 that these weaknesses were put to the test.

Three major weaknesses highlight the need for a better alternative:

1) *VaR as a number is not very useful.* It may have a meaning but it is not very useful. Recall that a 97.5% VaR is not the quantity you could lose with 2.5% chance—it is the *minimum* you could lose with 2.5% chance. The expected loss could be many times larger. You will be precisely inaccurate if you misunderstand this point! As an analogy: suppose you have a volcano warning system that tells you with precision that the *minimum* potential loss of life is 50,000 in the next eruption. The next day, the model says, due to a new tectonic reading, the minimum potential loss has gone down to 10,000. You would naturally feel relieved by this latest reading, but this information is not useful at all—in fact, it is outright dangerous and misleading. Due to extremistan, the real loss could be 11,000 or 10 million! There is no way to tell. Still, most bankers talk about VaR with an air of certainty and tangibility in boardroom meetings. Behavioral science reveals plenty of evidence that the human mind tends to associate and project when given some information, even when the information is completely irrelevant. In a sense, we are all wired to be "fooled by randomness". There is no way to get around this instinct.

2) *VaR is symmetrical (non directional).* It does not take into account the often richer information set contained in price levels. Valuable information is lost in the process of detrending or differencing to arrive at a stationary

time series. Consequently, as long as the return sample wiggles with the same degree of volatility, VaR will be the same, regardless of where we are in the business cycle—whether at the height of euphoria, in range-bound, or in the slump of a recession. To be fair, simulated VaR allows for skewed distributions, but we have seen in Section 7.1 that skewness is often a weak and incomplete measure of the asymmetry of price behavior.

3) *Modeling the tail of a distribution is futile.* Such modeling is futile since there is practically not enough data at the tail to make inferences in a statistically meaningful manner. Some methods such as CAViaR overcome this lack of observations by modeling the tail as being a function of some independent variables. These quantile regression models have to struggle with specification problems instead. In all likelihood, the "real" tail risk is a moving target and unstable due to the extremistan nature of extreme events.

Although not a very useful number, proponents may argue that VaR is at least a *consistent* estimate (in a statistical sense)—we can measure VaR with a given precision or confidence level. Precision has to do with reproducibility, but is reproducibility all important when the system we are measuring is dynamically changing with time and levels? History evolves—technological advances in trading, economic breakthroughs, emergence of program trading, regulatory changes to the rules of the marketplace, product innovation—are often irreversible regime shifts (or "game changers"). Recall the target analogy in Section 1.4, if we are dealing with a moving target, any attempt to be precise will surely render the outcome inaccurate. An accurate (though less precise) approximation is perhaps better in dynamical systems.

It is probably common sense to assume that the true expected loss E lies somewhere between VaR (a minimum loss) and the "maximum" loss. Due to extremistan, the maximum loss is elusive. In the absence of perfect foresight, a good workable number is the all-time historical largest loss[1]. It is also likely that E changes with time. We propose to make E dependent on the price level[2], specifically, on a function of the market cycle. We call this estimate *Bubble VaR* (buVaR).

BuVaR is a countercyclical method which gives a rough estimate of the expected loss between the maximum and minimum bounds, conditional on current

---

[1] This may not be as unreasonable as it seems. Consider the Dow Jones index, our maximum will then be a 25% one-day drop (the "Black Monday" crash in 1987). This is a *very* large number and given the circuit breakers put in place nowadays, single day losses in excess of 10% are highly unlikely (unless the shock is of a non-market nature such as World Wars, but that will be technically considered an operational risk). For this reason, we shall define a reasonably estimated upper bound for buVaR later.

[2] Conditional variance is not a new idea; it is just that it has never been made conditional on past price *levels*.

price levels. BuVaR is designed with regulatory capital in mind, and addresses the three weaknesses mentioned above—we expect buVaR to be less precise than VaR, more objective than stress testing, and likely more accurate than both. BuVaR is directional, in particular, long positions are penalized most at the peak of a market bubble (where crash risk is highest), and shorts are penalized most at the market trough (where risk of a bounce is highest). This countercyclical buffer protects against fat-tail events (crashes and bounces) in the *corrective* direction.

13.2 Classical Decomposition, New Interpretation

In Chapter 2, we introduced the concept of classical decomposition where a price series can be seen as being composed of a long-term trend, a cycle and noise component (see Figure 2-25). Conventional VaR exclusively models the distributional properties (i.e. moments and quantiles) of the noise component. Unfortunately, the phenomena of fat-tails, clustering and the leverage effect have so far eluded modeling. Quantile regression and EVT are some attempts at explaining these phenomena using tail data (i.e. exceedences) of the noise component. While some models are successful in explaining certain aspects of these phenomena, we still lack the tools to control their risks.

It is well-known in the classical decomposition that valuable information is lost in the process of differencing to derive the stationary data (i.e. in the simple act of taking returns). So, the scenarios used for VaR computation are informationally incomplete. This could suggest that modeling fat-tails and other phenomena using the noise component may be an exercise in precision but not accuracy. We conjecture that the answer lies in the cycle, not the noise component.

We suggest a *new interpretation* where the long-term trend is driven by real economic growth, the cycle is caused by speculative excess (bubbles) and the noise component is the realization of trading under normal efficient market conditions. The latter can be modeled using a normal distribution in the same way as VaR.

First, we posit that the fat-tail phenomenon is caused by a *break in the cycle*, which we identify as a market crash or a bubble burst. Crashes are just corrections in the cycle—asymmetric and sharp. Figure 13-1 illustrates the new interpretation idea and highlights a break in the cycle. Note that the three components add up to create the price series; differencing prices gives the return series in the lower panel. This model also explains the leverage effect by saying that a downward cycle break is more common than an upward cycle break.

Figure 13-1 Fat-tails caused by breaks in the cycle

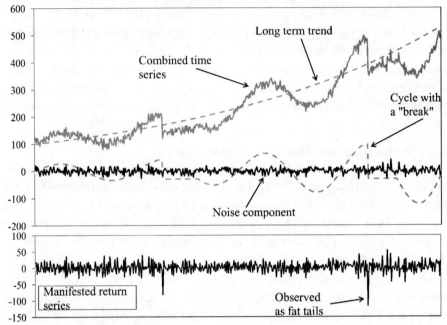

Figure 13-2 Cycle compression increases serial correlation and volatility clustering

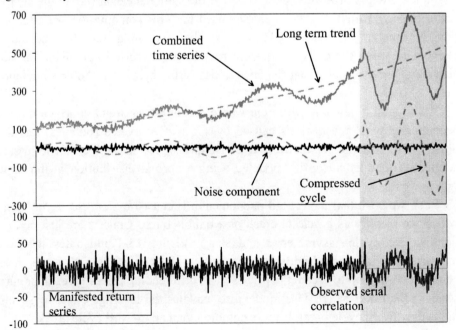

Second, we posit that a *cycle compression* causes increased serial correlation in the return series which could explain the volatility clustering effect. The notion is that cycles do not have a constant shape—in times of market stress both the frequency and the amplitude increase. This is illustrated in Figure 13-2 which shows compression in the last two cycles (the shaded zone). Notice the resulting increased serial correlation of returns is clearly manifested as a pattern in the noise (the lower panel). So during market stress, returns are less i.i.d. and stationary.

Figure 13-3 illustrates the situation where both cycle compression and cycle breaks are present. The return time series exhibits both serial correlation and fat-tailness. These rather stylized examples show that realistic market behaviors can be modeled using the new interpretation. Spreadsheet 13.1 lets the reader experiment with this concept.

The key benefit of the new interpretation is that the *distortions in the cycle can then be used to improve the distributional forecast.* By contrast, in the classical decomposition, only the stationary noise component determines the distributional forecast.

Figure 13-3 Cycle break and cycle compression combined effect

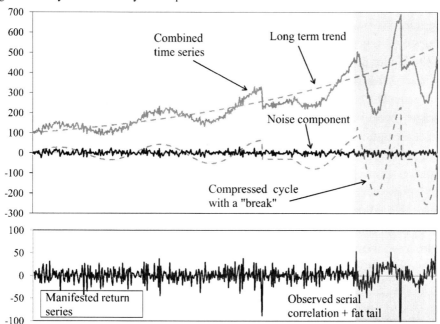

Our final objective is a countercyclical regulatory capital. What does this insight mean for regulatory minimum capital? Obviously we should not penalize the long-term trend; in fact, regulators should encourage participation in the economy. We should penalize the cycle but only to prevent a crash. In other words, the minimum capital should be asymmetrical depending on whether positions are long or short the "bubble" asset. In particular, minimum capital should discourage bubble-chasing.

We start with a premise that the tail is unknowable (not modelable) because of extremistan. We need to design a safeguard that is countercyclical. The noise component—representing trading during relatively stable market conditions—is already well-captured by conventional VaR. The idea is to use VaR (or a similar tail measure) and inflate it asymmetrically using the cycle, so as to penalize position-taking in the direction of the bubble.

13.3 Measuring the Bubble

The notion of equilibrium

To analyze the cycle we need to measure price deviation from some equilibrium level, which can be thought of as the *aggregate level of relative calm* during a long-term period, or *baseline growth trend* of the market economy. The further the price diverges away from this equilibrium, the larger the bubble has formed and the higher the crash risk. It follows that VaR should be inflated to reflect this heightened risk.

A natural choice is to represent the equilibrium as some kind of moving average[3] because we need a rolling-window to make buVaR responsive to market changes. The last three major crises (2007, 1997, 1987) occurred 10 years apart, so the window length must be shorter than 10 years in order to exclude distortion from previous crises. Yet, it must be long enough to contain the baseline growth trend of the most recent cycle. Empirically, a 1000-day window length, equivalent to four trading years, is workable and will be used here.

Let's test these ideas using a naïve 1000-day simple moving average (MA). Figure 13-4 shows a MA for the S&P500 index, the area plot shows the percentage price deviation from the MA.

---

[3] Arguably, we can also apply curve-fitting to determine this equilibrium, but this is less tractable-you will need to re-estimate daily and the fitted function is non-unique. Furthermore, the risk industry is already familiar with using rolling windows.

From here on, we shall call such deviation from equilibrium the *bubble*. The *bubble* is used to inflate VaR, for example if the *bubble* is positive (negative), we will penalize long (short) positions proportionally. To achieve this, we multiply the negative (positive) side of the return distribution used for VaR calculation by a factor called the *inflator*. The inflator is a function of the *bubble* after a calibration step.

First, in Figure 13-4 we would have penalized investments for a decade in the 1990's (the shaded area). As mentioned earlier, the minimum capital should not penalize the long-term trend. Otherwise, banks which use buVaR for minimum capital will under-invest during a period of sustainable growth; this is economically undesirable.

Figure 13-4 1000-day MA as the equilibrium line (S&P 500 index)

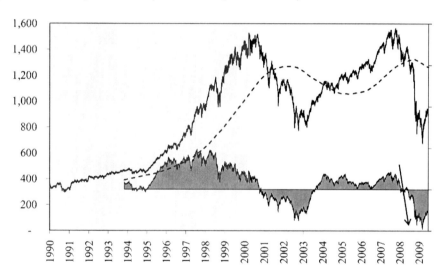

Second, in the July 2008 crash, the *bubble* turned negative too early because during a typical crash, the price falls sharply through the "slower" MA line. This means buVaR will penalize the shorts, when it really should penalize the longs during a crash. Put another way, it encourages buying during a crash. This is not prudent. Ideally, buVaR should detect that a crash in underway and continue to penalize the long side.

Third, notice that the area plot (in Figure 13-4) is choppy because we are taking the difference between a "jagged" price line and a smooth MA line. This means the *bubble* measure (hence, buVaR) will be too choppy and unsuitable for minimum capital.

Using a simple moving average clearly does not work, but it highlights the criteria required for a good buVaR design. In particular:

1. The measure must follow the market cycle.
2. The measure must not penalize investments during periods of sustainable long-term growth.
3. The measure must persistently penalize positions which are against a market crash *throughout* the crash episode.
4. The measure must not be too choppy for minimum capital purposes.

Adaptive moving average

To satisfy criteria (2), we introduce an *adaptive moving average* (AMA) where the average is taken over a variable window length *m* adapted to recent history.

$$m = Int[Min\left\{ \frac{Stdev(x_n, x_{n-1}, ..., x_{n-500})}{Stdev(x_n, x_{n-1}, ..., x_{n-1000})} *1000, 1000 \right\}] \qquad (13.1)$$

where x_n is the price on day-*n* and *m* ranges between [500,1000] days. Here, we will often write equations in the form of Excel functions similar to how they would appear in the spreadsheet.

Figure 13-5 Price "hugging" by AMA and EWMA (for S&P 500 index)

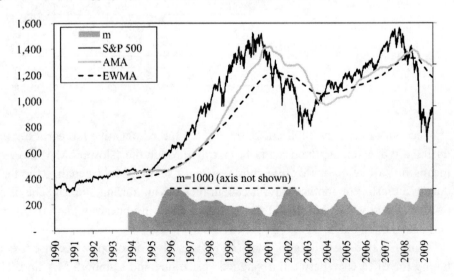

When market prices trend up (or down) for an extended period of time at constant speed, m is designed to adapt and shrink to about 500 days. With a shorter rolling window, the MA line will move closer to the price, thereby reducing the deviation (*bubble*). Put simply, the AMA "hugs" the price during periods of sustainable growth. As a comparison, Figure 13-5 shows the AMA and the EWMA (exponentially weighted moving average) of the S&P 500 index. It is well-known that the EWMA is more timely than a simple MA, but AMA performs even better.

Using rank filter

We propose the following methodology to derive a well-behaved equilibrium measure. To measure the equilibrium on day-n using prices x up to day-n:
1. Derive a vector of daily log returns $r_n = \ln(x_n/x_{n-1})$ for all previous days.
2. Apply an 8% *rank filter*[4] to r_n within the past 1000-day rolling window. That means we set $r_n=0$ whenever it is below the 8% quantile or above the 92% quantile of a rolling sample $\{r_n, \ldots, r_{n-1000}\}$. We have effectively filtered off the exceedences of the return distribution.
3. Create a vector of discount factors given by: $d_n=\exp(r_n)$ for each n.
4. At day-n, reconstruct a 1000-day new price vector $\{p_n, \ldots, p_{n-1000}\}$ "backward" iteratively using the "starting" price x_n. In order words, $p_n=x_n$ (the starting price) then calculate $p_{n-1}= p_n/d_n$ iteratively until p_{n-1000}. This vector is called the *alternate history*.
5. We defined the *equilibrium* μ_n as the adaptive moving average of the alternate history.

This rank filtering process effectively removes all extreme price movements due to crashes, euphoria, unsustainable rallies and breaks. We have recreated an alternate history in which bubbles and manias did not exist hypothetically and growth was gradual and sustainable. It is the adapted average of this new history that locates the *equilibrium* level. We define the *bubble* as the deviation from this *equilibrium*.

$$B_n = x_n / \mu_n - 1 \qquad (13.2)$$

---

[4] Rank filters are commonly used in digital image processing to enhance digital information. The method is a special case of a rank convolution process that has found wide application in technology and computer science. The choice of 8% cutoff is based on empirical studies. It is likely the "best" cutoff is slightly different for various asset classes, but would not be significantly different from 8%.

Figure 13-6 shows the *equilibrium* and the *bubble* for the S&P 500. The simple MA and its deviation are also shown for comparison. In the 1990's the *bubble* shrank (because of the adaptive "hugging") as the growth trend became established, while the MA deviation continued to penalize the longs. Another attractive feature is that the *bubble* is smoother than the MA deviation, because it is the difference between two jagged lines moving in tandem (the S&P and its *equilibrium*), whereas the MA deviation is the difference between a jagged line (S&P) and its smoother MA.

Figure 13-6 The *equilibrium* and the *bubble* (for S&P 500 index)

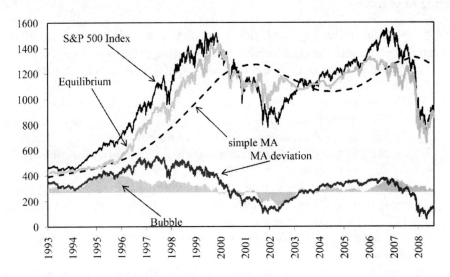

When there is a sharp price fall, as occurs in a crash, the *equilibrium* point falls by about the same magnitude also, because the "starting" price x_n used for its computation falls. As a result, the *bubble* is maintained and does not fall to the negative during a crash (unlike the MA deviation). Hence, the inflator (defined next) not only penalizes longs during bubble formation but also *throughout the crash*. Only *after* the crash, if a bearish bubble forms, will the inflator turn negative. The same reasoning applies to the bearish side as well, with "crashes" taken to mean upward spikes (bounces) in prices.

13.4 Calibration

To create a countercyclical VaR, we introduce the concept of an *inflator* that is designed to follow the market cycle. It is desirable to have a capital buffer that depends on what type of assets are being held by a bank, hence, the model has to be calibrated using previous episodes of crashes or crises, specific to that asset.

The *inflator* Δ is a multiplicative adjustment to *every* scenario on *one side* of the return distribution, penalizing the bubble side. On day t, if $B_t>0$, multiply every scenario of the negative side to penalize longs, and if $B_t<0$, multiply the scenarios on the positive side to penalize shorts.

First, we define the *maximum stress* Ψ as the average of the 5 largest positive and negative (absolute) daily returns in all history, capped by the circuit breaker size imposed by the exchange, if any[5]. For the computation of this average, we exclude large returns caused by regulatory changes (such as foreign exchange "depegs" and sovereign debt defaults—see Section 9.1) because such events are almost never repeatable and are not caused by the formation of financial bubbles.

Next, to derive the inflator, we assume a response function of the form:

$$\Delta = \exp[\omega_1 Abs(B_t)^{\omega_2}] \tag{13.3}$$

where ω_1, ω_2 are positive parameters. Aside from simplicity, equation (13.3) has some desirable features:
1. It is floored at 1.0. This is useful as this multiplier is supposed to inflate a scenario, not decrease it.
2. It grows exponentially with the *bubble*, B_t. In other words, the penalty should expand rapidly to restrain market euphoria.

However, we need to cap the exponential equation (13.3), so that Δ does not grow without bound. In other words:

$$\Delta = Min(cap, \exp[\omega_1 Abs(B_t)^{\omega_2}]) \tag{13.4}$$

Indeed, we want VaR to be inflated but not rise beyond Ψ. We define the *cap* as the shift that will bring the current VaR (which we approximate as $2\sigma_t$) to Ψ. This cap should correspond to the largest *absolute* observed *bubble* value B_{max} in history[6]. Using this boundary condition, equation (13.3) gives:

---

[5] Circuit breakers are safeguards introduced by exchanges after the 1987 crash. Once a circuit breaker is triggered, trading is halted for the day. Using the Dow Jones index as an example, the average is 9.92% and the initial circuit breaker instituted by the NYSE is 10%. So $\Psi=$ MIN(9.92%,10%) = 9.92%.
[6] There will be a $(B_{max}, \Psi)_i$ for every risk factor i. For securities that are newly-traded and there is not enough history to meaningfully determine (B_{max}, Ψ), we can benchmark to an index or proxy.

$$\psi/(2\sigma_t) = \exp[\omega_1 B_{\max}^{\omega_2}] \tag{13.5}$$

where σ_t is the standard deviation of returns of the VaR observation period of 250 days, ending day t. Substituting this inside (13.4), we can eliminate ω_1:

$$\Delta = Min\left(\frac{\psi}{2\sigma_t}, \exp\left\{\left(\frac{Abs(B_t)}{B_{\max}}\right)^{\omega_2} \ln\left(\frac{\psi}{2\sigma_t}\right)\right\}\right) \tag{13.6}$$

The *response function* (13.6) converts the measured *bubble* B_t to the inflator Δ_t. The reader can use Spreadsheet 13.2 to explore the behavior of the response function. The parameter ω_2 tunes the curvature of the response function (see Figure 13-7). We propose to set $\omega_2=0.5$. This is found by choosing the ω_2 that gives the smoothest day-to-day variation in buVaR, because a stable metric is useful for the purpose of risk capital.

Figure 13-7 Inflator response function of different ω_2 for σ=2.5%, $B_{\max}$=6, Ψ=10%

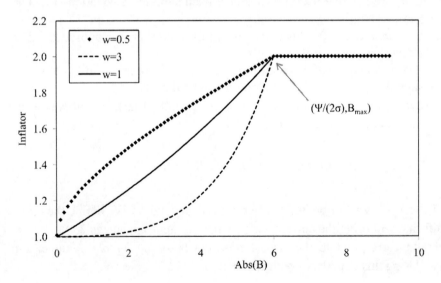

The *bubble* measure often peaks one step ahead of a market crash. Hence, the inflated VaR (buVaR) will rise well before the conventional VaR rises, often months in advance. The latter is known to spike up at the same moment as a crash, hence, too late for risk control. Ideally, Ψ should be determined by the regulator—a higher upper bound will give a more conservative (penal) buVaR. Here we set Ψ such that the resulting buVaR is slightly higher than the expected shortfall as witnessed *during* the 2008 crisis, but where this buVaR will be delivered (or charged) *ahead* of crises during the euphoria (run-up) phase.

The inflator is recomputed daily because B_t and σ_t vary with time. However, at any given day t, the constant Δ is multiplied to *every* return scenario on *one* side of the distribution (the side determined by the sign of B_t). See schematic in Figure 13-8.

Figure 13-8 Inflating the distribution on one side

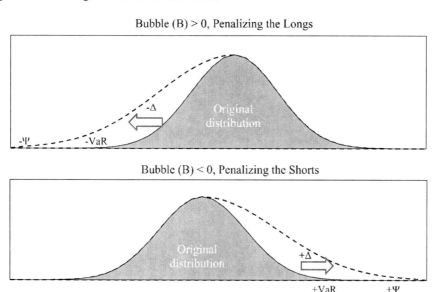

13.5 Implementing the Inflator

The inflator must be applied to the return distribution correctly. By design, buVaR does not allow negative prices (or rates), for reasons explained in Section 3.4. So negative rates, if any, will need to be floored at a small positive number.

Since buVaR inflates one side of the distribution, if the inflator is large enough, the negative returns (on the left tail) can cause shifted levels to become negative, an undesirable outcome. This problem is solved by using log return instead of the usual percentage return. Hence, instead of using equation (13.7), we use (13.8).

$$shifted\_level(i) = base\_level * (1 + \%return(i)*\Delta) \tag{13.7}$$

$$shifted\_level(i) = base\_level * \exp(log\_return(i)*\Delta) \tag{13.8}$$

where $i=1,\dots,250$ is the scenario number in the VaR observation period, and $\Delta \geq 1$ is the inflator computed earlier. We only penalize the bubble side i.e. if $B_i>0$ then $\Delta=1$ for all positive returns, if $B_i<0$ then $\Delta=1$ for all negative returns. Figure 13-9 shows the plots of equations (13.7) and (13.8). Left panel: when there is no inflation ($\Delta=1$), just as in VaR, it does not matter whether we used log return or percentage return—they are the same. Also shifted levels can never become negative.

Figure 13-9 Plot of shifted level vs. returns (*base level*=100. Left: $\Delta=1$, right: $\Delta=3$)

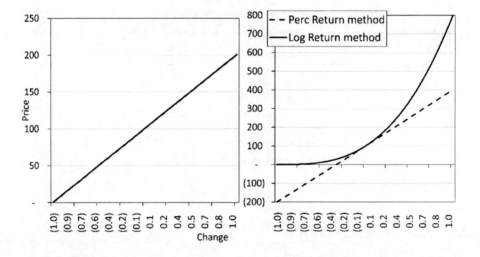

Right panel: when we inflate the returns three times ($\Delta=3$), the shifted level can become negative if percentage return is used. But if log return is used, the left tail shows a gradual fall to zero that avoids the negative territory. If Δ is large, the decline to zero will be steep. On the right tail, the shifted level rises in a convex way and may seem unnerving at first. But in practice, there is no concern that the resulting buVaR will blow up indefinitely because the shifted level is limited at some upper boundary—the inflator is capped at $\Psi/(2\sigma_i)$. Using the example in Figure 13-9 (base=100), and assuming Ψ=25% (a quantum similar to the fall on "Black Monday", 1987), the shifted level can barely go above 130 (=100exp(0.25)) even for a $2\sigma_t$ return scenario. As seen in the figure, the convex behavior is still not noticeable at price level of 130.

An advantage of buVaR is its ease of implementation. If a bank already uses hsVar, the infrastructure can be easily modified to compute buVaR. The historical simulated scenarios need to be multiplied on one side by today's inflator, a *scalar* which is computed independently. The bank also needs to ensure log returns are used as in equation (13.8). Once a vector of shifted levels is generated, the rest of the calculation steps (full revaluation and computing the tail measure) are almost identical to that of hsVaR.

In an ideal global regulatory regime, the inflators and return scenarios for all risk factors should be calculated by an independent and approved agency. The data could be downloaded daily by banks for their buVaR computation. Standardization would make risks comparable across the banking industry for supervision.

13.6 Choosing the Best Tail Risk Measure

After the operation in equation (13.8), the shifted levels will be used by a bank's risk engine to revalue deals in the portfolio. Just as in hsVaR, the dollar difference between values of the base case and the shifted scenario cases will give the PL vector for each deal. These PL vectors are aggregated to give the portfolio PL vector, which represents the PL distribution.

BuVaR is defined as the *expected tail loss* (ETL) of this PL distribution at a given confidence level. Let us explore the benefits of using ETL rather than quantile as our tail measure.

We simulate the GBM paths for two assets—A and B—which are inversely correlated. 600-day price paths are generated and a regime change is introduced on day-300, where the correlation changes from -0.9 to +0.9 *abruptly* and volatility increases three fold (see Figure 13-10). We wish to study the responses to the regime break for ETL, hsVaR and pVaR. All three risk measures use a 250-day window and a 97.5% confidence level.

The *implied* correlation ρ is backed-out from formula (13.9) given the other simulated variables, and is plotted in Figure 13-11.

$$\sigma^2_{portfolio} = \sigma^2_A + \sigma^2_B + 2\rho\sigma_A\sigma_B \tag{13.9}$$

where σ_A, σ_B, $\sigma_{portfolio}$ are replaced with the risk measures for assets A, B and the combined portfolio respectively. All three risk measures are tested in this way. Spreadsheet 13.3 provides a worked-out solution.

Figure 13-10 Two GBM paths simulating a regime break half way through the series

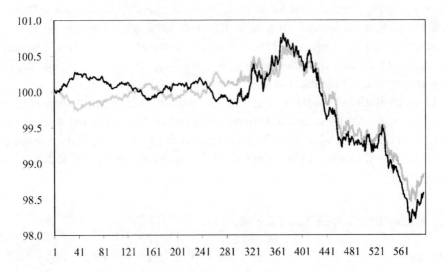

The result in Figure 13-11 confirms that the ETL is superior in three aspects:

Coherence

The implied correlation of hsVaR goes above +1 occasionally. From (13.9) it means the hsVaR of the portfolio can sometimes be larger than the sum of its components—subadditivity is violated. As expected, the implied correlation of pVaR stays below +1 because, by assuming a normal distribution, pVaR is subadditive. Interestingly, ETL is also subadditive—its implied correlation is always bounded below +1.

Responsiveness

Of the three risk measures, ETL is the most responsive to a regime switch. It takes less days for its implied correlation to move from -0.9 to +0.9 after the regime switch occurred on day-300.

To understand this, recall that for hsVaR, the 97.5% quantile corresponds to the 7th largest loss (after rounding up). Assuming the 6th largest loss is very close to the 7th largest loss, then, if a new extremely large loss (a Black Swan) enters the left tail, the 6th loss will now becomes the 7th loss (the new hsVaR). Hence, the dollar change in hsVaR is still small. However, by taking ETL, the *average* tail loss will increase sharply because of the inclusion of the new extreme observation.

The pVaR is the least responsive because standard deviation as a statistic is quite robust to outliers.

Stability

The fluctuation in Figure 13-11 gives some idea of the stability of the portfolio risk measure. After all, if ρ fluctuates a lot, by equation (13.9), $\sigma_{portfolio}$ will be less stable. Of the three risk measures, pVaR is the most stable because standard deviation is a smooth statistic.

Figure 13-11 Implied correlations computed from ETL, hsVaR and pVaR

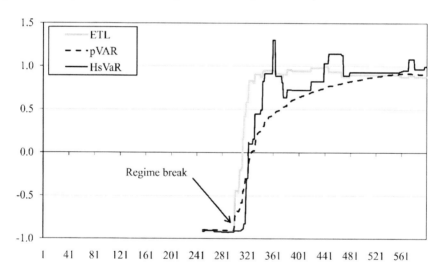

The ETL is marginally more stable than hsVaR. One can understand this by considering the case where the 8th largest loss is very far from the 7th largest loss (the hsVaR scenario). Then, if one of the left tail observations falls out of the 250-day rolling window, the 8th loss scenario will now become the new 7th loss (the new hsVaR). Hence, a large change in hsVaR will occur simply from data rolling off. However, for the ETL, the averaging of the 7 tail observations will soften the data roll off effect, making ETL more stable.

For these reasons, we choose ETL as the tail measure for buVaR. The q% buVaR is formally defined as the *ETL* of the *inflated* distribution over a 1-day horizon at $(1-q)$ quantile.

Spreadsheet 13.4 provides an example of how buVaR is calculated (for the S&P 500 index data). For comparison, both buVaR and ETL are plotted in Figure 13-12 for long versus short positions.

Figure 13-12 BuVaR vs. ETL for long and short positions (S&P 500 index)

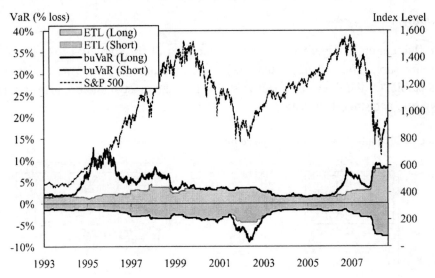

As seen, buVaR penalizes the long side at the market peak in Nov 2007 and penalizes the short side at the market trough in Nov 2002. In 1996, it penalizes the longs but when the rally proves to be sustainable, the inflator declines thanks to the adaptive moving average. Note that buVaR did not peak in 2000 for the S&P 500. This is because the dot com crash happened to the Nasdaq index (see Figure 15-3) and not to the S&P 500, which entered a bear market in a more gradual way. It is clear that buVaR has desirable countercyclical characteristics—it is usually one step ahead of market crashes. A full range of tests using different assets and various crisis episodes are performed in Chapter 15.

For the purpose of risk reporting, we recommend two important suggestions. Firstly, the mean-adjustment should be applied at the *aggregated* portfolio PL so that buVaR is expressed as a loss from the mean of a *joint* distribution. Secondly, buVaR at higher confidence (say 99%) should be derived using scaling by equation (6.10) because of data scarcity[7].

13.7 Effect on Joint Distribution

It is worthwhile to consider the big picture at this point and review what buVaR does to the distribution. Consider the bivariate normal case.

Figure 13-13 Inflator impact on joint distribution of two assets with zero correlation

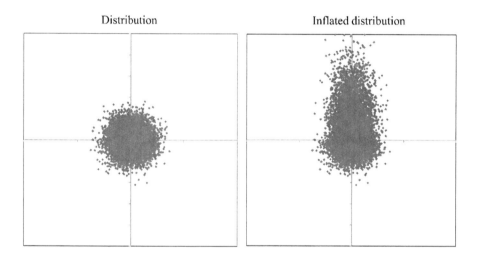

Distribution   Inflated distribution

Figure 13-13 shows a scatter plot of return samples (x, y), where the positive returns y (along the upper vertical axis) has been inflated by a factor of three on one side, to simulate the effect of the inflator. Mathematically, Y undergoes a variable transformation: $Y \rightarrow 3Y$ when $Y>0$. The bivariate example is simulated assuming zero correlation. Figure 13-14 is the case for correlation of +0.8.

As seen, the inflated distributions become *elongated* and are obviously no longer elliptical. Elliptical distributions are strictly symmetrical. However, this does not automatically rule out coherence. At the time of writing, it is not known whether the quantile of an inflated distribution is coherent or not, in general. The proof is non-trivial. In practice, we bypass the problem by using ETL (instead of quantile) for buVaR; it is then always coherent.

---

[7] One can debate whether the normal distribution assumption behind this scaling is justified. In the absence of adequate knowledge of the tail for extrapolation, we choose simplicity. It is after all nearly impossible to estimate the expected loss at the extremes with pinpoint accuracy.

Figure 13-14 Inflator impact on joint distribution of two assets with correlation of +0.8

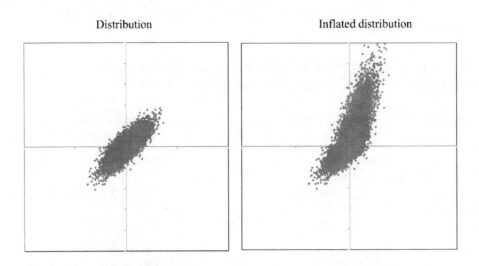

Distribution   Inflated distribution

13.8 The Scope of BuVaR

It is an appealing notion to apply buVaR to all asset classes, but empirical studies show that buVaR is not suitable for risk factors that are relatively stationary. This is not surprising because buVaR is designed to pick up cycles and trends. If the price series is range bound in a stationary way, the rank filtering process will still produce a cycle measure (the *bubble*) where no cycle exists. In other words, buVaR will inflate the risk measure even though there is no market bubble.

Different risk factor *families* show distinct market characteristics—not all fall under the scope of the buVaR methodology.

Price-based risk factors

Price-based risk factors originate from markets that trade using prices, for example, equity, index futures, commodities and foreign exchange markets. Characteristically, prices do not trade below zero, they show long-term trends and growth cycles. The leverage effect is often apparent, and retracements from a growth trend tend to be sharp and sudden. Higher prices tend to be more volatile; this "level effect" makes it necessary to take log returns for modeling. BuVaR can be used here.

Rates-based risk factors

These originate from markets that trade using yield quotation, such as interest rates and fixed income markets. Such risk factors have growth cycles that follow the interest rate policy cycles of central banks. Their time series rarely go below zero and often show long term mean-reversion. BuVaR can be used here as well.

Credit spread risk factors

These are spread quotations (in basis points) from credit derivative and corporate bond markets. They tend to be range bound and (in theory) mean-reverting with the business (credit) cycle. But, because of the risk of issuer default, credit spreads can become mean-fleeing once an issuer is under credit stress. This "credit escalation" phenomenon is often quick and asymmetrical (spread will spike upward only). If the issuer defaults, the spread becomes discontinued, otherwise, the spread drifts back to a range bound regime after some time. Such a complex behavior cannot be adequately captured by buVaR. In the next chapter, we will introduce *credit buVaR*, an extension of the basic buVaR method, which can incorporate both continuous spread risk and default risk.

Volatility-based risk factors

These are *implied* volatilities quoted (traded) in option markets including volatility indices (such as the VIX index). They tend to be highly stationary with occasional upward spikes and volatility clustering whenever there is unexpected news. Without trends, nor cycles, there is no need for buVaR—using conventional VaR (or setting inflator as 1) is sufficient.

13.9 How Good is the BuVaR Buffer?

Is a capital buffer based on buVaR adequate in covering extreme fat-tail losses? To answer this question, we need to look at the type of *market* losses that could threaten the solvency of a bank. Consider a simple back test chart for the Hang Seng index as per Figure 13-15. The vertical lines show the number and extent of VaR exceedences of long and short positions using a 1-day return as PL.

Using 1-day PL produces results which are "symmetrical"—breaches happen often in both directions—during a crash, even single day bounces after a sell-off often breach the VaR. However, risk managers should be more concerned about persistent losses (over many days) or *drawdowns* which could wipe out a bank.

Figure 13-16 shows that using a 10-day rolling return is more appropriate in modeling drawdowns (the VAR is also scaled to 10-days for consistency). Notice the VaR breaches are more intuitive—during a crash, drawdowns exceeding VaR occur more often and with larger magnitudes for *long* positions.

Figure 13-15 Back test exceedences based on a 1-day return vs. 1-day VaR

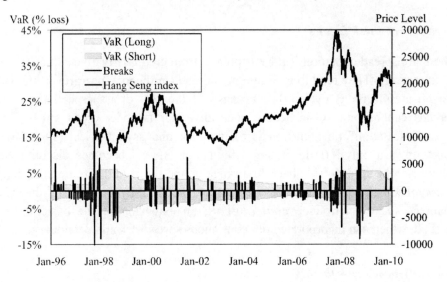

Figure 13-16 Back test exceedences based on a 10-day (rolling) return vs. 10-day (scaled) VaR

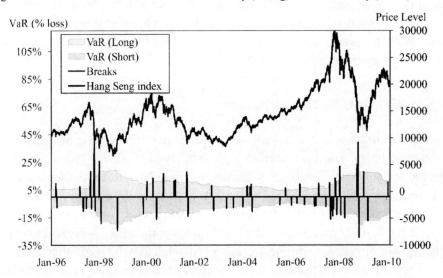

We can use this idea to check if a buVaR buffer adequately covers draw-downs during major crises. 10-day returns are used to back test against *ETL* (scaled to 10-days), the breaches are plotted alongside the buVaR in Figure 13-17. Note that during the Asian crisis (1997) and credit crisis (2007), the two sharp drawdowns are about twice the ETL! BuVaR is able to cover these exceedences and impose a buffer months ahead of the crisis. The buVaR buffer is also in the same direction as the drawdown, recognizing the asymmetry of risk.

Figure 13-17 buVaR as a buffer for extreme tail events

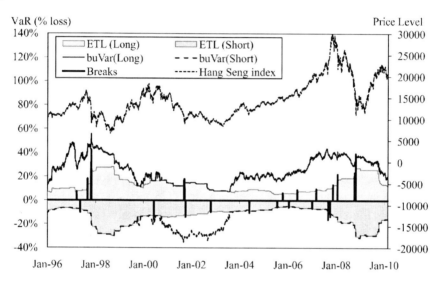

The above analysis suggests another way to calibrate the parameters of buVaR. A supervisor may choose an upper bound Ψ and parameter ω_2 such that past extreme events are sufficiently covered by buVaR (as in Figure 13-17). This does not guarantee, however, that an extreme event many times larger than buVaR cannot occur in the future. Modeling Black Swans is an oxymoron; there will always be a "surprise" element in risk modeling. The goal is not to have a capital buffer so large that it will encompass *all* Black Swans (that would be too uneconomical), but to have a reasonable cushion that works *most* of the time. The method in this section provides a tool for a supervisor to adjust this cushion based on his tolerance.

13.10 The Brave New World

"The difficulty lies, not in the new ideas, but in escaping from the old ones....",
(John Maynard Keynes, in the preface to *The General Theory of Employment,
Interest and Money*)

Hidden conditions

Models are created by man in an attempt to understand the world we live in.
Especially in social sciences, models are often mathematical abstractions laden
with simplifying assumptions. Such assumptions are necessary pillars upon
which knowledge can be built. Many "facts" that we take for granted are nothing
more than implicit assumptions.

For example, if someone asks what is the probability of getting heads in a
coin toss experiment. The natural answer (unless you are overly suspicious) is
50%. Yet this implicitly assumes that you are under the influence of gravity. The
answer will be indeterminate if the experiment is conducted in outer space. So
perhaps the real question should be—what is the probability *conditional* on the
experiment being done on earth.

Lest you consider that example pedantic, let's look at another—assuming the
average life span of an average human male is 75 years. If a 60-year old man
asks what his life expectancy is, one will be tempted to say 15 years. But what if
a 74-year old asks the same question? 1 year to live? One cannot arrive at the
right answer by asking the wrong question. The correct question should be—
what is his life expectancy *conditional* on living up to 74 years. This statistic is
found in the conditional distribution of the lifespan of men who had survived for
74 years. In other words, those who passed away before age 74 are excluded
from this sub-sample.

There really are two distributions here—a distribution for everyone, and a
distribution for 74-year olds. To answer the question correctly we have to pick
the latter. Likewise, one can think of VaR as having *two* distributions too—one
for normal times (which banks use), and one for stressful times (which lacks
observations). Suppose we have 1000 data points and suppose we define the
worst 5% of returns (50 points) as belonging to a stressed regime. If the 10th
worst loss is USD20 million, we will be tempted to think that this is the minimum loss with 1% probability (99% VaR). But if we knew that we were in the
stressed regime and use the latter distribution, the odds are really 20%! If we
think in terms of dual regimes, we can begin to see why crises happen more

often than suggested by Table 7-1—because we have been using the *unconditional* distribution[8].

There are many more hidden assumptions in the financial world that have been brought to light by crises. The time-honored assumption of normality widely accepted in financial modeling was debunked by the 2008 crisis. Other examples include the assumption of cointegration in statistical arbitrage (LTCM debacle), the assumption that major markets are liquid enough to weather a bank failure (credit crunch), the assumption that the government will defend its currency (pound devaluation) or guarantee a bank (Lehman bankruptcy), the assumption that the market is arbitrage free and will correct any misalignments, the assumption that many companies cannot default at the same time (CDO debacle), the assumption that a government will not default on local currency debt (Russian debt crisis); the list goes on. It is a truism in risk management that what you do not see (hidden assumptions) will hurt you the most.

VaR is loaded with assumptions too. Often its probability is unconditional. What is called conditional probability in the GARCH literature really means conditional on past returns (in an autoregressive sense) and that it *assumes* past returns contain *all* information as suggested by the efficient market hypothesis. Quantile regression is an important foray into introducing real conditional probabilities. As modeled in CAViAR, the quantile itself is made a function of (or conditional on) *other* variables. BuVaR is another initiative in conditional models—the return distribution is made a function of the market cycle directly.

Beyond i.i.d.

In Parts I and II of this book, we have seen how pervasive the assumption of i.i.d. is in time series modeling. Alongside the requirement of stationarity and the assumption of normality, this "gang of three" lay the foundation of risk modeling. These simplistic assumptions are well-established because they allow for consistent and precise estimation using known techniques such as OLS and MLE. While mathematical tractability is desirable, in VaR we are really interested in quantile extremes, the tail observations. All evidence suggests that the assumptions break down during times of crisis when VaR is most needed. In effect, we are sacrificing accuracy for precision.

---

[8] The example is admittedly contrived—there is obvious uncertainty in deciding which regime we are in, and neither is there adequate data on conditional probability. But, the example does highlight the reality of conditional probability and the folly of making careless probability interpretations. Interestingly, Satchkov (2010) introduced a VaR system that uses dual regimes, and weights that depend on external risk indicators.

Perhaps it is time to go beyond the i.i.d. paradigm. This idea is not new. Traders and investment analysts have long used methods that are seen as not very consistent and precise by mathematicians' standards. Yet, tools such as technical analysis and quant trading (more recently algo trading) have attracted a huge following. In the most capitalistic sense, such profit-driven research is less hampered by strict statistical requirements.

In this chapter, we proposed the new interpretation of decomposition which isolates the cyclical (non i.i.d.) component of a time series, and uses this information to correct known weaknesses in conventional VaR. In hindsight, it seems questionable that a stationary time series, detrended, and stripped of any directional information can be of any value in risk monitoring of extreme market situations. We hope that buVaR will open up a new path for future research, one that is admittedly less precise, but hopefully more accurate.

Living with extremistan

The realization of hidden conditions and the loosening of simplistic model assumptions will challenge the way we model risks. In particular, we have to admit how much we don't yet know about extreme events. A third element that adds to the difficulty is the extremistan behavior of financial markets.

The extremistan philosophy says that the tail is inherently unknowable. It's impossible to model the tail of market distributions because of data scarcity and extremistan; there is just no typicality in the tail that is amenable to statistical quantification. How can we quantify risks that cannot be perceived? The extremistan message is: stop being fooled by randomness, it cannot be modelled, learn to live with extremistan by protecting yourself.

Perhaps, the right question then is: is it possible to control risks without modeling the tail with precision? Dr. Taleb's fourth quadrant is an example of how one can broadly identify positions that are vulnerable to extremistan and take evasive actions, say by strategically hedging the tail.

In the same spirit, buVaR is *not* a solution to the fat-tail problem. It broadly identifies the phase of the business cycle we are in, and penalizes the VaR in a countercyclical way in recognition that a crash can only happen downwards. It acts as a *compensating control* so that regulators can have a sensible and workable metric for minimum capital. The added capital buffer compensates for what we do not know about fat-tail phenomena. Until the day we solve the extremistan conundrum, a practical paradigm is perhaps the most prudent approach.

13.11 Spreadsheet

13.1 The *new interpretation* of classical decomposition breaks down a time series into—the trend, the cycle, and the noise—for analysis, and posits that cycle breaks and compressions could explain well-known market behaviors such as fat-tailness, leverage effects, clustering. Aim: illustrates the new interpretation using a stylized time series. Action: use the scroll bars to manipulate the period and the amplitude of the cycle compression. Press the button to randomly simulate cycle breaks. Note: it is possible to generate price series of *any* patterns using the decomposition concept. According to *Fourier theory*, any signal can be decomposed into a series of sine and cosine waves of different wavelengths and amplitudes. This has widespread application in science and engineering.

13.2 Central to the buVaR idea is the inflator which functions to adjust the distribution. The response function (13.6) converts the measured *bubble B_t* to the inflator Δ. Aim: a toy calculator that plots the response function. Action: use the scroll bar to adjust parameter ω_2 and observe the behavior of the plot. Which ω_2 setting gives a reasonable response function in your opinion and why?

13.3 It is interesting to compare three tail-risk measures—ETL, hsVaR and pVaR—in terms coherence, responsiveness and stability. These are desirable properties of a risk metric. Aim: a Monte Carlo method is used to simulate a regime break (a drastic change in correlation) in the times series of two assets. The implied correlation is plotted for analysis. Action: press F9 many times to simulate many scenarios. Are you convinced ETL is a superior measure?

13.4 BuVaR is a new risk metric introduced in this book. Aim: the spreadsheet is a prototype calculator for buVaR which illustrates various aspects of its computation. For comparison and analysis, expected tail loss (ETL) is also plotted on the same chart.

Chapter 14

Credit BuVaR

The basic buVaR idea cannot be used in the credit world because trends and cycles are not well-behaved. Credit spreads often trade in a range during times of normalcy, determined by an issuer's cost of funds and ratings. Then, upon credit stress, the spreads break out and become mean-fleeing. This rare breakout behavior throws off the buVaR's *bubble* measure. Fortunately, with a modification to the buVaR framework, its usage can be extended to the credit world with interesting outcomes.

14.1 The Credit Bubble VaR Idea

Conventional credit spread VaR that uses historical simulation already captures the risk of (continuous) spread movements. On the other hand, the default risk (a discontinuous jump risk) is separately modeled using default migration models such as CreditMetrics, which use rating migration transition matrix and actual default statistics of companies collected by rating agencies. But, the historically-recorded default rates can be a misleading indicator of future default risk because it is procyclical, backward-looking and critically lags actual defaults.

For example, during the pre-crisis "golden decade" (1998 – 2006) the default statistics were very low and would underestimate the true default probability realized during the 2007 – 2008 credit crunch when credit quality rapidly deteriorated. And surely the default rates recorded during the credit crunch period would grossly overstate the future default probability after the economy has recovered. Credit buVaR overcomes this procyclicality problem by not requiring default statistics at all.

The credit buVaR model is an attempt to merge default risk into credit spread VaR. The weakness of the current fragmented approach is that there is no natural way to combine migrational credit VaR, spread VaR and market VaR in a diversifiable framework[1]. But with the credit buVaR approach, they can be aggregated in the Markowitz sense[2].

The intuition of credit buVaR originates from two empirical observations. First, actual credit defaults/stresses witnessed during the 2008 credit crisis revealed that defaults are not simply jumps, as modeled in academia. Figure 14-1 shows a few impaired issuers during the 2008 credit crisis. They do not look anything like Figure 14-2 which shows a theoretically modeled jump-to-default process (a stylized time series for spreads of a 5-year junk bond with a 30% default recovery). The phenomenology is patently different. Actual defaults are in fact *always* preceded by rapid *spread escalation* or widening (*credit escalation*), which acts as leading signals, often weeks to months earlier. This observation suggests a credit model conditional on spread escalation could be forward-looking.

Figure 14-1 Spread escalation of a few issuers during credit crisis

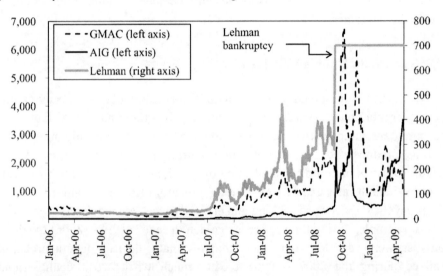

Source: Bloomberg Finance L.P.

---

[1] In the context of the new Basel II market risk capital, these are the IRC, specific risk charge and general market risk charge respectively.
[2] In Basel II, we have the dilemma of adding a 99.9%/1-year IRC to a 99%/10-day VaR. By contrast, credit buVaR captures both default and spread risks together using the same scale. It is essentially a short-term horizon model which is sensitized to also detect default risk in a forward-looking way.

A second observation is the asymmetry of credit default/deterioration—spreads can only escalate *upwards* and a default only hurts *long* credit risky positions. Such positions include (long) bonds, short protection default swaps (CDS) and generally, other credit-risky products which show negative credit01 (hence at risk to upward movements in spreads). This fundamental asymmetry is not reflected by the spread VaR model, which is just a function of spread return *volatility* without other market dynamics. Hence, spread VaR grossly underestimates skew/fat-tail risks. And since it is calculated using a rolling window, it lags significant market moves. Unfortunately, the 2008 crisis showed that the majority of the losses of banks came from trading spread risk (which is underestimated) rather than actual issuer defaults.

Figure 14-2 A modeled jump to default process

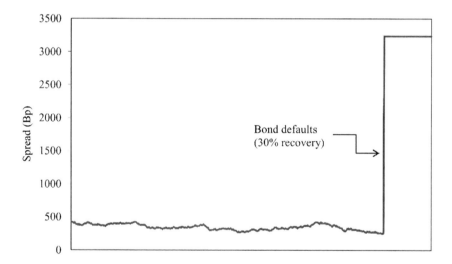

This asymmetry is not only a behavior of default risk, but also of spread risk. In theory at least, spreads are expected to trade in a range determined by ratings and with some cyclicality driven by business credit conditions. This pattern did not show up in recent history because of the overwhelming influence of product innovation. Figure 14-3 shows the 5-year CDS spreads for the Philippines. Until July 2007, the spreads showed a trending contraction as the euphoria for high-yielding credit products drove down spreads generally. This bubble burst when the US subprime crisis happened and spreads reversed direction sharply. For such issuers that were affected by the overall market distress, even if they did not eventually default, spreads became "mean-fleeing" to the upside.

The credit buVaR model will incorporate both the phenomena of rapid spread escalation and risk asymmetry. The plan is to detect the occurrence of spread escalation and to penalize spread VaR asymmetrically using an adjustment Δ_+ (the *inflator*). The adjustment is applied to the *positive* side of the return distribution (of spreads) since default risks can only hurt *long* credit positions.

Figure 14-3 Credit spread behavior—Philippines 5-year CDS

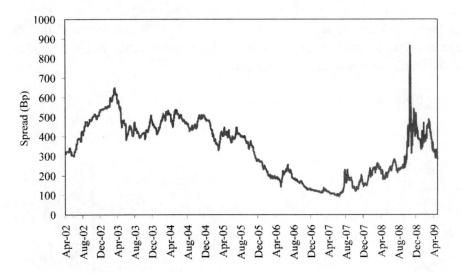

Source: Bloomberg Finance L.P.

14.2 Model Formulation

To derive the credit buVar inflator, Δ_+, we assume a response function of the form given by equation (14.1). It has some desirable properties:
1. It is floored at 1.0. This is useful as the inflator is supposed to increase a scenario return, not decrease it.
2. It grows exponentially with spread S. In other words, the penalty should expand rapidly during a credit escalation to recognize that a default event is becoming more imminent.
3. The inflator will be capped in a logical way such that as we move into default, a bond cannot lose more than its full notional (as we shall see).

$$\Delta_+ = \exp(\omega_1 S^{\omega_2}) \tag{14.1}$$

where the + sign means that only positive return scenarios are adjusted, S is the current CDS spread, and ω_1, ω_2 are positive parameters.

Obviously, spreads (unlike stock prices) cannot grow indefinitely—at some upper bound S_{cap}, the reference issuer will default. One simple way to determine S_{cap} is to use a bond pricing formula and assume a recovery rate of 10% upon default[3]. To derive the formula for S_{cap}, first we work out the yield of a defaulted bond using the Excel formula YIELD(.). The syntax is:

$$Y_{defaulted}=\text{YIELD}(COB, Maturity, Coupon, Price, Redemption, Frequency) \quad (14.2)$$

where the bracketed items are the inputs for the function. Equation (14.2) is for a specific issuer at a particular maturity (T)—it represents one credit spread risk factor. In credit trading, most banks use up to five benchmark risk factors on each credit curve for liquid issuers, i.e. $T=1, 2, 3, 5, 7$. Often, the 5-year point is the most liquid point observable and other tenor points are approximated.

Our primary interest is in designing an inflator which is representative of the *state of deterioration* of a particular credit name. Thus, it is superfluous to model the credit curve, and it suffices to choose a single benchmark, naturally at $T=5$, since this is the most reliable point. The computed inflator is then used to penalize all five risk factors of that issuer's curve. With the chosen benchmark the inputs for equation (14.2) are:

1. COB = close-of-business (today's) date
2. $Maturity$ = COB + 5 years
3. $Coupon$ = 5-year swap rate. This is a convenient assumption since the inflator result is not very sensitive to the coupon rate.
4. $Price$ = 10, the assumed recovery price of 10% par.
5. $Redemption$ = 100 or par.
6. $Frequency$ = 4, or quarterly coupon, consistent with the convention used in the CDS market.

Using these inputs, when a default occurs, the price will be floored at 10% of par, and its yield will be capped by (14.2). A credit spread is often defined as the yield premium over the risk free rate, thus, it will be capped at:

$$S_{cap} = Y_{defaulted} - \text{5-year swap rate} \quad (14.3)$$

---

[3] In practice, the regulator can stipulate a suitable recovery rate. Here we took guidance from Lehman's recovery value of 8.6% during its bankruptcy and rounded it to 10%.

S_{cap} will put a natural cap on the inflator in equation (14.1). We define the maximum inflator Δ_{max} to be the adjustment that will inflate the VaR (or two sigma)[4] to a loss at S_{cap}. Mathematically,

$$S_{cap} = S(1 + 2\sigma\Delta_{max})\qquad(14.4)$$

where the standard deviation of returns σ is taken over a 250-day window. This idea is illustrated in Figure 14-4. The original spread distribution is inflated to the right by Δ ($\leq\Delta_{max}$) in general, and the largest possible inflation is Δ_{max} shown in the schematic.

Figure 14-4 Inflator penalizing the credit spread distribution on the positive side

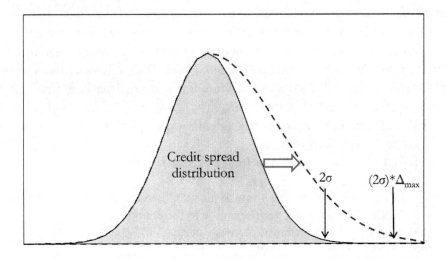

However, the maximum shift will also satisfy (14.1), hence:

$$\Delta_{max} = \exp(\omega_1 S_{cap}^{\omega_2})\qquad(14.5)$$

Substituting ω_1 from (14.5) into (14.1) and then eliminating Δ_{max} using (14.4), we obtain:

---

[4] We take a 2 standard deviation of returns as representing 97.5% VaR because it is more stable and easier to compute than other quantile measures.

$$\Delta_+ = \exp\left\{ \left(\frac{S}{S_{cap}} \right)^{\omega_2} \ln\left((\frac{S_{cap}}{S} - 1)/(2\sigma) \right) \right\}$$ (14.6)

We now have an equation with one parameter ω_2 that lets the risk controller tune the sensitivity of the response function. Setting a lower ω_2 makes the credit buVaR more conservative or punitive in terms of regulatory capital.

14.3 Behavior of Response Function

As an example, consider a 5-year corporate bond position and use the standard parameters mentioned earlier. S_{cap} works out to be around 5800bp by equation (14.3). Let's plot the response function (14.6) using ω_2=1.2 and σ=8% for two different volatilities.

Figure 14-5 Response function where swap rate=2.6%, ω_2=1.2, volatilities 1σ and 3σ

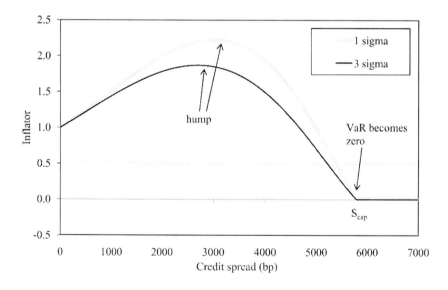

The response profile reaches its peak when spreads are at about half of S_{cap} after which the inflator would fall. The "hump" can be explained this way: at higher spreads close to S_{cap}, the inflator has to reduce in order to prevent the inflated spread (representing VaR) from overshooting S_{cap}. In theory, the bond defaults when S_{cap} is reached and there is no longer any price uncertainty, hence, VaR should become zero.

Note that the inflator, equation (14.6), is independent of the issuer; it is universal for all issuers with the same spread and volatility. This is appealing, as it implies that all information on default expectations is already contained in the spread, consistent with the efficient market hypothesis. Whilst we have set ω_2=1.2 for illustration, we will argue for a more conservative choice of ω_2 in Chapter 15.

The Δ_+ inflator will multiply only the *positive* returns in the scenario vector (or distribution). The incremental return is interpreted as coming from default risk (see Section 14.5). We use this inflated scenario vector to perform full revaluation of the credit portfolio to arrive at the PL vector. *Credit buVaR is formally defined as the expected tail loss taken on this inflated PL vector over a one-day horizon.*

Figure 14-6 illustrates the effect of the inflator on the VaR scenario. The horizontal axis is the current spread level (S) and the vertical axis shows the shifted spread level $S(1+2\sigma\Delta_+)$ after multiplying the VaR scenario (2σ) and the inflator Δ_+. Here σ is constant. The shifted scenario ($2\sigma\Delta_+$) is the scenario that produces the credit buVaR. The distance between the curve and the reference straight line is the degree of inflation applied to VaR; it shrinks to zero just as the bond defaults at 5800bp.

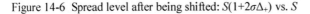

Figure 14-6 Spread level after being shifted: $S(1+2\sigma\Delta_+)$ vs. S

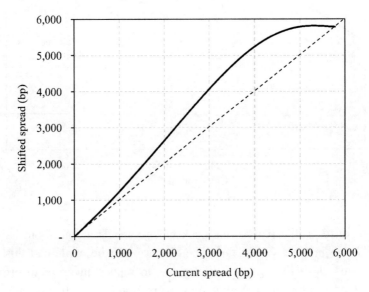

14.4 Characteristics of Credit BuVaR

Let's compare credit buVaR with conventional spread VaR. For illustration we will take credit buVaR as equal to $2\sigma\Delta_+$, in other words, as a simple inflation of parametric VaR. (In actual implementation, credit buVaR must be computed by taking the *expected tail loss* of the inflated PL vector.)

Figure 14-7 shows the credit buVaR calculated for a short-protection CDS on the Philippines. Because it is a *long* credit position, the buVaR is an inflated copy of the spread VaR (the shaded graph). If it is for a *short* credit position (or long-protection) no adjustment is needed; buVaR and spread VaR are identical. See Spreadsheet 14.1 for a worked-out example.

Figure 14-7 Credit buVaR vs. parametric VaR for 5-year Philippines CDS

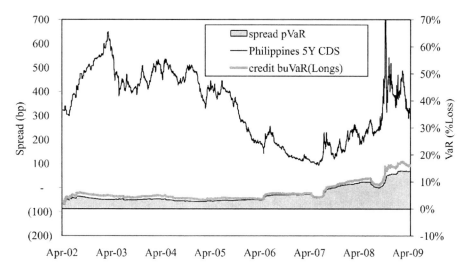

Source: Bloomberg Finance L.P.

It is important that credit buVaR is robust to the assumptions made in its derivation. Notably, S_{cap} is a function of *only* the 5-year swap rate in equation (14.3), all other parameters are assumed. It turns out the assumption on the coupon rate is not a sensitive one as long as the coupon is not *significantly* larger (say 5% more) than the swap rate. A bond is typically issued by a company with a coupon level set near to its yield (the company's cost of funds) and bond yields seldom trade far above swap rates during issuance.[5] Hence, assuming the bond's

---

[5] The exception is when the issuer is in distress, but under this circumstance it will not be able to issue a bond anyway.

coupon is equal to the swap rate is a reasonable standardization. It will not be a problem even for old bonds where coupons were fixed long ago (possibly at levels different from current yields). This is because banks use new bonds (*on-the-run* issues) for risk factor mapping, never old ones.

In contrast, S_{cap} is sensitive to the recovery rate assumption, especially if under 10%. From Figure 14-8, a very low recovery (<5%) will cause the hump in the response function profile to shift to the right significantly. Fortunately, this is less of a problem in practice—if the price of a bond is impaired to below 40%—a typical recovery rate assumed for CDS valuation—banks will most likely take the deal off the trading book and take a full reserve on the loss. The position will then be managed outside the VaR framework as a bad loan or asset under receivership.

But suppose that a bank chooses to keep the impaired asset on the trading book and the market quotes extremely high spreads in anticipation of a default with very low recovery (less than our assumed 10%), then buVaR will give zero (a discontinuity) since the bond has in theory defaulted with no further price uncertainty. This is shown as the thick line in the GM example (see Figure 14-9). To continue using buVaR, the bank can simply reset the recovery rate lower to say 1% and recompute buVaR as per the thin line. This bypasses the discontinuity problem.

Figure 14-8 Sensitivity of S_{cap} to recovery rate assumption

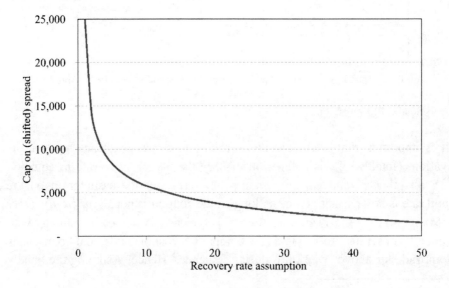

In summary, credit buVaR becomes larger than spread VaR whenever there is a credit escalation, but its increment is controlled so that a position cannot lose more than its principal (less recovery value).

Figure 14-9 General Motor 5-year CDS (long credit) position: handling of buVaR discontinuity

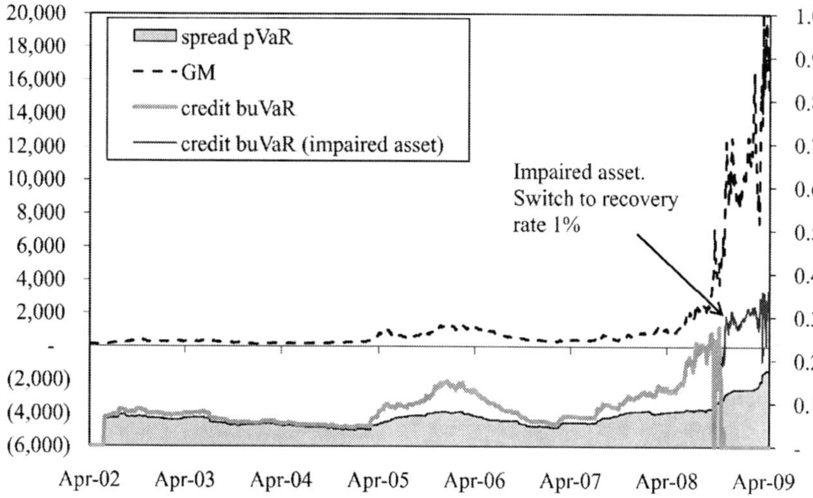

Source: Bloomberg Finance L.P.

14.5 Interpretation of Credit BuVaR

We posit that the additional portion of buVaR over and above conventional spread VaR represents default risk. To see this, we simulate a credit spread time series and let this spread increase gradually until the corresponding 5-year bond defaults. See Figure 14-10.

Note that the spread VaR is small, around 0.5% (this is daily, not annualized) compared to the inflated buVaR. At its peak (point A), buVaR of 10% is 20 times larger than spread VaR. With the prevailing spread at 4700, the buVaR will bring the shifted spread to 4700*(1+0.10)=5170, quite close to the default spread S_{cap}=5790 for our 5-year bond example[6]. As the spread escalates to 5500 (point B), the buVar goes *down* to 4.4% such that the shifted spread is 5500*(1+0.044)= 5742, almost reaching default. In short, as credit spread

---

[6] Our stylized bond is a 5-year bond with semi-annual coupon of 2.57%, default recovery rate of 10%. Swap rate at 2.57%.

escalates, buVaR (while falling) inflates the shifted spread towards the theoretical default spread S_{cap}.

To get a sense of magnitude, consider a $10 million bond of 5-year duration. At point A, the VaR loss is (5170-4700) = 470bp. In dollar terms, the buVaR works out to be 10000000/10000*5*470 =$2,350,000, compared to conventional spread VaR of 0.5%*4700*10000000/10000*5 =$117,000 that is due purely to volatility of spreads. The additional $2,232,500 loss in buVaR is attributed to *default risk*. In Section 15.4, we find further justification for this interpretation.

Figure 14-10 Stylized credit buVaR: approaching default

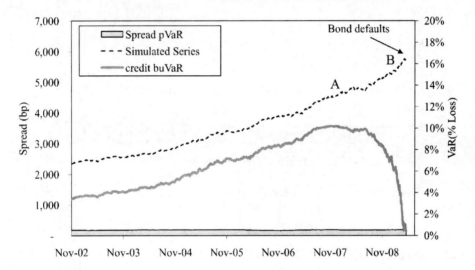

14.6 Spreadsheet

14.1 Credit buVaR is a new risk metric introduced in this book. Aim: the spreadsheet is a prototype calculator for credit buVaR which illustrates various aspects of its computation. For comparison and analysis, the pVaR is also plotted on the same chart. Note: for simple illustration, we simply inflate the pVaR for this single risk factor example. At a portfolio level, expected tail loss (ETL) should be used instead. This means that each issuer's inflator is different, and is multiplied to respective deals for all scenarios. Then, sum the PL by scenarios to get a diversified PL vector. Finally, ETL can be taken on this PL distribution.

Chapter 15

Acceptance Tests

The VaR models used in banks usually undergo the strict statistical tests found in Chapter 8. These "goodness of model" tests are a regulatory requirement. Passing all these tests proves that a bank's VaR distribution is i.i.d. and hence the quantile estimate is not biased or understated. Under these "peace time" conditions, the VaR model is a consistent metric. The great irony is that a risk manager should be more concerned about extreme conditions, which threaten the bank's survival. But these are the exact conditions under which such statistical tests would fail.

Unsurprisingly buVaR will fail these tests even under benign conditions since, by design, this metric is non-i.i.d. (its day-to-day distribution is conditional on the cycle). Hence, we will need to rely on other less consistent (and less precise) tests. We will test the *effectiveness* of buVaR by assessing its historical *performance* covering major financial assets and indices, over a long history and over specific stressful episodes.

15.1 BuVaR Visual Checks

Our test is similar to the way a trader would test his/her trading system—it is subjective, performance-based and is not based on strict hypothesis testing. First, and perhaps most importantly, we check visually to ensure that buVaR is generally doing what it is designed to perform. In particular, we look for evidence of:

1. Counter-cyclicality: the *bubble* measure must inflate to penalize positions of the correct side. Ideally, it should penalize the long-side most at price peaks and penalize the short-side most at price troughs.
2. If a rally becomes extended the *bubble* should ease off. The adaptive moving average is designed to produce this behavior which softens the penalty on long-term growth.
3. During a crash the *bubble* should continue to penalize the long-side the whole time instead of changing direction.

The test coverage as shown in Table 15-1 is chosen to broadly represent global financial markets. The buVaR is then computed with parameters as described in Chapter 13. Refer to Spreadsheet 13.4 for a worked out example. The *bubble* measure and the resulting buVaR are plotted for analysis. We also chart the expected tail loss (ETL) as a base case for comparison.

Table 15-1 Assets chosen for visual checks

Asset	Asset class	Benchmark representation
S&P 500 Index	Equity (US)	Global equity market driver
Nasdaq 100 Index	Equity (US)	Technology sector
Nikkei 225 Index	Equity (Japan)	Asia equity
Hang Seng Index	Equity (HK)	Greater china
USD/JPY	Forex	Major currency
AUD/SGD	Forex	A popular cross currency
USD 10-year swap	Interest rates	Long term global rates
USD 5-year swap	Interest rates	Medium term global rates
USD 3-month Libor	Interest rates	Short term global rates
Gold spot	Commodity	Inflation hedge, metals
Brent crude oil futures	Commodity	Energy

Figure 15-1 *Bubble* measure for S&P 500 index

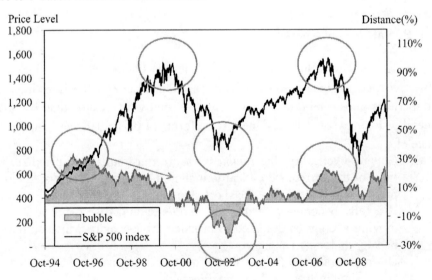

Figure 15-1 shows the *bubble* measure for the S&P 500 Index. The *bubble* peaked at the end of 1995 but it turned out to be a false signal—the rally developed into a long term uptrend that lasted until mid-2000. Due to the adaptive nature of the *bubble*, it eased off and maintained a moderately positive level up to 1999 (see arrow). Generally, the *bubble* peaked and troughed in tandem with the index (see circles in Figure 15-1).

Figure 15-2 shows the buVaR and the ETL of S&P 500 index. Using our definition of upper bound Ψ, the buVaR's peak during the run-up to the 2008 credit crisis is slightly higher than the ETL's peak during that crisis. As seen buVaR leads ETL (or any conventional VaR measure) significantly and peaks almost one year ahead of the crash.

Figure 15-2 BuVaR and ETL for S&P 500 index

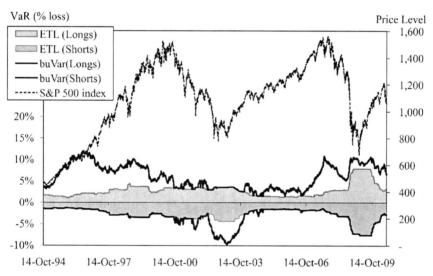

Figure 15-3 shows the *bubble* measure for the Nasdaq 100 index. The peak/trough of buVaR corresponded to the peak/trough of the index. The Nasdaq crash in 2000 was extremely sharp; had we used a simple moving average to construct the inflator, the *bubble* meter would have flipped to a negative reading when the price collapse reached 50% of the full crash amount and buVaR would have wrongly penalized short positions instead. Figure 15-4 shows the resulting buVaR for Nasdaq.

Figure 15-3 *Bubble* measure for Nasdaq 100 index

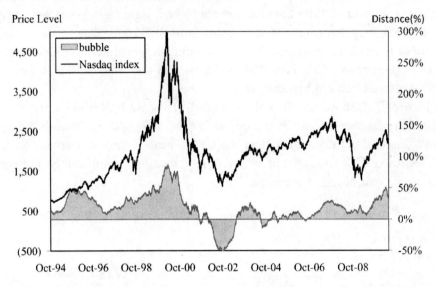

Figure 15-4 BuVaR and ETL for Nasdaq 100 index

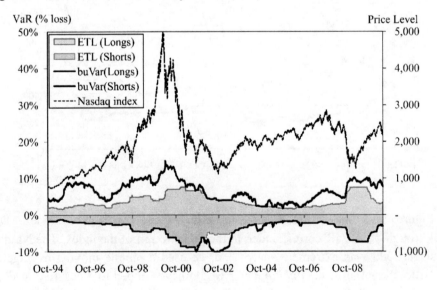

Figure 15-5 shows the *bubble* measure for the Nikkei 225 index. The *bubble* significantly penalized positions in a countercyclical way at major peaks and troughs (see circles in Figure 15-5). This is less obvious in the buVaR chart in

Figure 15-6 because the level of the ETL was ultra-low in 1989, which lessened the impact of the inflation.

Figure 15-5 *Bubble* measure for Nikkei 225 index

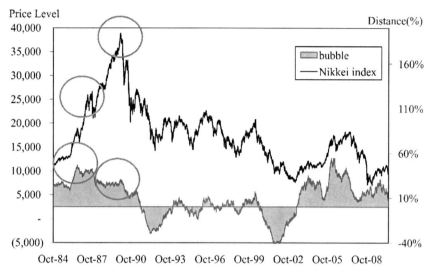

Figure 15-6 BuVaR and ETL for Nikkei 225 index

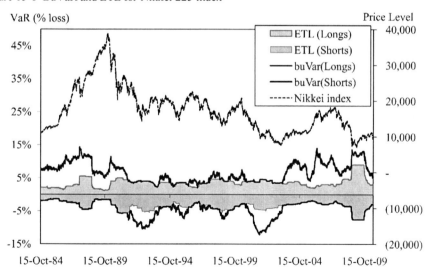

Figure 15-7 and Figure 15-8 show the *bubble* measure and buVaR for the Hang Seng index. The *bubble* penalized positions in a countercyclical manner ahead of peaks and troughs (circled). Notice that the *bubble* did *not* penalize every peak and trough, only the major unsustainable ones normally associated with crashes and manias. The circles correspond to the Asian crisis and the credit crunch.

Figure 15-7 *Bubble* measure for Hang Seng index

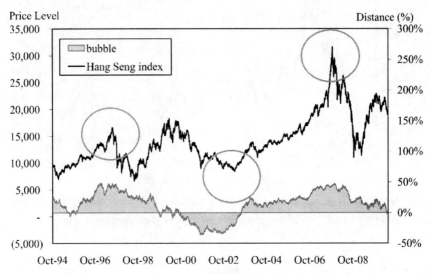

Figure 15-8 BuVaR and ETL for Hang Seng index

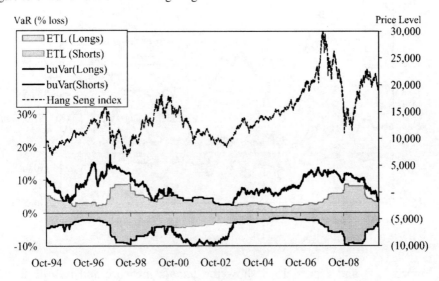

Figures 15-9 and 15-10 show the *bubble* measure and buVaR for the USD/JPY exchange rate. Major peaks and troughs were strikingly detected by the *bubble* measure. The buVaR was highest during the period in 1997–98 when the Bank of Japan (BoJ) actively defended the yen against speculators as a policy.

Figure 15-9 *Bubble* measure for the USD/JPY exchange rate

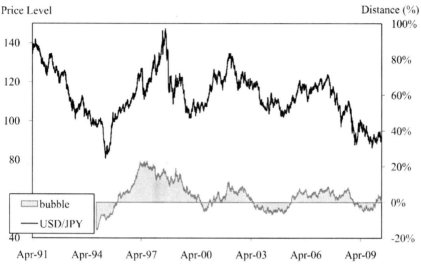

Figure 15-10 BuVaR and ETL for the USD/JPY exchange rate

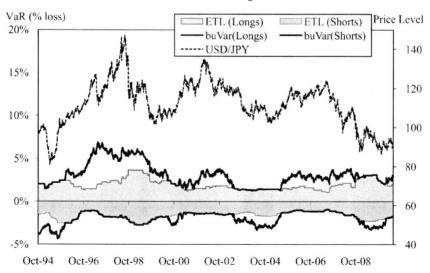

Source: Bloomberg Finance L.P.

Figure 15-11 *Bubble* measure for AUD/SGD exchange rate

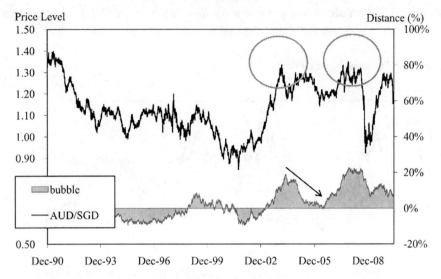

Source: Bloomberg Finance L.P.

Figure 15-12 BuVaR and ETL for AUD/SGD exchange rate

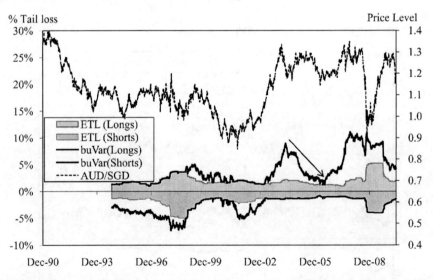

Source: Bloomberg Finance L.P.

Due to the exponential function *exp*(.) in the response function, *minor* peaks/troughs in the *bubble* will translate into immaterial buVaR enhancement, and should not be our focus. Instead, buVaR is designed to catch *major* crashes and manias. This is apparent in Figures 15-11 and 15-12 which show the *bubble* measure and buVaR for the AUD/SGD exchange rate. The left circle shows a major bubble but when it failed to burst the measure rapidly tapered off by design (the arrow). The right circle shows the "carry trade" bubble finally burst, triggered by the 2008 crisis, and was forewarned by buVaR.

Swaps and treasury bonds of major currencies tend to be highly correlated because central banks of major countries often coordinate their monetary policies to maintain economic and market stability. Hence, for the purpose of testing, we can use USD swap rates as a benchmark for global interest rates. Figures 15-13 and 15-14 show the *bubble* measure and buVaR for the 10-year USD swap rate. The major peaks and troughs are circled in Figure 15-13.

Figures 15-15 and 15-16 show the results for the 5-year USD swap which looks similar to that for the 10-year USD swap. This is because the mid-section and long-end of the same curve are expected to be highly correlated as they are influenced by common risk drivers.

Figures 15-17 and 15-18 show the results for the 3-month Libor rate which, in contrast, does not look at all like the 5-year and 10-year swaps. In fact, the Libor rate chart looks toothed and irregular because the short-end of the curve (overnight rate to 3-month rate), which acts as an *anchor* for the entire yield curve, seldom moves. Central banks control the overnight rates. The only time short rates really move is when there is an actual (or perceived) central bank rate cut or rate hike. And since such actions usually come in dosages of 25bp or multiples of it, the short rate time series becomes toothed. The problem with unsmooth time series is that it throws off most continuous-time modeling. As such, the *bubble* measure becomes ineffective—for example, the peak in Libor rates in Jun 2007 was utterly missed out by the model.

The solution to this problem is a simple one—since it is inconceivable that different parts of the same yield curve are at different business cycles (after all, they relate to the same economy), we really only need one single liquid benchmark from the curve for the purpose of deriving the *bubble* (which will be used for all tenors). The 5-year point is preferred for two reasons: most companies raise medium term funds by issuing corporate bonds in this part of the curve, and default swaps are also the most liquid for 5 years.

Figure 15-19 shows the *bubble* measure for the gold spot price (in $US). BuVaR did well by penalizing the longs markedly on three occasions (see

Figure 15-20) during the bull run, but when the rally proved unstoppable, the buVaR subsided temporarily.

Figure 15-13 *Bubble* measure for USD 10-year swap

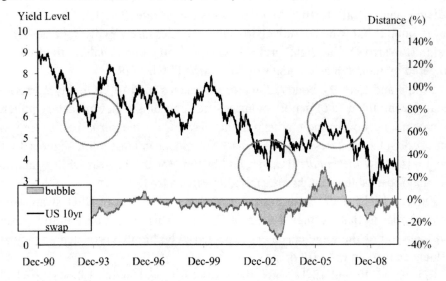

Source: Bloomberg Finance L.P.

Figure 15-14 BuVaR and ETL for USD 10-year swap

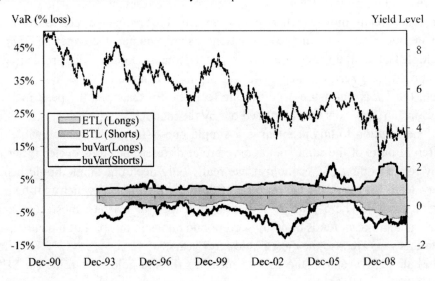

Source: Bloomberg Finance L.P.

Figure 15-15 *Bubble* measure for USD 5-year swap

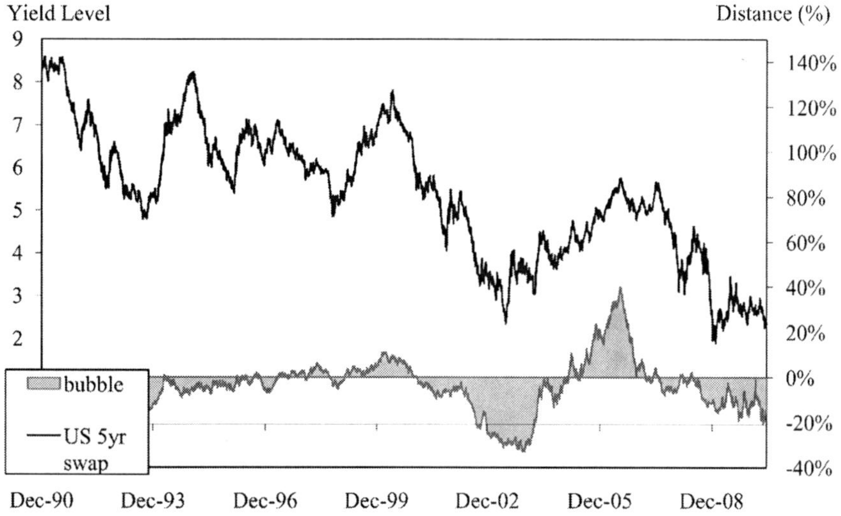

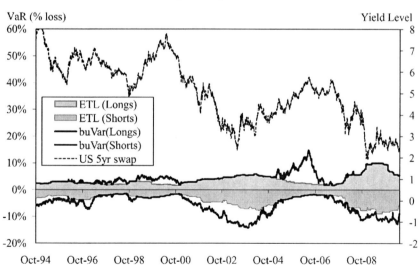

Source: Bloomberg Finance L.P.

Figure 15-16 BuVaR and ETL for USD 5-year swap

Source: Bloomberg Finance L.P.

Figure 15-17 *Bubble* measure for USD 3-month Libor

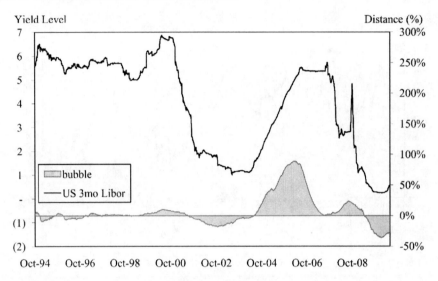

Source: Bloomberg Finance L.P.

Figure 15-18 BuVaR and ETL for USD 3-month Libor

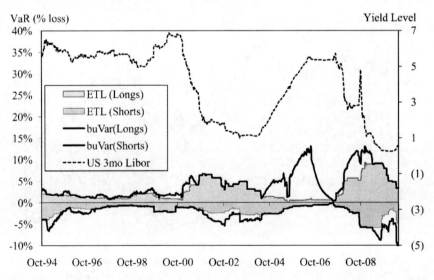

Source: Bloomberg Finance L.P.

Figure 15-19 *Bubble* measure for gold spot price ($US)

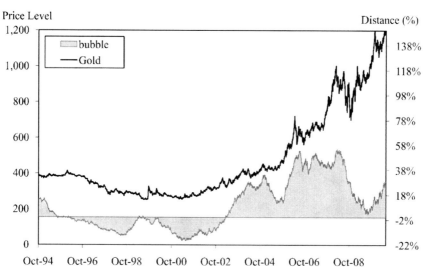

Source: Bloomberg Finance L.P.

Figure 15-20 BuVaR and ETL for gold spot price ($US)

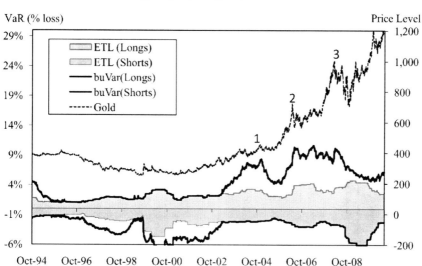

Source: Bloomberg Finance L.P.

Figure 15-21 *Bubble* measure for Brent crude oil futures price

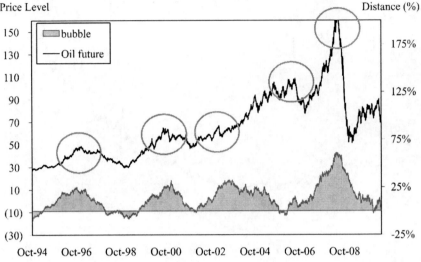

Source: Bloomberg Finance L.P.

Figure 15-22 BuVaR and ETL for Brent crude oil futures price

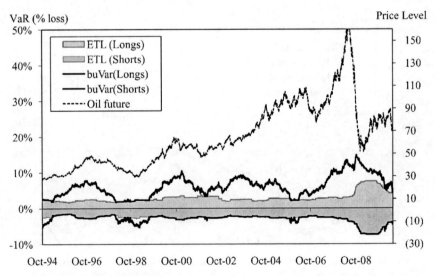

Source: Bloomberg Finance L.P.

Figures 15-21 and 15-22 show the *bubble* and buVaR for Brent crude oil futures (of the near month contract). Remarkably, the *bubble* measure preempted *every* major oil price spike in recent history (circled in Figure 15-21).

15.2 BuVaR Event Timing Tests

BuVaR is designed to anticipate market bubbles and provision against an impending crash. In this section, we look at major crises and extreme events in the history of financial markets, to test if buVaR was able to penalize players ahead of the crash. The test is deemed successful if the *bubble* measure inflates and buVaR peaks before the crash occurs. The infamous events in Table 15-2 are tested.

Table 15.2 Key negative events found in recent financial history

Asset	Asset class	Crash events
S&P 500 Index	Equity	2008 Credit crunch
Dow Jones Index	Equity	1987 "Black Monday" crash
Nasdaq 100 Index	Equity	2000 Internet bubble burst
Nikkei 225 Index	Equity	1989 Japan's asset bubble burst
Hang Seng Index	Equity	1997 Asian crisis
USD/JPY	Forex	1998 Bank of Japan intervention
AUD/SGD	Forex	2008 "Yen carry" unwind
Brent crude oil futures	Commodity	2008 Oil price bubble burst

Figure 15-23 shows the buVaR of the S&P 500 index during the 2008 credit crunch. It is not easy to pinpoint exactly when the crash formally occurred since it cascaded down. The arrow indicates the lead time from when the *bubble* peaked to when the price collapse was steepest. The *bubble* peaked in Jul 2007 just as the S&P index (and the buVaR[1]) reached its high, one year ahead of the crash, and maintained a significant penalty on the long side.

Figure 15-24 shows the buVaR of the Dow Jones index around the "Black Monday" (1987) crash, which registered a 25% single day freefall. Again, the arrow indicated a one-year lead time. The *bubble* measure was preemptive and the penalty was maintained until after the crash.

---

[1] The buVaR does not always peak at the same time as the *bubble* since, if conventional VaR is very small, its inflation may not produce a sizable buVaR. In such cases, the *bubble* peak often leads the buVaR peak.

Figure 15-23 The 2008 credit crunch and the buVaR of S&P 500 index

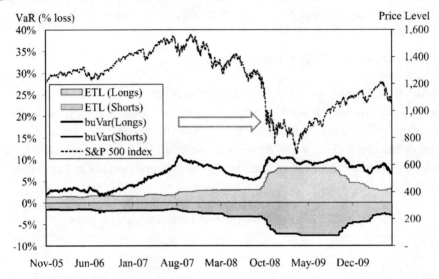

Figure 15-24 The 1987 "Black Monday" and the buVaR of Dow Jones index

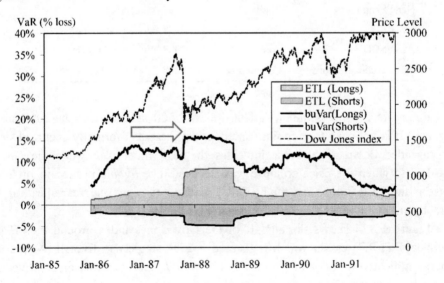

Figure 15-25 shows the buVaR of the Nasdaq index when the internet bubble burst in 2000. It may appear that buVaR peaked *after* the initial collapse, but the *bubble* measure actually peaked just as the Nasdaq made its high (Figure 15-3).

Figure 15-26 shows the buVaR of the Nikkei 225 index during the 1987 stock market crash and Japan's asset bubble burst in 1989. It would seem in 1989 (circled in Figure 15-26) buVaR did not significantly penalize the long side. This is because the ETL itself is ultra-low, even though the *bubble* measure peaked (see circle in Figure 15-5) its multiplicative effect is diluted.

Figure 15-27 shows the buVaR of the Hang Seng index during the 1997 Asian crisis. The buVaR peaked about 6 months ahead of the crash. In fact, the dotted vertical line indicates where the *bubble* measure peaked just before the crash (see also Figure 15-7).

Figure 15-28 shows the buVaR of USD/JPY exchange rate during the BoJ intervention period in 1997 – 1998. There were multiple rounds of BoJ purchases of yen; three of the largest collapses were picked up by buVaR, including the famous yen carry unwind on 7 and 8 Oct 1998 that was triggered by the Russian debt default (Aug 98) and LTCM collapse (Sep 98). The inflation of VaR was significant and preemptive, and would have discouraged (bank) speculators from shorting the yen during that period.

Figure 15-29 shows the buVaR of the AUD/SGD exchange rate during the "yen carry" unwind in 2008. The credit crunch sparked a massive flight-to-safety and exiting of "yen carry" trades[2], a favorite yield pick-up trading strategy among institutional investors. Because of the large differential between AUD and SGD interest rates, the AUD/SGD was a favorite choice for such trades. BuVaR peaked almost 6 months ahead of the AUD/SGD collapse.

Figure 15-30 shows the buVaR of crude oil futures during the bursting of the oil bubble in 2008. Both the *bubble* measure (Figure 15-21) and buVaR peaked ahead of the crash by about 3 months.

We can draw some general conclusions from the tests in Sections 15.1 and 15.2. BuVaR peaks and troughs ahead of the market, often with a comfortable lead time for banks to trim positions. In rare situations of ultra-low and declining volatilities, buVaR's effectiveness may be hampered. In contrast, conventional VaR is *always* one step behind the market in a crisis.

---

[2] The trader invests in a high-yielding currency using funds borrowed in a low-yielding currency. If the exchange rate remains unchanged, the trader stands to earn the interest difference between the two currencies as an accrual "carry" profit. The strategy is dubbed "yen carry" because yen, with near zero rates, is traditionally used for this strategy.

Figure 15-25 The 2000 internet crash and the buVaR of Nasdaq index

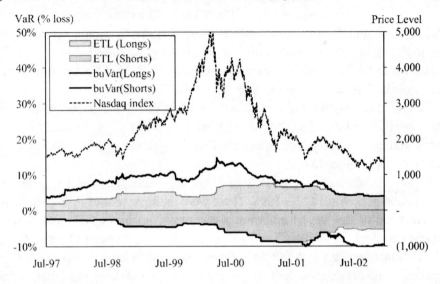

Figure 15-26 Japan's asset bubble collapse (1989) and the buVaR of Nikkei index

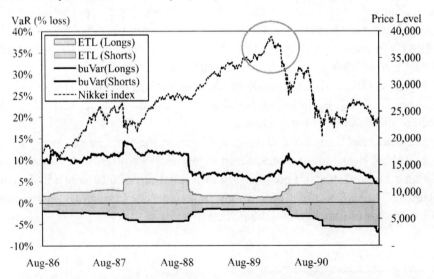

Figure 15-27 The Asian crisis (1997) and the buVaR of Hang Seng index

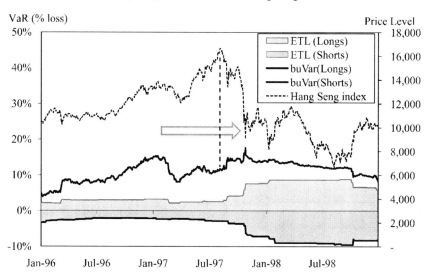

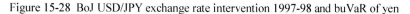

Figure 15-28 BoJ USD/JPY exchange rate intervention 1997-98 and buVaR of yen

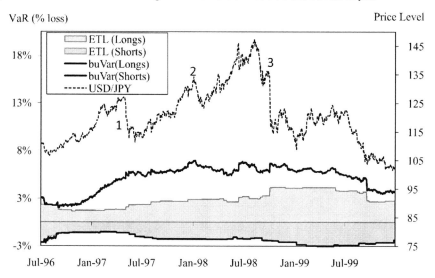

Source: Bloomberg Finance L.P.

Figure 15-29 "Yen carry" unwind in 2008 and buVaR of AUD/SGD exchange rate

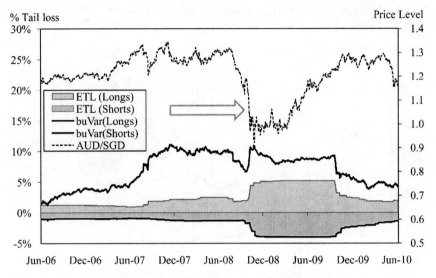

Source: Bloomberg Finance L.P.

Figure 15-30 Oil bubble burst in 2008 and buVaR of Brent crude oil futures

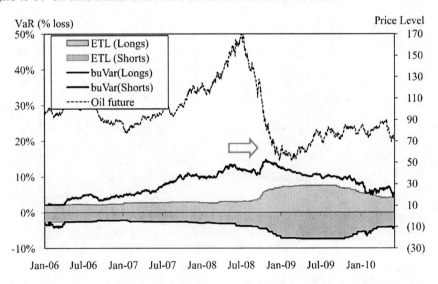

Source: Bloomberg Finance L.P.

15.3 BuVaR Cyclicality Tests

BuVaR is designed to act as a countercyclical measure of risk. To qualify, we need to test if the inflator synchronizes with the business cycle. There are many ways in the statistical literature to measure the business cycle. One popular method is the *HP filter* which assumes that a time series x_t can be divided into two components: the trend (l_t) and the cycle (s_t), such that $x_t = l_t + s_t$. Hodrick and Prescott (1981) proposed that the trend can be backed out by optimizing the following equation:

$$\min_{l_t} \sum_{t=1}^{T}(x_t - l_t)^2 + \lambda\sum_{t=1}^{T}(l_{t+1} - 2l_t + l_{t-1})^2 \qquad (15.1)$$

where λ is the smoothing parameter. The business cycle is derived by simply taking the ratio between the price series and the cycle, hence x_t/s_t. Hodrick and Prescott suggest setting $\lambda = 1600$ for quarterly data. Ravn and Uhlig (2002) proposed a way to adjust λ for data of different frequencies—it is optimal to multiply λ with the fourth power of the observation frequency ratio, for example, since we use daily data[3], λ should be $(90)^4.1600 = 104,976,000,000$.

Specifically, we want to test if the *bubble* indicator moves in correlation with the business cycle. Since there is no fundamental reason to expect the relationship to be a linear one, we use all three measures from Section 2.4: linear correlation, Kendall tau and Spearman rho.

Correlation should be calculated on changes rather than on price levels otherwise effects from long term trends can result in extremely misleading correlation values. For example, if one price series oscillates around a long term bullish trend and the other price series oscillates around a bearish trend, the correlation of *prices* would imply that the variables are inversely correlated, even if the timing of the upswings and downswings are perfectly in step. The computation is done using *monthly changes* (data from Dec93 to Jun09) because daily changes can be noisy.

As per Table 15-3, the correlation results are generally positive for all three measures and significantly different from zero (or no relationship). This suggests that the buVaR methodology can produce a risk metric that is correlated to the

---

[3] We assume one quarter is 90 days. Free shareware implementation of the HP filter is available from the internet. The reader can easily show that the result of the HP filter is similar to that of a low order (such as a cubic) polynomial fit, which is also commonly used by economists.

business cycle. Therefore, buVaR can be used for the computation of counter-cyclical capital buffers.

Table 15-3 Correlation tests of *bubble* measure vs. business cycle (Dec 93-Jun 09)

Test asset	Kendall tau	Linear correl	Spearman rho
AUD/SGD exchange rate	0.38	0.53	0.55
Gold (spot)	0.19	0.24	0.26
Hang Seng index	0.38	0.52	0.53
USD/JPY exchange rate	0.41	0.58	0.57
Nasdaq index	0.40	0.58	0.55
Nikkei 225 index	0.39	0.51	0.55
Crude oil futures	0.38	0.50	0.55
S&P 500 index	0.31	0.42	0.43
USD 5y swap	0.24	0.32	0.32
USD 10y swap	0.32	0.38	0.45
USD 3m Libor	0.35	0.25	0.49
Yen 1y swap	0.37	0.42	0.53

The correlation result in Table 15-3 is not perfect because the *bubble* is designed to not just track the cycle faithfully, but to also adapt to changing conditions automatically. In particular, it must widen when a market bubble is forming, it must not follow when the price crashes and it must shrink during extended periods of gradual growth. These adaptive benefits mean that the correlation, while reasonably positive, will not be very high.

15.4 Credit BuVaR Parameter Tuning

As seen in the few examples in Chapter 14, credit buVaR is *non*-cyclical in the sense that there is no dependency on the business cycle. It is designed to detect the occurrence of credit escalation and then penalize long credit positions in a sensible way.

There is no purer measure of default *expectation* than credit spread itself. Since expectations are forward-looking, a spread escalation is preemptive of a default. Because the spread is used to inflate credit buVaR, there is no issue with timing, the effects of inflation will always be immediate—thus no timing test is required. The crucial issue is then the setting of ω_2. How conservative (or penal) should one make credit buVaR?

To answer this question, let's look at credit buVaR for five selected issuers that have experienced the credit crunch in 2008. We convert 5-year spreads to bond prices using the same model assumptions as in Chapter 14, in particular, the 5-year swap rate and the bond's coupon are taken to be 2.57%. Two sets of results are calculated, for ω_2=1.2 and more conservatively, for ω_2= 0.5.

Table 15-4 revisits the conditions during the 2008 crisis, particularly the spreads are recorded on those dates when (credit) buVaR reached its peak for each issuer. The buVaR and VaR are expressed as shifted price level and dollar loss. For example, in the case of Toyota, on 16-Dec-08, its VaR is a loss of $1.27 from 90.09 to 88.82 for $100 standard notional.

For each individual issuer, its spread is tabulated. Assuming a 5-year bond for the issuer, its prevailing price and shifted price are computed using Excel function PRICE(..). For example, to calculate the AIG bond price after being shifted by buVaR of 69.2%[4] (with ω_2=0.5) use:
PRICE(TODAY(),TODAY()+5*365,0.0257,0.0257+2670*(1+0.692)*0.0001, 100,4)=15.31.

Table 15-4 Summary calculation when Credit buVaR is at its peak

	Toyota	Philippines	Lehman	AIG	General Motor
Date	16-Dec-08	02-Mar-09	15-Sep-08	22-Apr-09	04-May-09
Current Spread	224	488	701	2,670	15,445
Current Price	90.09	79.81	72.42	31.01	1.77
Price (at VaR)	88.82	77.36	68.10	24.30	1.44
Price(at buVaR,w=1.2)	88.68	76.76	66.73	19.67	1.23
Price(at buVaR,w=0.5)	86.61	71.50	58.41	15.31	1.11
VaR loss	1.27	2.45	4.32	6.71	0.32
buVaR loss (w=1.2)	1.41	3.05	5.69	11.35	0.54
buVaR loss (w=0.5)	3.48	8.31	14.01	15.70	0.66

As expected, ω_2=0.5 produces more conservative buVaR results than ω_2=1.2 i.e. the dollar loss is larger. As we shall see, the rapidity of credit deterioration (when it occurs) calls for a penal minimum capital regime. Let's look at a few examples.

---

[4] The calculation of 69.2% buVaR (which will shift the spread) is not shown here.

Figure 15-31 shows the buVaR for Lehman 5-year CDS. Its spread broke the 200 level on 15 Feb 08 and then again on 22 May 08, and deteriorated rapidly. Lehman defaulted 16 weeks later when spreads were at 701. Two important lessons for modeling are: 1) default is not a jump process, there is always a warning signal in the form of spread escalation, 2) it can happen very quickly and sometimes discontinuously (in this case at 701). If a 5-year bond were to deteriorate *continuously* until default, Lehman would have escalated to 5,800bp (assuming 10% recovery). However, the market expected a Fed bail-out so spread widening was not drastic. When the rescue plan failed the bankruptcy surprised the market and trading stopped abruptly.

The same pattern is shown in the case of General Motors (see Figure 15-32). Its spread broke 1000 on 23 May 08 (the same time as Lehman's breakout!). It took the market 11 months to reach the high of 21,000bp. The same observations here: 1) there is ample warning time, 2) the spread escalation was rapid. In practice, once spreads escalated to above 4000bp – 5000bp, there is very little a bank can do to trade out of the position since liquidity will dry up and most counterparties will treat it like an impaired asset and look for off-market settle-ment. While the time series was not disrupted, the bond has effectively defaulted on a MTM basis (see the last column of Table 15.4). Notice the buVaR started coming off as the spread went above 15,445. This is to constrain the shifted price from falling below zero.

Figure 15-31 BuVaR for Lehman 5-year CDS spread

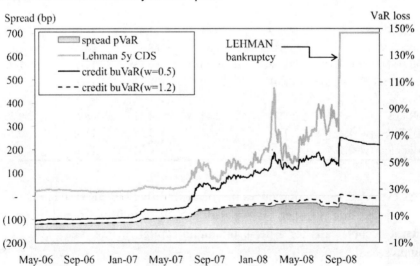

Source: Bloomberg Finance L.P.

A notable observation is that conventional spread VaR is a poor measure of default risk. The VaR for GM moved up very little throughout the crisis—it is capturing changes in volatility while ignoring the rapid rise in spread levels. It is possible for spreads to trade at high levels but with low volatility. Spread VaR completely missed the warning signs.

Figure 15-32 BuVaR for General Motors 5-year CDS spread

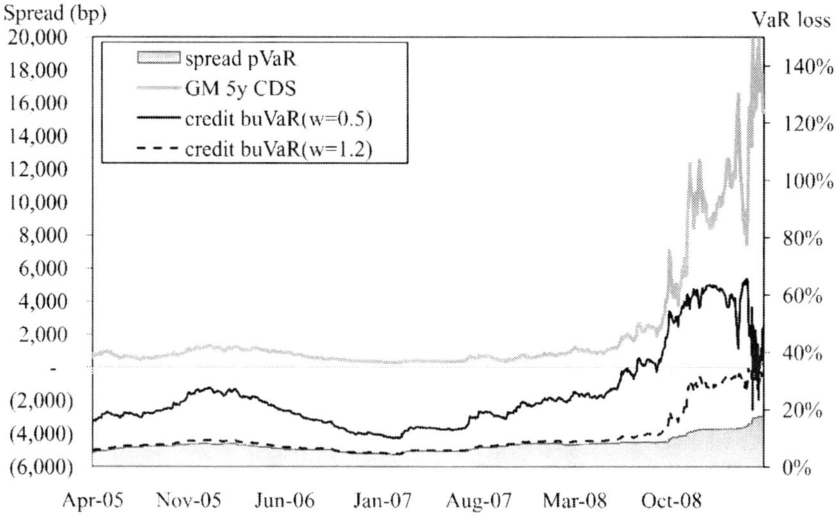

Source: Bloomberg Finance L.P.

Figure 15-33 shows the spread of AIG which did get a government bail-out package. The spread broke 500 on 11Sep08 and reached 2500bp just 7 weeks later. From these examples, it would seem that banks may have as little as 2 months to react to a credit deterioration say by cutting positions.

Figure 15-34 and Figure 15-35 are two examples of issuers that were negatively affected by the sentiment during the credit crunch, but were never in danger of default. (It is inconceivable that the Philippines government would declare a debt moratorium because of contagion from the sub-prime crisis; the economics are too far apart.) The spread escalation was equally rapid but the magnitude was many times smaller.

These five examples have highlighted a common theme, credit deterioration is very rapid when it occurs. Figure 15-36 shows the response function for $\omega_2=1.2$, $\omega_2=0.5$. The shaded region is the "normal" trading zone when the market is not in distress. When credit escalation occurs, the credit spread accelerates rapidly above 500bp (for instance) to outside the normal zone.

Figure 15-33 BuVaR for AIG 5-year CDS spread

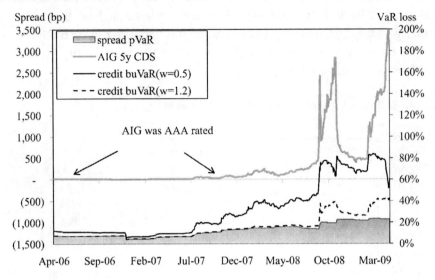

Source: Bloomberg Finance L.P.

Figure 15-34 BuVaR for Toyota 5-year CDS spread

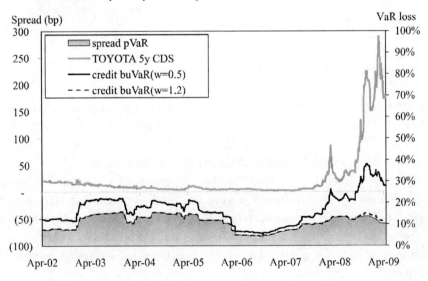

Source: Bloomberg Finance L.P.

Figure 15-35 BuVaR for the Philippines government 5-year CDS spread

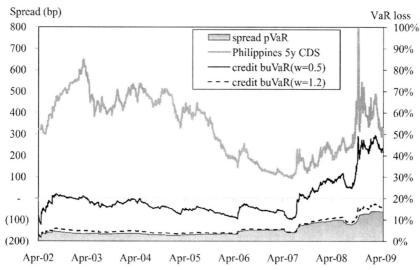

Source: Bloomberg Finance L.P.

Figure 15-36 Response function for two settings of ω_2=1.2, ω_2=0.5

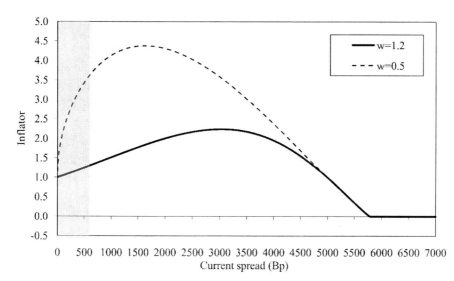

This phenomenon argues for a more penal setting (ω_2=0.5) since it will be too late (and counter-productive) to raise minimum capital only when the issuer company is rapidly falling apart. A capital buffer for default risk needs to be built up when spreads are still trading in the normal zone, but showing signs of widening.

Using ω_2=0.5 (dotted line) as an example, let's examine how penal buVaR is. When the spread is at 20 (AAA-rated levels) the inflator is at 1.5, which means that for the best corporate issuers a long credit position is taken to be 50% more risky than a short credit position. When the spread is at 350, the average 5-year spread of Philippines CDS during the period shown in Figure 15-35, the inflator is at 3.0. This means for high-yield issuers, a long credit position is 3 times riskier than a short credit position. For ω_2=0.5 the inflator is capped at 4.4 times.

It is true that a short credit position has no risk of *default* unlike a long position. But is it reasonable to penalize the long side multiple times more than the short side from the default risk standpoint? We offer a heuristic argument.

The "credit spread puzzle" was well-researched as discussed by Amato and Remolona (2003)—it refers to the fact that corporate credit spreads are much wider than what expected default would imply. The latter is derived from historical default statistics available from rating agencies. Studies by Elton et al. (2001) confirmed that expected default risks contributed no more than 25% of observed spreads. Georges et al. (2005) showed that results can differ widely depending on the methodology, the default cycle, and recovery rate assumptions. In particular, for the period of high default cycle, the proportion for Baa bonds can go as high as 71% of estimated spread, assuming a recovery rate of 49%. For this case, when the recovery assumption is reduced to 40%, the proportion increases to 83%.

Hence, depending on the severity of the default cycle, the proportion of default risks in credit spreads can be as high as 83%. The rest is explained by risk premium (arising from spread volatility), liquidity premium and difficulty in diversification of tail-risks. We argue that a short CDS position is free from default risk, hence, should have non-default risks portion that can be as low as 17%. We can then infer the ratio of risks between long and short CDS.

As a rough guide, if up to 83% of the spread is contributed by default risks (i.e. at least 17% by non-default risks), then, a long CDS is up to 100/17=6 times riskier than a short CDS. Hence, the inflator should range from 1 to 6 depending on the extent of credit deterioration, in general agreement with our cap of 4.4 times. Put another way, the incremental loss of buVaR over and above spread VaR (which just measures volatility) can be attributed to default risks.

In summary, credit buVaR provides an add-on buffer to conventional spread VaR on the long side to account for default risks. The response function is theoretically appealing and we justified its interpretation by referring to research on the "credit spread puzzle".

Chapter 16

Other Topics

This last chapter deals with miscellaneous topics relevant to buVaR. First, we discuss the effects of implementing buVaR at the portfolio level. Are diversification, aggregation and decomposition similar to that of conventional VaR? Is basis risk well-captured? Second, we look at how buVaR as a new framework for measuring risk is able to meet the ideals proposed by the Turner Review. Lastly, we reflect that buVaR can be seen as a potential new direction in the quest to create a good riskometer.

16.1 Diversification and Basis Risks

A risk measure is of limited use if it cannot be aggregated in a diversifiable way. BuVaR preserves the correlation structure even after incorporating countercyclicality, which means that the benefits of diversification are maintained. PL vectors of different positions, portfolios and even of different banks can be aggregated. The reverse process of decomposition is best achieved using the method of incremental VaR of Section 6.3.

Recently there has been a lot of pressure from regulators for banks to include and improve on the measurement of basis risk, which is seen as under-represented in current VaR systems. Basis risk arises from long-short and spread positions. Since such positions are intended to be *market-neutral* (not sensitive to general market movement) one can expect the basis to be not volatile almost all the time except for exceptional days where there is idiosyncratic news that specifically moves the basis. This makes basis risk fat-tailed (high kurtosis) by its very nature. Consider Figure 16-1 which compares the kurtosis of 5-year and 4-year USD swaps and their spread position over a four year period. The kurtosis is measured using a 250-day rolling window. The basis return shows high kurtosis in general.

A further complication is that in a typical VaR observation period, there are just too few idiosyncratic observations for adequate quantification of tail-risk or true kurtosis. BuVaR compensates for this weakness by making basis buVaR more sensitive.

Figure 16-1 Kurtosis behavior: 4-yr swap, 5-yr swap and their basis

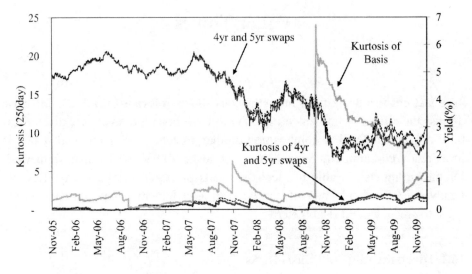

Source: Bloomberg Finance L.P.

We illustrate this in Exercise 16.1 using Dow Jones and S&P 500 index data during the credit crisis period, Nov 07 – Oct 08. Their returns are highly correlated during stressed markets with coefficient +0.99. Since the *bubble* measure was positive during this period, we multiply the left side of both distributions by a factor of 3 (as a simple illustration). We look at a hedged basis position or long-short strategy, with $1 million notional on each side of the deal.

Table 16-1 Comparison of buVaR vs. expected shortfall for $1 million outright and basis positions

	Expected shortfall (ES)	buVaR	buVaR/ES
Long postion (Dow)	(58,009)	(174,026)	3.0
Short position (S&P)	(51,073)	(51,073)	1.0
Hedged position (basis)	(6,824)	(17,702)	2.6

Table 16-1 shows the resulting buVaR vs. the expected shortfall (ES). The long position risk measure is inflated by 3 times as expected while the short position is not penalized, since it is not chasing the bubble. More interestingly, the basis buVaR risk is small ($17k) and is reflective of a hedged position, but is larger than the basis risk as measured using ES. This indirect inflation of basis risk (by 2.6 times) compensates for the underestimation of fat-tailness.

Furthermore, buVaR increases the basis risk measure whenever bubbles are building rapidly or when there is a crash. This is a desirable property because spread relationship has a heightened risk of breaking during such times. In comparison, under conventional VaR, basis risk VaR will only creep up slowly after the start of a financial crisis as idiosyncratic observations roll into the observation window.

16.2 Regulatory Reform and BuVaR

The Turner Review highlighted two dangers of using VaR as a risk measure and metric for minimum safety capital—its inability to capture fat-tail risk and its susceptibility to procyclicality. The Review goes on to lay down the requirement of a future metric for risk capital—first, it must be overtly countercyclical and second, it must provide a much higher capital level to buffer against extreme tail events. We have developed the idea of buVaR in this book. Let's see how buVaR is able to satisfy these criteria.

Cushioning fat tail losses

From the author's own research, it is found that buVaR is asymmetrical. This innovation recognizes that fat-tail losses can only happen in one direction during any given period—crashes can only happen downwards in a bull market, and bounces can only happen upwards in a bear market. BuVaR inflates the distribution in a unidirectional way to create a more realistic buffer against fat-tail events. Hence, for the bank that is short, the bubble asset will require less capital than for a bank that is chasing this "hot" asset.

In the same way, in credit buVaR, a bank that is short credit risk (i.e. the protection buyer) can hold less capital than a bank that is long credit risk (i.e. the protection seller). This recognizes that credit default risk is asymmetrical and hurts only the long side.

With buVaR in place, one can expect risk capital to be multiples of the current VaR and in the direction which penalizes imprudent investment. And capital will be largest when the bubble is largest just when the risk of a fat-tail crash event is highest.

Overtly countercyclical

BuVar evidently has a countercyclical quality—it can rise and peak up to several months ahead of the actual peak in an asset bubble. In other words, unlike VaR, it is a *leading* (not a lagging) risk measure and can provide an "early warning" of market distress.

BuVaR creates buffers for *individual* assets depending on the extent of bubble formation in that asset. In other words, it is not a one-size-fits-all method for minimum capital and is thus superior to a naïve method of multiplying a countercyclical factor to a bank's overall VaR without differentiating between assets held. Suppose the general market index is rallying towards the peak of a boom cycle (bubble), and a bank is short the index or is exposed to some other market (non-bubble) for the same amount of VaR, the bank will be unduly penalized under the naïve approach. This may create a perverse incentive where banks will favor "hot" assets over benign ones for the same amount of risk (or VaR) exposure, since the cyclical charges for both are the same.

We now realize that VaR does not just *measure* but also *influences* market risks. With hard-wired procyclicality at play to pressure mandatory risk capital and consequently, the bank's ability to leverage, the banking system can collectively increase the likelihood of extreme events. It increases the frequency and magnitude of the boom-bust cycle.

The countercyclical alternative buVaR, if used on a global scale, will not only build buffers against large losses but may actually decrease the likelihood of systemic crashes. It makes it painful (or expensive) for banks to chase hot assets even before the bubble can burst, and effectively acts as a cycle dampener. If all regulated banks, "too big to fail" institutions and shadow banks are required to use buVaR for regulatory capital, a much safer financial system can be created.

Other advantages

Aside from the two criteria proposed by the Turner Review, buVaR has other merits:

Firstly, buVaR is a lot more responsive to regime breaks in correlation and volatility compared to conventional VaR, thanks to the choice of using expected shortfall for the tail estimate.

Secondly, credit buVaR is able to account for default risk in a forward-looking way by making itself a function of credit spread *level*. This is because the spread reacts quickly to trading and is forward-looking when it comes to credit deterioration as compared to conventional spread VaR. The latter is nothing more than a rolling standard deviation of spread changes and is thus backward-looking. From back-testing using 2008 crisis data, credit buVaR often reacted weeks ahead of credit deteriorations. More interestingly, because it is a function of *both* spread volatility and spread level, buVaR is able to integrate spread and default risks into a single measure. There is then no longer a need to rely on credit ratings to model default risks separately. Rating signals were found to be grossly late during the credit crisis.

Finally, under the current capital regime, supervisory multipliers are applied on the "outside" after the VaR has been computed (see equation (11.5)). This means the VaRs for market risk, credit risk and other risk classes may only be added as lump sums and thus will not account for diversification. In contrast, for buVaRs, the supervisory parameters are built "inside" the risk model itself. The regulator can penalize harder a weakly-managed bank by tuning the buVaR parameters. The advantage is that the market buVaR and credit buVaR can be sub-added while retaining the feature of diversification in the process. The supervisor can even sub-add buVaR across banks for example to perform CoVaR and other systemic risk analysis. This gives the systemic risk regulator a unified, powerful and centralized tool to detect and monitor pockets of risk concentration and network effects in the financial system.

16.3 BuVaR and the Banking Book. Response time as Risk.

BuVaR is designed for trading book capital, and is less suitable for the banking book. The calculation of buVaR requires daily price data. Hence this metric is only applicable for markets that show good price discovery, including tradeable credit markets, but excluding actual loans.

In contrast, banking book loans are modeled by LGD and PD using historical statistics of loan delinquencies—daily prices are not readily observed. The new Basel III contains a countercyclical capital buffer designed to protect against procyclicality of credit growth which directly affects the banking book (see Section 11.5).

With the exception of pure investment firms, most lending institutions would have a much larger banking book in terms of notional compared to the trading book; thus the credit risk charge is generally higher compared to the market risk charge for a typical bank. However, the author argues that the risk of the trading book is actually much higher (for the same notional) compared to the risk of the banking book. This has to do with the element of "response time to calamity" seldom considered in modern risk management and measurement.

As an analogy, consider the proposition that a bush fire is less dangerous than a tsunami, even though the former may cause relatively more devastation to a wider geographical area. This is because a bush fire provides more "warning time" for people to take evasive action. In short, *a risk that affords plenty of warning time is actually less risky!*

We can rank the various risk categories faced by a bank in terms of response time that they allow:

1. Operational risk, little to no warning time. For example, in a rogue trading incident, or during the 9-11 tragedy, top management has almost no time to react rationally.

2. Funding liquidity risk, in a matter of days (when there is a liquidity squeeze). This is a function of information efficiency. The interbank money market dealers operate in a relatively small community, where any news or rumors are quickly translated into market prices and bid/ask spreads. Fortunately, during exceptional times, the central bank often acts as lender of last resort to ensure that there is no disruption in the payment system.

3. Market risk, in weeks. While liquid markets react to news at internet speeds, the massive number of buyers/sellers with opposing views, mean that price falls are often "supported", and price movements, albeit large, are orderly. For example, Figure 15-31 shows that even in the Lehman bankruptcy, the credit spread took 16 weeks to escalate after it broke the 200 level for the second time. An investor with the correct foresight would have had enough time to liquidate or hedge his position.

4. Credit risk of loans, in months. Real deterioration of credit conditions takes time to affect borrowers; hence, NPL (non-performing loans) take time to rise in the banking book. This long lead time allows a prudent institution to take evasive actions to avert a fall out, such as by raising fresh capital or by hedging, etc. It also provides time for borrowers to look for alternate source of funding, or to reduce debt.

The unequal response time afforded by different risk types, means that trading book losses can be higher than banking book losses. This is supported by evidence from the credit crisis. The IMF report[1] estimated a mark-to-market loss of USD720bln from derivatives of loans (such as CDO, ABS, MBS) as of March 2008, compared to an actual loss of USD225bln from whole loans in the US. Hence, for the purpose of capital buffers, some form of scaling to account for unequal response time to risk is probably prudent.

---

[1] "Global Financial Stability Report", April 2008, IMF.

16.4 Can buVaR pick tops and bottoms perfectly?

Many empirical studies have shown that markets are efficient, hence, forecasting models cannot profit from the market *consistently*. Markets can be inefficient in the *short run* which could explain why some traders do make money using strategies/insider information. However, the usefulness of strategy/insider news is often short-lived, and the trader either goes bust subsequently, or finds himself modifying his strategy to survive. Thus, a model that performs like a money-making machine—the "holy grail" of trading—just doesn't exist.

If you believe in efficient markets, the *bubble* indicator should not *consistently* pick the exact occurrence of market tops and bottoms, otherwise trading profits can be generated by exploiting this indicator.

While buVaR cannot be used for profit-making, it can be used for risk management or loss avoidance. We have tested in Chapter 15 that buVaR will provide an additional capital buffer ahead of crashes most of the time. One drawback is, at times, the *bubble* may rise in a rally even though the frenzied rally subsequently proves to be a long-term trend. This will make the buVaR too conservative; the adaptive moving-average is a device to mitigate this weakness. If used for trading, such early signals will lead to losses, but used as a risk management tool, a conservative buffer during periods of heightened risk is a prudent approach.

Another drawback is, on very rare occasions, at the height of a bubble, prices may advance at ultra-low volatility (what I call "the calm before the storm" effect). This was observed for the Nikkei 225 index in the period leading up to the Japanese asset bubble burst at the close of 1989. The unusual calmness made buVaR small even though the *bubble* indicator was reaching a peak. Despite this weakness, buVaR is still much larger (and more conservative) than normal VaR or expected shortfall in this case when the market is brewing with danger.

16.5 Post-modern Risk Management

The Markowitz framework is also called modern portfolio theory. Its greatest contribution is in providing a formalized framework for investment decision-making which incorporates a proper risk measure (variance), correlation relationships and risk diversification in an elegant way. Its major weakness lies in its assumptions of variance as a risk metric and normal distribution of asset returns—both of which are symmetric notions. As modern risk management adopted the Markowitz framework, our risk measurement is inherently symmetric.

In 1959, Markowitz suggested that a model based on *semi-variance* would be preferable but in light of the formidable computational challenge at that time, his model was based on mean-variance. Simplistically, semi-variance is the same as variance except that only returns which are below the mean are selected for the computation. Hence, it reflects dispersion or risk on the downside. This asymmetric measure of dispersion opened up an area of modeling which subsequent researchers termed *post-modern portfolio theory.*

In the same spirit, buVaR is an "asymmetric" quantile where one side of the distribution is inflated to reflect the influence of the market cycle. More importantly, buVaR is also a breakaway from conventional frequentist thinking. It adopts a perspective that extreme tails are inherently unknowable. Questions of "true risk" are empty, and a risk metric's value lies in its usefulness. The crucial question to ask is: used in a given application, will buVAR promote prudence and desirable behavior at financial institutions?

16.6 Spreadsheet

16.1 The basis risk of a long-short portfolio often contains large kurtosis which is understated in VaR because of the lack of tail data. BuVaR compensates this weakness. Aim: the spreadsheet illustrates that buVaR gives a more aggressive result for basis risk as compared to expected shortfall.

Chapter 17

Epilogue: Suggestions for Future Research

This book hopes to pave the way for a new approach in measuring risks, one that is unrestrained by ingrained notions of i.i.d., stationarity and normality of financial variables. Without such assumptions, mathematical risk models will lose a degree of tractability but will gain a practical ability to handle the risk of fat-tails and procyclicality. Essentially, we have lost precision but have gained accuracy, and hence become less "wrong" in our assessment of risks.

The removal of these strict mathematical conditions leads to an open arena for further development of the basic buVaR framework beyond what is described in this book. Some potential directions for further research include:

a) Calibration: Determining a more elegant theoretical upper limit for buVaR calibration. In this book, we used an average of the largest daily changes encountered in all history capped by a possible circuit-breaker (cap on day loss) imposed by the exchange. The weakness is that some markets do not have circuit-breakers (such as commodities and FX markets) and nascent markets will not have enough history of downturns for proper calibration. Ideally, the upper limit should be based on some natural limit imposed by the financial system environment. Such a limit should be intuitively justified and should not come from mathematical abstractions.

b) Benchmarking: The computation of the *bubble* measure is highly dependent on the availability of continuous data. For some emerging markets, illiquid prices make the measure inaccurate. In such cases, using benchmarks may be a better alternative, for example, using an equity index as a benchmark to derive the *bubble* measure for an illiquid stock. A potentially better idea is to use a group of suitable benchmarks to derive the *bubble* measures for *all* assets in the financial markets. Using benchmarks can be appropriate because we are actually interested in the cycle of the *general* market. And benchmarking will certainly lead to more stable results.

c) Performance testing: Because buVaR is "non-i.i.d.", back tests and most statistical tests will not be meaningful, which leaves us to rely on performance testing not unlike that done for trading systems. In such tests, the practitioner is more concerned with accuracy (shown up as positive performance) than with statistical precision. Hence, one area of research is in designing a better gauge of "goodness" or effectiveness for the buVaR model. A well-defined test metric will be useful for the purpose of optimizing the parameters in buVaR.

d) Systemic risk: One advantage of buVaR is that it outputs *PL vectors*, which makes it compatible for use with other new risk tools such as CoVaR and network models. These new models attempt to measure the spillover and transmission of systemic risks (see Chapter 12). Given that buVaR itself preempts many major sell-offs in history, it will be interesting to explore its effectiveness when used in combination with network models and CoVaR. Will it provide an early warning of systemic events?

e) Risk indicators: It is worth exploring whether risk indicators can be used to create an alternative *bubble* measure for application in buVaR. A risk indicator is a proprietary indicator which banks use to gauge market sentiment, hence, it is usually very cyclical[1]. Applying rank filter (see Section 13.3) to it may produce the necessary counter-cyclical quality.

f) Ultra-low volatility problem: We observed in the tests in Chapter 15 that on a few occasions (see Figure 15-26) the buVaR peaked and then *fell back* just before the crash, even though the *bubble* measure correctly timed the crash. This was due to the extremely low volatility that preceded the crash—the ETL (and VaR also) was so low and much-decreased that despite the multiplier effect, the buVaR came off. This is not ideal. Future research may attempt to offset this "calm before the storm" effect. Under this rare circumstance, the buVaR will dip from its peak before the crash, but VaR in comparison will always be too late (it will register a big reading when the crash occurs).

g) By looking at the result charts in Chapter 15, it is apparent buVaR inherited the "plateau" effect problem (see Section 2.7) from using the equally-weighted historical simulation approach. It is proper to use decaying weights so that data rolling-off the observation window will have a smaller impact. We abstain from including a decay factor in Chapter 13 because we wish to simplify the illustration of the buVaR idea, and because the author does not have a strong view on the choice of decay schemes. We leave this to future research.

---

[1] A risk indicator is typically a normalized formula with constituents such as: the VIX, credit spreads, T-bill yields, Treasury-eurodollar (TED) spread, FX option's skew (called *risk reversal*) and implied volatility, etc.

REFERENCES

Adrian, T. & Brunnermeier, M.K. (2009). CoVaR. Princeton University and FRB of New York Working Paper.

Adrian, T., & Shin, H.S. (2008). Liquidity, monetary policy, and financial cycles. *Current Issues in Economics & Finance*, 14(1), 1-7.

Alexander, C. (2008). *Market risk analysis: Practical financial econometrics.* Chichester, England: Wiley.

Amato, J., & Remolona, E. (2003). The credit spread puzzle. *BIS Quarterly Review* (December), 51-63.

Artzner, P., Delbaen, F., Eber, J., & Heath, D. (1999). Coherent measures of risk. *Mathematical Finance*, 9(3), 203-228.

Balkema, A. & de Haan, L. (1974). Residual life time at great age. *The annals of probability*, 2(5), 792-804.

Bank for International Settlements. (2008). *Principles for sound liquidity risk management and supervision.*

Bank for International Settlements. (2009). *International convergence of capital measurement and capital standards: a revised framework-comprehensive version.*

Bank for International Settlements. (2009). *Revision to Basel II market risk framework-final version.*

Bank for International Settlements. (2009). *Findings on the interaction of market and credit risk.* (BIS Working Paper No.16).

Bank for International Settlements. (2010). *Countercyclical capital buffers: exploring options.* (BIS Working Paper No.317).

Bank for International Settlements. (2010). *Guidance for national authorities operating the countercyclical capital buffer.*

Bank for International Settlements. (2010). *Basel III: International framework for liquidity risk measurement, standards and monitoring.*

Bank for International Settlements. (2010). *Basel III: A global regulatory framework for more resilient banks and banking systems.*

Beveridge, S. & C. R. Nelson (1981). A new approach to decomposition of economic time series into permanent and transitory components with particular attention to measurement of the business cycle. *Journal of Monetary Economics* 7(2), 151-174.

Billio, M., Getmansky, M., Lo, A. & Pelizzon, L. (2010). Measuring systemic risk in the finance and insurance sectors. Working paper.

Black, F., & Scholes, M. (1973). The pricing of options and corporate liabilities. *Journal of Political Economy*, 81(3), 637. Retrieved from Business Source Premier database.

Bollerslev, T. (1986). Generalized autoregressive conditional heteroskedasticity. *Journal of Econometrics* 31(3), 307-327.

Boudoukh, J., M. Richardson & Whitelaw, R. (1998). The best of both worlds. *Risk*, 11, 64-67.

Breuer, T., Jandacka, M., Rheinberger, K. & Summer, M. (2008). Regulatory capital for market and credit risk interaction: Is current regulation always conservative? *A Discussion Paper Series 2*: Banking and Financial Studies 2008 (14), Deutsche Bundesbank, Research Centre.

Brockmann, M. & Kalkbrener, M. (2010). On the aggregation of risk. *Journal of Risk*, 12(3).

Brunnermeier, M., Crockett, A., Goodhart, C., Persaud, A. D. & Shin, H.S. (2009). The fundamental principles of financial regulation: preliminary conference draft. *Geneva Reports on the World Economy 11*. Geneva, Switzerland: International Center for Monetary and Banking Studies.

Campbell, S. D. (2005). A review of backtesting and backtesting procedures. Finance and economics discussion Series 2005-21, Board of Governors of the Federal Reserve System (U.S.).

Coleman, R. (2010). A VaR too far? The pricing of operational risk. *Journal of Financial Transformation*, 28, 123-129.

Cox, J.C., & Ingersoll, J.E, Jr & Ross, S.A. (1985). A theory of the term structure of interest rates. *Econometrica*, 53(2), 385-407.

Crouhy, M., Galai, D. et al. (2000). A comparative analysis of current credit risk models. *Journal of Banking & Finance*, 24, 59-117.

Danielsson, J., Embrechts, P., Goodhart, C., Keating, C., Muennich, F., Renault, O. & Shin, H.S. (2001). An academic response to Basel II, Special paper no. 130, FMG and ESRC, London, May.

David, D.A. & Fuller, W.A. (1981). Likelihood ration statistics for autoregressive time series with a unit root. *Econometrica*, 49(4), 1057-1079.

Diebold, F., Schuermann, T. & Stroughair, J. (1999). Pitfalls and opportunities in the use of extreme value theory in risk management. *Journal of Risk Finance*, 1(2), 30-35.

Dionisio, A., Menezes, R. & Mendes, D.A. (2007). Entropy and uncertainty analysis in financial markets. *Quantitative Finance Papers*, arXiv.org.

Eisenberg, L., & Noe, T.H. (2001). Systematic risk in financial systems. *Management Science*, 47, 236-249.

Elsinger, H., Lehar, A. & Summer, M. (2006a). Risk assessment for banking systems. *Management Science*, 52 (9), 1301–14.

Elsinger, H., Lehar, A. & Summer, M. (2006b). Using market information for banking systems risk assessment. *International Journal of Central Banking*, 2 (1),137–65.

Elton, E.J., Gruber, M.J., Agrawal, D. & Mann, C. (2001). Explaining the rate spread on corporate bonds. *Journal of. Finance*,56(1), 247-277.

Embrechts, P., Klüppelberg, C. & Mikosch, T. (1997). *Modeling extremal events for insurance and finance*. Springer, Berlin.

Embrechts, P., McNeil, A. & Straumann, D. (1999). Correlation and dependency in risk management: properties and pitfalls. ETH Preprint.

Engle, R.F. (1982). Autoregressive conditional heteroscedasticity with estimates of the variance of UK inflation, *Econometrica*, 50, 987-1007.

Engle, R.F. & Granger, C.W.J. (1987). Co-integration and error correction: representation, estimation and testing. *Econometrica*, 55(2), 251-276.

Engle, R.F. & Manganelli, S. (2004). CAViaR: Conditional autoregressive value at risk by regression quantiles. *Journal of Business & Economic*, 4(2-3), 187-212.

Financial Service Authority. (2009). *The Turner Review: A regulatory response to the global banking crisis.* Financial Service Authority Corporate Document.

Financial Service Authority. (2010). *The prudential regime for trading activities: A fundamental review* (FSA Discussion paper 10/4).

Finger, C. (1997). A methodology to stress correlations. *RiskMetrics Monitor*, 4th Quarter, 3-11.

Finger, C. (2009). Comment on the Basel committee on banking supervision's consultative document entitled guidelines for computing capital for incremental risk in the trading book. RiskMetrics Group.

Finger, C. (2009). IRC comments. *RiskMetrics Research Monthly*, February.

Finger, C. (2008).The once holy grail. *RiskMetrics Research Monthly*, January.

Fisher, R. & Tippett, L. (1928). Limiting Forms of the Frequency Distribution of the Largest or Smallest Member of a Sample. Proceedings of the Cambridge Philosophical Society, 24, 180–190.

Frankland, R., Smith, A.D., Wilkins, T., Varnell, E., Holtham, A., Biffis, E., Eshun, S & Dullaway, D. (2008). Modelling Extreme Market Events. (Working paper presented to the Institute of Actuaries, UK).

Georges, D., Geneviève, G. et al.(2005). Default risk in corporate yield spreads. *Financial Management*, 39(2), 707-731.

Ghysels, E. & Osborn, D. (2001). *The econometric analysis of seasonal time series.* Cambridge University Press.

Gnedenko, B. (1943) Sur la distribution limite du terme maximum d'une s´erie al´eatoire. *Ann. of Math*, 44, 423–453.

Hallerbach, W.G. (2002). Decomposing portfolio value-at-risk: A general analysis. *Journal of Risk*, 5(2).

Heston, S. (1993). A closed form solution for options with stochastic volatility with applications to bonds and currency options. *Review of Financial Studies*, 6(2), 327-343.

Hodrick, R. & Prescott, E. (1981). Postwar U.S. business cycles: an empirical investigation. Reprinted in: *Journal of Money, Credit, and Banking*, 29, 1–16.

Hua, P., & Wilmott, P. (1998). Crashmetrics Technical Report: Basic methodology: worst-case scenarios and platinum hedging.

Hull, J. (2008). *Options, futures and other derivatives* (7th ed.). Upper Saddle River, NJ: Prentice Hall.

Hull, J. & White, A. (1998). Incorporating volatility updating into the historical simulation method for VaR. *Journal of Risk*, 1, 5-19.

International Monetary Fund. (2008). Containing systemic risks and restoring financial soundness. *Global Financial Stability Report*, April 08.

J.P. Morgan/ Reuters (1996). *Riskmetrics technical document* (4th ed.).

Johansen, S. (1988). Statistical analysis of cointegration vectors. *Journal of Economic Dynamics and Control*, 12, 231-254.

Jorion, P. (2003). *Financial risk manager handbook* (2nd ed.). Hoboken, NJ: Wiley.

Jorion, P. (2007). *Value at Risk* (3rd ed.). New York: McGraw Hill.

Jorion, P. (2002). Fallacies about the effects of market risk management systems. *Financial Stability Review*, 115-127.

Koenker, R. & Bassett, G.W. (1978). Regression quantiles. *Econometrica*, 46, 33–50.

Lavine, M. (2008). *Introduction to statistical thought.* Published at http://www.stat.duke.edu/~michael/book

Lo, A. (2009). The feasibility of systemic risk measurement: Written testimony for the House Financial Services Committee hearing on systemic risk regulation. October.

Mandelbrot, B. (1963). The variation of certain speculative prices. *Journal of Business,* 36, 394-419.

Markowitz, H.M. (1952). Portfolio selection. *Journal of Finance,* 7 (1), 77–91.

Merton, R. C. (1974). On the pricing of corporate debt: the risk structure of interest rates. *Journal of Finance,* 29(2), 449-470.

Mini, J. & Xiao, J.Y. (2001). Return to Riskmetrics: the evolution of a standard. RiskMetrics Group.

Morris, S. & Shin, H.S. (1999). Risk management with interdependent choice. *Oxford Review of Economic Policy,* 15, 52-62.

Nelson, D.B. (1991). Conditional heteroskedasticity in asset returns: A new approach. *Econometrica,* 59, 347-370.

Oest, T. & Rollbuhler, J (2010). Detection and Analysis of Correlation Clusters and Market Risk Concentration, *Wilmott,* July.

Pérignon, C. & Smith, D.R. (2010). The Level and quality of value-at-risk disclosure by commercial banks. *Journal of Banking & Finance,* 34, 362-377.

Pickands, J. (1975). Statistical inference using extreme order statistics. *Ann. Statist,* 3, 119-131.

Ravn, M. & Uhlig, H. (2002). On adjusting the HP-filter for the frequency of observations. *Review of Economics and Statistics,* 84 (2), 371–376.

Rebonato, R. (1999). The most general methodology to create a valid correlation matrix for risk management and option pricing purposes. Quantitative Research Centre of the NatWest Group.

Rebonato, R. (2003). Theory and practice of model risk management. In *Modern Risk Management: A History* (Ed.). London: RiskWaters Group.

Rebonato, R. (2007). *Plight of the fortune tellers: why we need to manage financial risk differently.* UK: Princeton University Press.

Rebonato, R. (2010). *Coherent stress testing: A Bayesian approach to the analysis of financial risk.* Chichester: Wiley.

Samuelson, P. (1947). *Foundations of Economic Analysis.* Cambridge, MA: Harvard University Press.

Satchkov, D. (2010). When swans are grey: VaR as an early warning signal. *Journal of Risk Management in Financial Institutions,* 3(4), 366-379.

Sebastian, S. & Christoph, K. (2009). Market liquidity risk- an overview. *CEFS Working Paper Series* No. 4.

Shannon, C. E. (1948). A mathematical theory of communication. *Bell System Technical Journal,* 27, 379-423, 623-656.

Sharpe, W. (1964). Capital asset prices: A theory of market equilibrium under conditions of risk. *Journal of Finance,* 19, 425-442.

Speth, H. - Th. (2004). *The BV4.1 procedure for decomposing and seasonally adjusting economic time series,* Methodenberichte 3 (ed. Federal Statistical Office).

Taleb, N. (1997). *Dynamic hedging: Managing Vanilla and exotic options.* NY: Wiley.

Taleb, N. (2009). Errors, robustness, and the fourth quadrant. *International Journal of Forecasting,* 25(4), 744-759.

Taleb, N. (2009a). Common errors in interpreting the ideas of the Black Swan and associated papers. Working paper.

Taleb, N. (2007). *The black swan: the impact of the highly improbable*. NY: Random House.

Thomas, H. & Wang, Z.Q. (2005). Interpreting the internal ratings-based capital requirements in Basel II. *Journal of Banking Regulation*, 6, 274–289.

Vasicek, O. (1991). Limiting loan loss probability distribution. KMV Corporation

Wilde, T. (1997). Credit Risk+, A credit risk management framework. Credit Suisse Financial Products.

Wilmott, P. (2007). *Paul Wilmott introduces quantitative finance* (Second Edition). England: Wiley.

Zangari, P. (1996). An improved methodology for measuring VaR. *RiskMetrics Monitor*. Reuters/JP Morgan, 7-25.

Zumbach, G.O. (2006). The Riskmetrics 2006 methodology. RiskMetrics Group.

INDEX

A

accuracy 12, 267, 319
across scenarios, summation of PL .. 98, 130
arrow of time................................. 144
asset & liability management (ALM) 185
asset allocation 48
asynchronous data......................... 173
augmented Dickey-Fuller (ADF) test . 42
Austrian Nationalbank (OeNB) 232
autocorrelation............................... 35
    function (ACF) 36
    joint test.................................. 168
Autoregressive Conditional
    Heteroscedasticity (ARCH) model 43
autoregressive model...................... 36

B

bad loan... 280
balance sheet................................. 222
    spillover risk 230, 234
Bank of England (BOE)................... 236
Bank of Japan................................ 289
banking book 204
Basel
    Committee of Banking Supervision
    201
    formula for MRC....................... 136
    III 213
    three pillars 203
baseline growth trend.................... 248
basis risk
    of proxies 81
    types of..................................... 109
Bayesian 17, 149, 153
behavioral finance 7, 48, 243
Berlin procedure 60
bespoke product
    bid-ask spread......................... 187
    data problem........................... 173

    implied correlation 107
    liquidity risk.............................. 185
beta approach............51, 110, 134, 226
beta coefficient............................. 110
bid-ask cost..............................184–86
bid-ask spread............................... 187
bi-modal, distribution.................... 221
Black Monday 153, 221, 297
Black Swan.................................6, 153
Black-Scholes formula 89, 104
block maxima method.................... 123
BoJ..........................See Bank of Japan
    currency intervention 299
brute force, method of.............55, 227
bubble, modeling of 251
bunching test 167
business cycle
    forecast................................58, 303
    procyclicality of 7, 207
buVaR
    and basis risk............................ 312
    and capital regime...............313–16
    and coherence.......................... 261
    and credit ratings 315
    calibration 319
    correlation test......................... 304
    diversification........................... 311
    scope of 262

C

calibration..................................... 96
cap/floor... 77
capital
    base 214
    buffer....................................137, 155
    conservation buffer 215
    countercyclical buffer 208, 215, 216, 248, 304
    double counting 217
    minimum...........................202, 214
    regime...................................... 215

risk-based............................ 202
rules-based approach............... 202
Tier 1............................. 214
Capital Adequacy Directive (CAD)... 202
Capital Asset Pricing Model (CAPM) 110
CDO debacle 185
CDS spread 188
central bank
    capital control 171
    eligible collateral 213
    governor 201
    monetary policy 291
    policy cycles 263
central limit theorem 27, 123
Cholesky matrix 57, 92
circuit breaker................... 253
classical decomposition............. 58
    new interpretation of 245–48
clumping effect, of random sampling 97
coherence........................ 258
cointegration 52
comprehensive risk capital charge.. 210
conditional autoregressive value-at-risk
    (CAViaR)....................118–21
conditional probability 267
    in EVT............................ 124
constant proportion portfolio insurance
    (CPPI) ....*See* Portfolio insurance
contagion default risk.................. 236
Contagion VaR (CoVaR)............229–32
convexity 101–3
copula............................. 34
corporate governance................... 177
correlated random number.........57, 94
correlation
    historical 76
    implied....................76, 107
    linear........................... 31
    matrix adjustment schemes......... 94
    matrix failure.................... 93
    of default 182
    Pearson's....................... 31
    products........................ 107
    proxy risk factor 109

rank............................... 34
risk clusters 239
spurious 39
stochastic....................... 108
trading 109, 211
weaknesses of 33
correlogram 36
cost-of-carry 75, 101
counterparty risk...........180, 233
    capital 214
    concentration.................. 239
covariance 31
crash coefficient............... 226
Crashmetrics..................224–27
credit default swap 78
    benchmarking 110
credit escalation..*See* Spread escalation
credit rating
    agencies 180
    simulation 182
credit risk
    asymmetry of 273
    banking book.................. 179
    charge (CRC)..................203–5
    definition..................... 179
credit scores 180
credit spread puzzle 310
credit spread VaR................ 209
    weakness of 307
credit valuation adjustment (CVA).. 214
Creditmetrics 180–84
critical value,of hypothesis testing.... 41
cumulative distribution function (CDF)
    25
currency
    Asian crisis.............171, 195
    controls....................... 171
    pegged 172
    speculators.................... 171
cycle
    component.................... 245
    distortion 247

D

data scarcity 76, 118, 139, 197
data snapping 72, 173
decay factor...................................... 44
delta approach................................. 90
delta-gamma approach 90
delta-gamma approximation.......... 103
delta-hedge, continuous 224
destruction of wealth..................... 145
deterministic trend process............. 56
detrending...................................... 21
differencing 21, 53
    information loss 245
discrete differences........................ 90
diversification 49, 194
    ratio 131
drawdowns, of PL........................... 263

E

Economic Cycle Reserve................. 208
efficient frontier............................. 50
efficient market 317
    hypothesis..........................174, 267
    theory 205, 220
eigenvalues..................................... 92
elliptical distribution 33, 159
endogenous, risk drivers 220
Engle-Granger regression................. 53
Enron, unauthorized trading 179
enterprise risk management 74
entropy.. 143
    asymmetry of........................... 144
    information theory................... 144
    Shannon................................... 144
equilibrium level, modeling of........ 251
estimate
    biased 38
    consistent................................. 23
    inconsistent............................. 39
EVT .... *See* Extreme value theory
    Classical..............................121–24
    limitations 126
    multi-variate 127
EWMA .... *See* exponentially weighted

moving average
    use in Hybrid VaR 115
    volatility 88
exceedence.............................31, 124
    clustering 169
expected shortfall 160
expected tail loss (ETL) .....*See* Expected
    shortfall
    advantages of........................... 257
exponential GARCH model (EGARCH) 46
exponentially weighted moving
    average 44
extreme event 6, 153, 297
extreme loss 121
extreme value theory..................... 121
extremistan.......................6, 153, 268

F

fat-tailed
    cause of.................................... 150
    distribution.........................96, 106
    EVT... 122
feedback loop 222–23
Fisher-Tippett theorem 122
forecasting...................................... 61
foreign currency loan, risk of.......... 195
forward rate agreement (FRA).......... 78
Fourier series 60
fourth quadrant, Nassim Taleb ..154–55
frequency back test....................... 165
frequency distribution.................... 153
frequentist...................................... 17
front-to-back, risk management
    architecture............................... 71
full revaluation, method of.............. 96
fungible, of cash flow 188

G

game theory 220
gaming, of risk system................... 176
gamma, of option........................... 105
Gaussian distribution 25, 154
general equilibrium theory............. 220
general market risk charge 204

Generalized Autoregressive Conditional
    Heteroscedasticity (GARCH)......... 45
generalized extreme value distribution
    (GEV)... 122
generalized Pareto distribution (GPD)
    124
geometric Brownian motion (GBM). 56,
    95
global minima 225
Goldman Sachs commodity index..... 78
Greeks 88

H

hedge fund, VaR for 176
hedge ratio 51, 175
herding behavior............................ 220
Heston, stochastic volatility model.. 95,
    150
hoarding of liquidity............... 185, 229
holding period...... *See* Liquidity horizon
HP filter 303
Hull-White VaR 117
hypothesis testing........................... 41

I

i.i.d. .....*See* Independent and identically
    distributed
    paradigm............................206, 268
    test of 163
    violation of assumption 149
idiosyncratic risk 51, 79, 137
impaired asset 280
incremental risk charge (IRC).......... 209
independent and identically distributed
    ....11, 21
index-tracking funds......................... 52
information
    arrival (news) 149
    asymmetry of 238
integrated, time series 53
intelligent VaR engine design 73
Internal Model............................... 203
internal ratings based (IRB) approach
    203

internet bubble............................. 299
inverse transformation.................... 55
issue-specific securities ....*See* Name-
    specific securities

J

Johansen method............................ 54
JP Morgan...............................88, 180
jump-to-default process................. 272

K

Kendall's tau 34
Keynes, John 266
    animal spirits 4
    dictum...................................... 12
Knightian uncertainty.................... 207
kurtosis...............................20, 106
    and fat-tails 154
    Excess....................................... 21
    of basis position 311

L

lagging, indicator........................... 156
Law of Large Numbers..................... 22
law of one price 175
Lehman, bankruptcy...................... 306
leptokurtic 20
leverage effect..........................46, 145
leverage ratio................................ 214
leverage targeting....................222–23
likelihood function 51
limit order book 186
limit, trading 130
limiting distribution..................27, 123
linear approximation
    approach............*See* delta approach
liquidity horizon 137, 210
liquidity ratios............................... 212
liquidity risk
    add-on/ reserve....................... 189
    firm... 184
    funding.................................... 185
    market 185
liquidity-adjusted VaR 186

Ljung-Box statistic 168
lobbying 177, 238
local risk measure 92, 104
log-likelihood function 51, 125
lognormal distribution 56

M

macro hedge 155
marginal default rate 188
market "anomalies" 143
market crash, asymmetry of 9
market momentum 24
market risk 74
    charge (MRC) 136, 203–5
    contagion 239
    total charge 211
Markowitz
    Harry 48
    mean-variance framework 48
    portfolio theory 91
    problem 49
mark-to-market 72
    accounting 158, 222
    uncertainty 185
    vs. Mark-to-model 175
mark-to-model 174
maturity transformation, banking
    function of 238
maximum likelihood estimation (MLE)
    51
mean 19
mean excess function, EVT 124
mean-adjustment, of VaR ... 84–85, 100,
    117
mean-fleeing, of credit spread 263
mean-variance framework 48
median 28
mediocristan 6
Merton's model 182
minimization problem 225
mixture of normal, distribution 106, 150
model misspecification 96
modern portfolio theory 48
modified duration 102

moment 20
moments matching 96
Monte Carlo method 55
Monte Carlo simulation
    multi-step 210
    Quasi 98
    weaknesses of 96
moving average
    adaptive 250
    deviation from 250

N

name specific securities 110
negative rates 82
network
    Austrian model 234
    effect in CoVaR 229
    externalities 220
    model of funding liquidity risk
        (RAMSI) 236
    model of interbank 233
non-deliverable forwards (NDF) 82
non-linear
    products 90
    risk profile 104
non-market risks 74
non-performing loan (NPL) 316
normal distribution 25
    forecast using 153
not identifiable model 62
null hypothesis 42

O

off-the-run, bonds 109
one-factor model 95
one-sided alternative hypothesis 42
on-the-run, bonds 110
operational risk
    actuarial approach 190–94
    Basel guidelines 190
    loss distribution approach 194
    taxonomy 189
    VaR (OpVaR) 190–94
optimization algorithm 227

optimization problem............ 48–50, 63
option
   decay 111
   exotic.. 105
   flooring of risk 104
   premium 111
optionality risk............................... 105
ordinary least squares (OLS)
   regression 38
outsourcing mania 71
overnight rate................................ 291

P

pair trading..................................... 52
parallel computing 73, 97
peaks-over-thresholds (POT) method
   124
percentile 28
performance, tests..................283, 319
pillars........................*See* tenor buckets
plateau effect 45
platinum hedging........................... 224
point estimate..........................31, 159
point-in-time, behavior 215
ponzi schemes 6
portfolio insurance.................175, 220
portfolios, hierarchical 72
positive semi-definite problems 92
post-modern portfolio theory 318
precision...................................12, 244
   measure of..........................40, 163
prehedge 139
premium, risk of............................ 111
preprocessing step, data 72
present value per basis point . *See* PV01
pricing engine 71
pricing model
   risk.. 174
   standard..................................... 174
principal-agent problem................. 176
probability density function (PDF) 25
problem of aggregation, of risks 194–95
procyclicality......................8, 158, 222
pseudo random numbers................. 97

pseudo-arbitrager 175
put-call ratio 9
PV01.......................................90, 102

Q

QRM ..... *See* Quantile regression model
quantile 28
   interpretation............................ 169
quantile function............................. 88
quantile regression
   line.. 63
   model (QRM)..........................62–63
   used in CAViaR 120
   used in CoVaR............................ 231
quantitative modeling.................... 143

R

random generator, Excel.................. 55
random walk, process 56
rank filter, technique...................... 251
rate curves, types of........................ 77
rates cleaning................................ 173
recovery rate 182
   assumption........................275, 280
   of bank in network 235
reflexivity..................................... 220
regime break................................ 108
regime shift.................................. 100
   simulated 156
regulatory arbitrage 203
relationship
   lead-lag 39
   linear.. 37
   quantify...................................... 37
reserve, PL.................................... 81
residual
   error term 38
   serial correlation of 39
response time to calamity.............. 315
return, types of 81
risk communication........................ 133
risk drivers, study of...................... 136
risk engine .... *See* VAR engine
risk factor

mapping 74–79
proxy 79
stressing 228
universe 76
risk sentiment index 64
risk weighted asset (RWA) 202
Riskmetrics 44, 88
risk-netting, rules 209
riskometer, ideal 5
risk-return tradeoff 48
rolling window 43

S

scaling
    problems of 197
    square root of time 137
    VaR 139
scatter plot 152
scenario generation 81
seasonal decomposition .....*See* classical
    decomposition
second law of thermodynamics 143
securitized credit product 210
semi-convertible currencies 82
semi-variance 318
sensitivity
    approach to VaR 88
    risk factor .... *See* Greeks
serial correlation 35, 138, 247
shadow banking system 238
short rate models 95
skewed incentives 176
skewness 20, 147
slippage, loss 50, 175, 185, 187
Sobol sequence 98
social wealth gap 3
Soros, George 219
Spearman's rho 34
special investment vehicles (SIV) 238
specific risk 111
specific risk charge (SRC) 137, 204
spillover risk 229
spread escalation 272
spread option 108

Standard Approach, Basel 203
standard error 40
standard normal deviate 91
standard normal distribution 27
standardized maxima, EVT 122
static hedge 224
stationarity test 42
stationary, time series 21
statistical arbitrage 52
statistical bootstrapping 163
stochastic trend processes 55
stop-loss, strategy 175, 222
stress test 5, 172, 211
    in network model 236
    non-frequentist 229
    reverse 228
    weaknesses of 217
student-t distribution 41
subadditivity 49, 159
supervisory multiplier, of Basel Rules
    137
support functions 72, 176
swaption 77
switching strategy 221
systemic risk regulator 238

T

tail profile, of hsVaR 132
Taleb, Nassim 6
Taylor expansion 89, 102, 225
technical analysis 24, 156
technical breach, of limit 130
tenor buckets 76
theta effect 100
through-the-cycle, credit modeling. 208
time decay ....*See* theta effect
time series 21
trading book 204
trading strategy 175, 299
traffic light approach 165
transition matrix, ratings 180
    criticism 180, 271
transition probabilities ... *See* Transition
    matrix, ratings

translation invariance.................... 112
t-ratio 41
trend-following indicator 156
Troubled Asset Repurchase Program
   (TARP)...................................... 185
Turner Review............................8, 205

U

unbiased estimate, of quantile 165
unconditional coverage test............*See*
   Frequency back test
underwriting and securitization deals
   139
uniform distribution......................... 55
unknowable, risk..................... 154, 268

V

VaR
   advanced methods 115
   Component.................................. 133
   conditional 64
   Conditional (cVaR)..................... 160
   confidence level 29
   Credit.. 184
   data integrity............................. 173
   decomposition 133–35
   diagnostic.................................. 132
   diversified 131
   engine.. 72
   formal definition 87
   historical simulation (hsVaR)........ 98
   hybrid historical simulation........ 115
   Incremental........................100, 135
   interpretation.............................. 28
   margin spiral 223
   Monte Carlo (mcVaR) 94
   observation period 29
   parametric (pVaR) 88

portfolio level............................ 130
reports 129
risks not in................................. 101
sampling error...................101, 164
standalone 91
stressed (SVaR)........................... 211
undiversified 131
variance-covariance (VCV) ....*See*
   parametric VaR
weaknesses of........................... 243
variance... 20
   conditional 44, 52
   portfolio...................................... 48
vendor data 173
VIX index..................145, 227, 232, 263
vol cube.. 78
volatility... 43
   clustering 45, 149
   implied... 47
   of volatility .. *See* Stochastic volatility
   skew.. 145
   smile 47
   stochastic 150
   surface 77

W

weakly stationary............................. 21
whipsaws, trading.......................... 156
whistle-blowing.............................. 177
white noise 23
wholesale funding......................... 212
WorldCom, accounting scandal 179
worst-case scenario loss................. 224
write-off, of premium.................... 111
wrong-way trades..................195, 214

Y

yen carry, unwind 221, 299

226843LV00003B/93/P